THE PLEASURE SEEKERS: The Drug Crisis, Youth and Society

by JOEL FORT, M.D.

Grove Press, Inc., New York

Contents

TO MY PARENTS, CHILDREN, WIFE MARIA, AND THE
FEW TEACHERS, WRITERS, ARTISTS, AND TRUE LEADERS
WHO HELPED IN DIVERSE, DIRECT AND INDIRECT, WAYS
TO DEVELOP MY INDEPENDENCE, CREATIVITY, AND
KNOWLEDGE OF DRUGS, YOUTH, AND SOCIETY; AND TO
MY EDITOR, ROBERT OCKENE, WHO WITH GENTLENESS
AND PATIENCE ENCOURAGED AND NURTURED THIS
BOOK, WHICH I HOPE REFLECTS THE QUALITIES OF
INDIVIDUALISM, RATIONALITY, AND COMPASSION
WHICH I CHERISH.

CHAPTER I

The Truth Shall Make You Free

> "Every ambiguity, every misunderstanding, leads to death; clear language and simple words are the only salvation from this death."   CAMUS

THE SEMANTICS OF DRUGS

Conventionally honorable men and traditional sources of information tell us that the word "drugs" refers only to marijuana, LSD, and narcotics, and that these substances are so destructive and dangerous that anyone who comes near them or thinks of using them must be handled as a criminal. Most efforts, whether literary or political, are concentrated on upholding widely accepted stereotypes and mythologies, selling newspapers or books, aggrandizing existing expensive and unsuccessful agencies, rescuing many people from well-deserved obscurity, and, in general, hiding real problems and the real world.

Mankind, and perhaps most particularly Americans, seems to be in a constant quest for oversimplification and pseudosolutions, a trend avidly fostered by the advertising industry, the mass media, and politicians. As with most phenomena of contemporary life, whether foreign policy, drug abuse, or any other, we continue to take certain elements out of context, distort and polarize in a one-dimensional way, and substitute rhetoric and passion for knowledge, logic, and rationality. The false and incomplete word goes out in ghost-written speeches and books, often scissors–and–paste jobs, which after decades of citing each other as experts or authorities turn falsehoods into "facts."

In marked contrast to the present mindless hysteria over drug use and abuse, let us look at some of the questions formulated in the 1890s by a royal commission of British and Indians empowered to study marijuana (hemp, cannabis): *"What opportunities have you had of obtaining information regarding the matters connected with hemp drugs in regard to which answers are framed? What classes and what proportion of the people drink or smoke hemp drugs, and in what localities? Is the use of these drugs on the increase, or on the decrease? What proportion of the consumers are (a) habitual moderate, (b) habitual excessive, (c) occasional moderate, (d) occasional excessive consumers? To what extent is the consumption of each of these drugs practiced in solitude or in company? Is there a tendency for the moderate habit to develop into the excessive? If not beneficial, do you consider the moderate use to be harmless? Give reasons for your answer. Does the habitual moderate use produce any noxious effects — physical, mental, or moral? Do you think the cultivation of the plant should be in any way controlled; would this be feasible; if so, indicate the method by which such control could be exercised. Would it be feasible to prohibit the use of these drugs; would the drug be consumed illicitly; how could the prohibition be enforced; would the prohibition be followed by recourse to alcohol or other drugs?"*

Actually, the word "drug" refers to any biologically active substance used in the treatment of illness or for recreation or pleasure. Thus included are aspirin, penicillin and other antibiotics, antihistaminics, antacids, as well as the mind-altering or psychoactive drugs that we are primarily focusing on in this book.

Although it might seem so to some, this fuller definition of drugs is not just of theoretical interest, for it reveals what is almost an axiom of pharmacology, that any drug can be dangerous, depending on how much is consumed and how often, its purity, and numerous other factors. Just as no drug or chemical can be said to be totally harmless, it cannot be said to be inevitably or uniformly harmful or vicious.

The broader definition certainly shows the impossibility of ever "controlling" drug usage by all of us making criminals of those who use a particular drug. Finally, the total

picture illustrates how easy it is to select certain qualities
of a drug out of context and, with carefully constructed
propaganda, to incite fear and hysteria. As an example, one
of the substances mentioned above has been massively
used for decades; its mechanism of action on the brain and
other body organs is unknown; it accounts for thousands of
deaths and illnesses each year, and it produces not only
chromosomal breakage, but actual birth defects in *lower*
animals. (If one wanted to be consistent with the distorted
conclusions circulated about LSD, it could be implied that
this substance was responsible for the 250,000 physically
deformed children born each year in America.) On the basis
of the foregoing, an ambitious politician or other dema-
gogue could call for a march on the Capitol to urge a legislature always willing to enact new, albeit harmful and
expensive, laws to make criminals out of those who use this
chemical. The substance described is aspirin, and of course
when one looks at the full picture, it is easily recognized
that millions of people regularly and beneficially use tons
of this drug without untoward consequences.

THE DRUGS SOUGHT FOR PLEASURE

Having touched upon a few of the common sources of
ignorance and confusion about drugs in general, we can
begin to look in detail at the mind-altering segment. This
begins with the most widely used and abused, by both
young and old, legally and illegally (remembering age prohibitions): the drug alcohol. Not far behind comes nicotine
in tobacco cigarettes, followed by sedatives; stimulants;
tranquilizers; marijuana; LSD-type substances, and narcotics. Yet the list is still not complete, for there is an
almost unlimited number of miscellaneous substances that
people throughout the world seek out for altering their
consciousness, including glue, gasoline and cleaning solvents; asthma inhalers; nitrous oxide and other gases in
aerosol containers; morning glory and other plant seeds;
nutmeg and other kitchen spices; amyl nitrite; over-the-

counter pseudosedatives; and numerous synthetic chemicals manufactured in recent years.

Perhaps the most commonly used term applied particularly by police and newspapers to users of a few of these drugs is "dope fiend" or "addict," the drugs themselves being described as "dope" or "narcotics" or the "hard stuff." In actuality, the law, which as Dickens said "is an ass," has incorrectly and harmfully lumped together a number of dissimilar substances as narcotics because of the urgings of police and prosecutors. The word "narcotic" scientifically refers to opium or its derivatives, morphine, heroin, and codeine, or synthetic equivalents such as meperidine (Demerol) and methadone, used in medical practice to treat severe pain and other specific conditions. It is false and deliberately misleading to apply this term to other drugs or to subdivide the term into so-called "soft" and "hard" narcotics. Such subdividing may be good from a public relations or propaganda standpoint because it seems to say that, even though a given drug, for example, marijuana, is not a narcotic, it is still a narcotic but it is somehow softer than some never defined concept of hardness. "Soft narcotic" makes as much sense as "soft pregnancy."

The same or different substances can at different times be conceptualized as beverages, tonics, medicines, drugs, intoxicants, poisons, narcotics, etc., and result in completely opposite attitudes and reactions.

If one wishes to view with alarm, a popular and well-rewarded practice in America, the vocabulary of fear moves on from "narcotic" to "hallucinogen," used to describe LSD, other similar synthetic substances, mescaline, and sometimes marijuana. Taken literally, the term implies that the drug will inevitably and consistently produce hallucinations, meaning false perceptions of reality, in the user. Conversely, the much smaller group who choose to point with pride to certain illegal drugs refer to them as "psychedelics," meaning "mind-expanding" or "mind-manifesting," implying that this effect can be expected by all. Without going into further detail, suffice it to say that the simplest and most precise way to refer to, or designate, a drug is by its specific name, so that one would talk about alcohol, marijuana, heroin, LSD, without the luxury of generic categories that seem to communicate a great deal more than they actually do.

The process of taking, ingesting, or consuming any of these psychoactive (psychotropic) drugs can be referred to as "getting high," "turning on," "getting a glow," and progressively as "getting stoned" or "loaded." The regular user can be called, if one prefers, a "head," but it is highly questionable whether such designations as "alcohol-head," "tobacco-head," "pot-head," or "acid-head" add any more to human understanding than the long-standing stereotype of the "(dope) fiend," or the more recent "(speed) freak." Parenthetically, any mind-altering drug can be associated with "fiendish" behavior, but the drug most implicated in such behavior is far and away alcohol. Most dangerous, bizarre, antisocial, unpleasant, or crazy behavior has nothing at all to do with drugs, although many like to think otherwise.

With certain socially disapproved or illegal drugs, usually no distinction is made with regard to use, abuse, or addiction. Contrariwise, with the approved and encouraged drugs such as alcohol and tobacco, almost all use, including abusive and addictive use, is thought of as wholly normal use. Actually, the use of any such substance can be one time, experimental, or occasional, and is only sometimes regular. Any regular pattern of use would itself have to be subdivided into monthly, weekly, daily, etc., with only some daily use involving excessive amounts, and only some of that (with a few drugs) involving actual addiction, meaning physical dependency.

Sometimes any nonspecific, nonmedical, or nondiscriminate use of a drug is referred to as "misuse." The term is mainly of value to communicate that the majority of use of mind-altering drugs, and a good deal of the use of other drugs, is not for very specific or necessary reasons.

Drug abuse is a concept that can be used precisely, although many use it to refer to any use of a drug not used by them, or anyone whom they don't like who uses a particular drug. Properly used, "drug abuse" refers to the use of a drug, usually chronic excessive use, to an extent that produces definite impairment of social or vocational adjustment or health. In subsequent chapters, the main drug abuses (including alcoholism and drunken driving, barbiturate addiction, tobacco smoking, and narcotics addiction) are covered in depth.

DRUG DEPENDENCY

Addiction—or in more contemporary language, physical dependency—can occur pharmacologically only with certain drugs, all depressants: alcohol; narcotics, such as morphine or heroin; and sedatives, such as barbiturates or meprobamate (Miltown, Equanil). The two components of physical dependency are tolerance and a withdrawal illness, or abstinence syndrome when the drug is discontinued or sharply reduced in amount. "Tolerance" refers to a physiological process whereby with daily heavy use of one of these drugs over many weeks, the body cells adapt in some homeostatic manner to the chemical so that it requires more and more to produce the same effect obtained on the first day with a moderate dosage. Following such a process, when the drug is no longer available objective physical symptoms appear, some of them quite severe and serious. With alcohol or sedatives, this withdrawal illness (commonly referred to as DT's or delerium tremens with the alcoholic) can include generalized convulsions, hallucinations and delusions, as well as the lesser symptoms of restlessness, irritability, nausea, and vomiting. These latter symptoms, as well as gooseflesh, sweating, tearing of the eyes, running of the nose, and often severe muscular pain, occur as part of the withdrawal illness of narcotics addicts, but paradoxically, in view of the public impressions that have been created, the alcohol-withdrawal illness is far more dangerous.

In recent years, as a few individuals have sought to bring truth to bear on this subject, it has become clear that some drugs falsely talked about for decades by drug policemen and their associates as "addicting" are not truly in that category, and hence, a new type of name-calling concept has been put forward, "psychological dependence." This is more commonly known as "habituation," and refers to someone becoming psychologically accustomed to something, drug or otherwise, through regular usage so that, when that thing is no longer available, the person becomes restless, irritable, ill at ease, and perhaps doesn't know what to do with himself. Readers will readily recognize that such habituation quite often occurs with a wide range of commonly used substances, including coffee or Coca-Cola, tobacco, alcohol, as well as with more complex phenomena, such as baseball, one's wife or husband, and television. Thus, there are many millions of Americans who have become so accustomed to watching television several hours each evening that, when a tube suddenly burns out, they become restless, irritable, and do not know what to do with themselves.

No blanket generalizations can be made in any case about the implications or significance of psychological dependence or habituation when it does occur. All the mind-altering drugs, including the ones already mentioned and certainly including marijuana, amphetamines, and barbiturates, can with regular use lead to psychological dependence, but it would always have to be decided on an individual basis whether the dependence on a drug, the spouse, or television was significantly impairing one's life functioning, self-development, or social contributions; whether it was enhancing these; or whether it was having no effect whatsoever. Again, we see that reality is far more complicated than the fairy tales of the simple-minded and, perhaps for that reason, more difficult to understand, accept, and deal with.

HOW M.A.D.'S WORK

If any single concept can be thought of as the core of the confusion and hysteria about drugs, it is the concept of *drug effect*, i.e., just how a mind-altering drug (M.A.D.) produces its effects, and what those effects are. This is the heart of the demonology and the basis for our inaccurate categorizations of problems and how to deal with them. Drug overkill rests upon this insubstantial foundation with many parallels to the weapons overkill and its justifications.

A faulty, one-dimensional concept of how the drugs sought after for pleasure work is revealed in an ancient Persian anecdote about three men who decided to travel to a neighboring walled city. Of the three, one was a chronic alcohol user, one a chronic cannabis (marijuana) user, and the third a chronic user of opium. After a long day's walk, they reached their destination just after dark and found the gates to the city already closed. As they discussed what to do, the opium user proposed that they lie down and sleep until the next morning, when the gates would be opened; the alcohol user, that they break down the gate; and the cannabis user, that they go through the keyhole.

A more accurate perception of how mind-altering drugs exert their effects is demonstrated by the most common such experience in American society, the cocktail, or other drinking, party. At such a gathering, people of approximately the same age and body size consume the same amount of the drug alcohol over the same time period and yet behave in markedly different ways. Some become boisterous or even aggressive; some passive, withdrawn, or sleepy; some amorous, flirtatious, or lascivious; and some show no particular change from their nondrug state.

What we loosely call the "drug effect" and magically attribute to certain supposedly inherent properties of a few drugs while commonly ignoring others is in truth a complex interaction between three main factors. One of these is the physical or pharmacological properties of the drug. A second is the social and cultural setting in which the drug is consumed, including the immediate environment. But the most important determinant of the drug effect is the personality and character structure of the person consuming the drug, including mood, attitude, and expectations. Although dosage, purity, method of ingestion (mouth, inhalation, or injection), body size, purpose, and chance factors all enter into the process, what comes out of the mind-altering drug experience primarily depends upon what you are as a person. This means that no drug can be considered inherently or inevitably vicious, and none totally innocuous. Understanding this basic concept, one can immediately cut through the bizarre statements of what we might metaphorically call the right wing extremist, who constantly tells us that within a short time after using marijuana, or other drugs (depending upon the agency or position for which such men speak), the user will become a murderer, rapist, heroin addict, and a lifelong institutionalized psychotic. An equally polarized and absurd position, although one that has had little influence except negative on public policy, is what we could by contrast call the left wing extremist view that, within minutes or hours following such drug usage, the individual will become a fully self-actualized, creative genius, living happily and productively ever after. A major source of drug repression is Puritan or Victorian values while drug advocacy may stem from a utopian ethic.

There are, as might be expected, many other kinds of bias which keep us from finding or hitting the real target. We have many people masquerading in ghost-written speeches or books as "experts" in this field although totally lacking relevant training and experience. There are, for example, specialists in psychiatry, or even infectious diseases and anesthesiology, who have not worked directly or extensively with any phase of use or abuse of the drugs about which they declaim, but who hold what are incorrectly considered to be prestigious political or medical-political titles, giving them a platform from which to pontificate. Traditionally and presently, most so-called information and education about drugs has come from the same drug or narcotics police who created the mythology, successfully lobbied for the passage of our present laws, and have no training or experience in any of the areas of knowledge necessary for an understanding of drugs: pharmacology, psychology, sociology, anthropology, philosophy, and public health, to name the most important. Bureaucrats, whether doctors or police, moving in the remote worlds of administration rarely speak with truth or knowledge.

Then we have those who have worked only in laboratory situations, usually just with lower animals in pharmacological experiments; those who have worked with only one drug, such as heroin; those who have seen only individuals in hospital emergency rooms or jails and who generalize from those very limited pathological perspectives to the broader situation and communicate a very distorted and incomplete picture of reality. There is also the bias of the chronic drug user: the individual who regularly uses and in various ways is attached to marijuana or alcohol or other drugs often fails to accept or recognize that his drug is a drug or can have detrimental effects. While commonly thought of only in connection with advocates of "psychedelic" drug usage, this bias has actually had far more significance in connection with the chronic use of alcohol and tobacco by lawmakers and opinion-formers, which (combined with their dependency on the financial resources of these industries) often leads them to excluding these substances from any discussion of social, health, or criminal problems.

Let us remember as we move ahead to other dimensions of drug use and abuse to think in multiple dimensions about each drug and when comparing drugs, e.g., to separate average doses and excessive doses; single doses and multiple doses; durations of action; potential for producing dependence or abuse; the reasons the drug is sought by users; short-term effects and long-term effects; the many different concepts of normality and abnormality or deviance; and the many kinds of problems with numerous possible ways of attempting to control or regulate these problems.

CHAPTER 2
Around the World

"It should be our earnest intention to insure that drugs not be employed to debase mankind, but to serve it."

JOHN F. KENNEDY

The ethnocentrism or provincialism indulged in, or implicitly accepted, by most of mankind helps to give a narrowness of perspective in regard to the drug issue. To be able to look back over centuries or millennia and to examine diverse countries and continents in the twentieth century is a harbinger of understanding, if not hope.

The world's three and a half billion people of highly diverse religions, races, languages, cultures, climates, geographies, education, and economic status use most of the same drugs and have many of the same problems and pseudoproblems that we talk about in America. Mind-altering-drug use and abuse occurs in communist and capitalist, free and totalitarian, rich and poor societies, and like the situation in the United States, which drug or which aspect of its use is singled out for attention depends not only on the objective situation, but also the vagaries of politicians and the mass media; and the poverty, disease, war, illiteracy, and suppression of human rights which pervade most of the world.

ALCOHOL

Alcohol, in terms of available evidence, has the longest history of use of any mind-altering drug. This, along with its relative ease of preparation, probably accounts for its present worldwide preeminence as a source of escape, relaxation, and trouble. Since some Neanderthal or Cro-

Magnon man first imbibed this drug some one million years ago, take or leave several hundred thousand years, its use in the forms of wine, beer, and distilled preparations, both manufactured and homemade, has spread to probably one third of the world's population including in most countries between 70 and 90 percent of adults. At an early stage, use came to be linked with religious practices, but the social and recreational uses presumably came to the fore quite early in the evolutionary process, and some 2,000 years ago Horace was saying, "What wonders does not wine! It discloses secrets, ratifies and confirms our hopes; thrusts the coward forth to battle; eases the anxious mind of its burden; instructs in arts." A statement not dissimilar to some of the paeans of praise we hear presently about it and other drugs.

The origins of alcohol were attributed to a number of different gods, or sometimes devils, and it was not until 1857 that Pasteur discovered the process of fermentation in which yeast converts sugars into carbon dioxide and alcohol. Organized production of the drug dates back at least to Egypt in 3700 B.C., where a brewery is described in historical records. About a thousand years later, the ruler of Crete was already collecting wine taxes. The Arabs introduced distilling into Europe in the Middle Ages and whiskey originally meant "water of life."

More people are drinking more alcohol in more forms and in more places than ever before, to such an extent that in the United States alone the legal alcoholic-beverage industry in all its facets grosses 12 billion dollars per year, which is more than is spent on education, medical care, or religion. In round numbers, Americans are consuming several gallons of the equivalent of pure alcohol per capita per year (a figure including a very large child and youth population, most of whom presumably are not using this drug, at least during infancy). Pouring down American throats yearly are roughly 650 million gallons of distilled spirits, 100 million barrels and 6 billion bottles or cans of beer, 200 million gallons of wine, 100 million gallons of moonshine (illegal) whiskey, and vast amounts of legal homemade wine and beer.

Governments receive large revenues from this drug industry: millions of dollars for most states, several billion per year for the U.S. government, and proportionately large amounts for most other countries.

As far as abuse is concerned, conservatively there are at least 25 million alcoholics around the world, with the highest rate in France, where as much as ten percent of the population is estimated to be alcoholic. Other countries with major known alcoholism problems include the United States, Russia, Sweden, Denmark, Belgium, Switzerland, Canada, Australia, Chile, and Japan. These and other countries, of course, have situations parallel to America's with deaths and injuries from drunk driving, disability and death from cirrhosis of the liver, divorces, crimes, and job losses associated with problem drinking, but many as yet have failed either to recognize or to define this as a "problem" and give specific or adequate attention to it.

CANNABIS-MARIJUANA

Caffeine and nicotine apart, second only to alcohol in worldwide popularity, despite its illegality, is *Cannabis sativa*, known variously as marijuana, kif, ganja, maconha, dagga, bhang, charas, and hashish. The plant was christened by Linneaus in 1753 and is a close relative of hops and the fig plant. Historically, cannabis, or what seems to be cannabis, was first mentioned in 2500 B.C. in a Chinese pharmacoepia. Not surprisingly, even at this relatively early stage of civilization those who considered pleasure or happiness immoral began to speak of the plant as the "Liberator of Sin," while others who found it a desirable euphoriant or apparently effective medicament for ailments such as arthritis, malaria, or constipation began speaking of it as the "Giver of Delight." Somewhere between 1500 and 800 B.C., the plant came to be used in India for its mind-altering effect, being used primarily for religious and medical pur-

poses. Hindus came to speak of the drug as "the heavenly
guide" and "the soother of grief." It was considered holy
and described as a sacred grass during the Vedic period.
One legend speaks of the guardian angel of mankind living
in the leaves of the plant, and another account describes the
plant as springing from nectar dropped to earth from heaven.

Use of cannabis spread throughout the Indian subcon-
tinent and other parts of Asia, probably developed independently in Africa and South America, and was brought to
Europe by Marco Polo, although there is some question
about this since Herodotus writes of the Scythians inhaling
the fumes of burning hemp seeds and then "shouting
for joy."

In any case, there seems to have been little use of the
drug in the West until the middle of the nineteenth century,
when it was taken up by a number of French and American
writers including Baudelaire, Gautier, Taylor, and Ludlow,
who in a sense popularized it, as hemp or hashish.

In the form of hashish, it has been widely used for
hundreds of years in the Middle East, and in the early
1900s it came to the United States as marijuana, used by
Mexican laborers.

Growing easily in diverse climates, it is now used by
some 250 million people in all parts of Africa, North
America, Brazil, the West Indies, India and Pakistan, the
Middle East, and other regions and countries.

OPIUM-MORPHINE-HEROIN

Exactly when the mind-altering effects of the use of the
opium poppy, later named *Papaver somniferum*, was discovered is rather vague. Some attribute its discovery to the
ancient Egyptians because of a papyrus written around
1600 B.C. which appears to refer to a tincture of opium for
preventing the excessive crying of children. In any case, it
was known to the Greeks and Romans, and was widely
used by these peoples, being the active principle of the
nepenthe talked about by Homer as the "destroyer of grief."
It is thought to have been carried to Persia and China in

the ninth century by Arab traders. It reached India through
the Portuguese in the early 1500s, soon achieving widespread popularity; not only was its use widespread in India,
but the cultivation reached sufficiently large proportions
that it became the most valuable crop of export. Although
there is some evidence that the Portuguese first imported
opium into China, it was the British East India Company
that made it a large-scale enterprise, progressively increasing from 30,000 pounds per year in the first part of the
century to 750,000 pounds per year in the first part of the
nineteenth, and six million pounds by mid-century. American traders were also sending in Turkish opium, which
was inferior in morphine (the active ingredient of crude
opium) content.

At least nominal efforts were made by Chinese rulers to
suppress opium use and trade in the fourteenth century, in
1729, in 1800, and in 1879. Between 1834 and 1858, two
so-called Opium Wars were fought and won by the British
when Chinese officials attempted to stop the trade and seize
the chests of opium. As a by-product of this, Hong Kong
was ceded to England, China became open to the West,
and opium importation was fully legalized.

Competition over political and cultural superiority was
certainly involved in these Western-Chinese clashes, but
probably most significant was the prevailing belief which
continued into the twentieth century, that as expressed by
one Britisher whatever the effects of opium might be on
Westerners, "there is something about Chinese physique
and character that seems to make the use of opium not only
relatively harmless, but even necessary to his happiness
and well-being." Prohibitionist views existed in England
but were a minority position, and there was also a scientific
question as to how damaging opium smoking actually was.
For example, in 1891, the Colonial Surgeon commented
that "opium smoking does not do one thousandth of the
harm to either the individual or his family that alcohol does
at home," and he went on to state that it was also less inju-
rious than tobacco smoking.

In the early twentieth century, it was estimated that eight

million Chinese were using opium with an annual consumption of 22,500 tons; in the 1920s, an official committee stated 25 percent of the adult population of China and
Hong Kong (including two percent of the females) were
using opium with general public acceptance or support of
this use; and in the mid-1930s, it was said that ten million
people were users. This use was not only through legal distribution, but also involved considerable smuggling which
had gone on since the nineteenth century.

During the period of the Chinese Civil War in the 1930s,
and the later Japanese occupation, there was little information available about fluctuations in either use or traffic, but
presumably the long-standing cultural acceptance continued, although availability of the drug was often interfered
with. The Japanese at first banned opium after occupying
Hong Kong in 1941, but later made it available again, reg-
istering and selling to smokers, and permitting divans
or dens.

In present-day mainland China, the sketchy information
available from translated press reports and the observations
of the few Westerners allowed in, suggests a dramatic de-
cline in opium use and addiction, probably due to a combination of the cutting off of opium imports; a transformation
of cultural attitudes; peer-group pressures in local com-
munes; anti-Western feelings; and strict, implemented
penalties.

Following abrupt American-inspired post-World War II
bans on the traditional opium use, such use by the middle-
aged or elderly by smoking has been largely replaced by the
far more serious heroin addiction among the young by inhalation or injection, along with extensive crime and corruption. Currently, Hong Kong has an estimated 150,000
to 250,000 illicit heroin and opium users or addicts out of a
population of perhaps four million; Macao, some 6,000; and
Taiwan (Republic of China), some 40,000.

Returning to India, including the portion that was later
to become Pakistan, opium use by eating or drinking became very common among all sorts of classes and both

sexes without any social stigma. For a time opium distribution was a state monopoly; later it came under the control of private merchants; then the British East India Company; and finally back to government control. In 1893, a Royal Commission concluded that the main use was by a "small" percentage of the total population of adults and children; was generally moderate; gave no evidence of harmful physical or moral effects; and that it would be impractical, unenforceable, and lead to increased consumption of alcohol if the use were to be prohibited or severely limited. They felt that the use was due to the universal tendency of mankind to take some form of "stimulant" to comfort or distract themselves, to a popular belief in the medical effectiveness of the drug, the ceremonial and social uses to which it was put, and its acceptance by Hindus, Moslems, and general public opinion.

The drug was introduced into the Hindu system of Ayurvedic medicine in the fourteenth century and probably into the Moslem system of Unani medicine not long after. The materia medica of each contain some eight basic preparations which were, and are still, used for diarrhea, pain, increased sexual power, and pleasure. Some states of India continue to maintain official opium shops to supply licensed addicts; opium continues to be grown for both legal medical and illegal social use; and the number of users, whether for social, religious, or indigenous medical reasons, certainly numbers in the millions in the country of 600 million people.

In Persia, now Iran, opium use was mentioned as far back as 850 B.C., and it was introduced into medical therapeutics in the tenth century. It was commonly believed that the Arabs, using the drug to allay their hunger during desert crossings, brought it to Iran. A beverage made from the boiled opium poppy was widely drunk in the sixteenth century and later extensively used as a remedy for many diseases and for recreation, and a lucrative export trade developed. The Persian or Farsi word for the drug translates as "panacea." Legal efforts to prohibit or control cultivation or use occurred in 1910, 1928, and in 1938 without significant effect. By the 1950s, there were an estimated 1,500,000 opium users (as in other countries, usually referred to as "addicts"); an annual harvest of 700 to 1,200 tons; daily smoking of 2,000 Kilograms; widely available public smoking houses; frequent prescribing of the drug by physicians; and general social acceptance. An abrupt and more complete ban was instituted in the 1950s but the number of users presently would be between 250,000 and 500,000 with an additional (and growing) 10,000 heroin users.

Other countries with significant known opium or heroin use and/or addiction include Japan, Korea, Laos, Thailand, Burma, Indonesia, Canada, and the United States.

Western use of opium does not seem to have moved beyond limited experimentation until the eighteenth and nineteenth centuries, when as laudanum, the drug came to be taken as a medicine for practically all complaints.

Such writers as Coleridge and DeQuincey wrote romantically of the pains and pleasures to be derived from opium. The latter in one such passage: "I had heard of it as I had heard of manna or of ambrosia, but no further. How unmeaning a sound was opium at that time! What solemn chords does it now strike upon my heart! I was necessarily ignorant of the whole art and mystery of opium taking; and what I took, I took under every disadvantage. But I took it, and in an hour oh heavens! What a revulsion! What a resurrection from its lowest depths of the inner spirit! What an apocalypse of the world within me!" He went on to talk glowingly about opium as revealing an abyss of divine enjoyment, as a panacea, or pharmaconepenthe for all human woes, the secret of happiness which might now be bought for a penny, a portable ecstasy, and a source of peace of mind.

The isolation of morphine from *Papaver somniferum* in 1800; the invention of the hypodermic needle in the 1840s; the production of diacetylmorphine (heroin) in 1898; widespread narcotics use during and after the American Civil War; extensive distribution and use of patent medicines and tonics such as Lydia Pinkham's containing opium and/or alcohol; and the importation of opium by Chinese immigrants all led to the spread of narcotic use and addiction in the United States (and other Western countries). Also heroin (and later Demerol) was for years touted as a safe, nonaddicting substitute for morphine.

Appearing much more recently in human history, receiving considerable early vilification, and becoming probably the most widespread of all the mind-altering drugs, because of, or possibly even despite, their relative mildness as drugs, are caffeine and nicotine.

TOBACCO (NICOTINE)

Exactly when the Indians of the New World began using tobacco will probably never be known, but in 1492 when Columbus arrived, he and his men first witnessed the practice in a small Cuban village. A rolled tobacco leaf was placed in one nostril, lit up, and inhaled several times to get a "pickup" by relieving tiredness and monotony. Within half a century, Spaniards were almost totally converted to tobacco. In the meantime, in the sixteenth century, English explorers had observed Nicaraguan Indian women smoking in the same manner and had causally related this practice to the sexual ardor and passion they experienced with these women. So they shipped it (the tobacco) home, and by 1614, there were 7,000 tobacco shops in London alone, although there is no evidence that passion was successfully transmitted across the ocean or between sexes. With the development of cigarette mass production, distribution techniques, advertising, and the emancipation of women, smoking quickly spread throughout the Western world and later to other regions. Perhaps because the plant *Nicotiana tabacum* requires, like corn and bananas, careful cultivation, its production and use have become most widespread in the (southern) United States, where it now constitutes an eight-billion-dollar-a-year industry, and where Americans alone smoked 544 billion cigarettes in 1968.

Probably the full history of nicotine and tobacco use goes back at least hundreds of years prior to the events mentioned above, since archeologists have found what appear to be tobacco pipes dating back long before 1492, and there is also evidence of tobacco drinking by certain South American tribes. Nevertheless, it is striking that in less than 500 years, the substance has swept the world, being used by the vast majority of the adult population of the industrialized or economically overdeveloped world, a significant proportion of those in underdeveloped nations, and millions of children in addition to adult men and women. All of this despite the fact that nicotine, besides being a stimulant, is one of the most potent poisons known, and despite the toxic substances in cigarette paper and the overwhelming evidence of death and disability from the tobacco coal tars. Additional vast quantities of the drug are consumed throughout the world in the form of hand-rolled cigarettes and cigars, pipe tobacco, manufactured cigars, snuff, and chewing tobacco.

COFFEE-TEA-CHOCOLATE (CAFFEINE)

In one sense, probably the most widely used of all the mind-altering drugs is actually caffeine in the form of coffee, tea, chocolate, and colas because of the regularity and multiple doses involved in even ordinary use, wide availability, relative mildness, and low cost. It became an important commodity of trade by the fifth century A.D. and spread to Japan around A.D. 600, where it led to the development of probably the most elaborate religious use of a mind-altering drug, the tea ritual or tea ceremony of Buddhism-Shinto. An exponent of this once wrote: "Teaism is a cult founded on the adoration of the beautiful among the sordid facts of everyday existence. It inculcates purity and harmony, the mystery of mutual charity, the romanticism of the social order. It is essentially a worship of the imperfect as it is a tender attempt to accomplish something possible in this impossible thing we know as life." Later named *Thea sinensis* by Linnaeus and related botanically to the camellia, the plant first reached Venice (and thereafter the rest of Europe) in 1559 and led to the development of the East India Company, of notoriety for the already described opium trade. Tea reached America in 1665 through Dutch importation to New Amsterdam and was, of course, involved in still another international conflict associated with drugs, the Boston Tea Party. Although generally popular throughout the world, in modern times tea consumption has achieved its greatest heights in England, where in the 1950s a medical member of the House of Commons stated that "the national intake of pure caffeine is about 50 million pounds annually. Some persons consider ten cups of tea per day a normal consumption. It is apparent that some people who would never think of drinking beer intoxicate themselves by taking an excessive amount of caffeine through their tea. They then pose before us as virtuous people, forgetting that they are the truest type of drug addicts, because caffeine is a true cerebral stimulant." As might be expected, like comparable and in fact far more serious complaints relating to cigarettes, this received little attention and per capita consumption of tea in England is now in excess of ten pounds per year for every man, woman, and child, or roughly 15 to 20 grains of caffeine per day. Not only chocolate, but other plants, such as guarana and kola nut, are sources of caffeine, but for a variety of reasons the *Coffea arabica* plant has become the most widely cultivated drug or beverage plant since its misty origins in ancient Ethiopia or Abyssinia. Its use as a medicine for keeping the sleepy awake is mentioned in an eleventh-century Arabian medical text, and it quickly came to be used by Catholic monks and by Moslems to keep from dozing during periods of scheduled religious reverence. In 1554 the first known coffeehouse was opened in Constantinople, in the 1580s coffee reached northern Europe through the German explorer Reuwolf, and in the early 1600s it reached England via Persia. Its use generally, and in coffeehouses, rapidly spread (there were eight in Leipzig alone in 1725), particularly after the pleasures of mixing it with sugar were discovered. Bach in his satirical *Coffee Cantata* describes great parental concern and strict measures to get a young girl to give up coffee, but love and coffee triumph in the end.

As has seemingly occurred with all substances sought after for (and sometimes giving) pleasure throughout history, religious zealots, moralists, reformers, kings, and politicians unsuccessfully sought to ban coffeehouses and to condemn the drug and its users, in England (and its American colonies), Germany, and elsewhere. Others, as in contemporary life, welcomed it as a source of revenue. Despite this, and because of it, it rapidly spread, particularly in the twentieth century, to enormous worldwide use by all age groups, now amounting to 40 million bags (each weighing 132 pounds) per year and in the United States alone, 20 pounds per year for every man, woman, and child. Other widely used stimulants, of a milder type, are betel nut in Asia, khat in Africa, kava in the Pacific islands, and the more potent ephedrine found in "Mormon Tea" and used 5,000 years ago in China.

COCAINE-AMPHETAMINES

The most potent (plant) stimulant, and one with a very long history, is cocaine, obtained from *Erythroxylon coca*, the divine plant of the Incas, whose rulers had made extensive use of it. The leaves of this plant are now regularly chewed by as many as ten million Andean Indians (sometimes as many as 90 percent of adult males) in Peru, Boliva, Colombia, and Argentina. This is done to better tolerate the cold of these mountainous areas, to alleviate fatigue, and reduce hunger. In the form of the leaf, and also the purified cocaine, there is limited quasilegal and illegal use of this drug in the large cities of South America, North America, and Western Europe and somewhat more extensive use in India and Pakistan. Perhaps paradoxically, the cocaine bush is grown primarily for the Coca-Cola Company, which uses the leaf (all drug extracted in recent decades) as a flavoring agent. Of the more potent stimulants (those considered "drugs" or "medicines" as opposed to "beverage"), amphetamines synthesized in 1933 are the most widely used in the Western world, both by prescription and illicitly. In 1965, the last year for which complete figures are available in America (the country most productive of these and other drugs), 153,000 pounds of amphetamines were produced, along with thousands of pounds of other central-nervous-system stimulants.

SEDATIVES-TRANQUILIZERS

Another popular and widely used and abused family of mind-altering drugs are the sedatives, hypnotics, and tranquilizers. Alcohol actually is in this family and is, of course, the most widely used and self-prescribed sedative, but of those synthesized as medicinal chemicals, the bromides are the oldest, dating back to 1857. At one time the latter group, particularly potassium bromide, was being used by millions in the West, and although now superseded by other sedatives, it is still a common ingredient of the over-the-counter "sedative"-headache remedy-nerve tonic often along with such ingredients as belladonna or scopolamine, an antihistaminic, and aspirin. Chloral hydrate (1869) and paraldehyde (1882) were other early and still widely used chemicals, but the most commonly used prescription sedatives are the barbiturates, which were first synthesized in 1912. One striking illustration of the quest for pleasure and relief of anxiety and tension is the 1965 production figure for barbiturates, 971,000 pounds. A more recent sedative, meprobamate, popularly known as Miltown or Equanil, had a production of 1,179,000 pounds in 1965 and the overall production of this family of drugs includes chlordiazepoxide (Librium) and the phenothiazine tranquilizers such as Thorazine, Compazine, and Stelazine, all produced and used in large quantities. Together, the sedatives and tranquilizers account for about 20 percent

of all physicians' prescriptions and are also the most commonly refilled of prescriptions. Then there are more than
a hundred popular over-the-counter pseudosedatives and
pseudotranquilizers.

LSD-TYPE DRUGS

Finally, with only passing mention of such miscellaneous
psychopharmacological, or mind-affecting, substances as
nitrous oxide and carbon dioxide, glue and gasoline fumes,
nutmeg and mace which are used by additional numbers of
people, we come to the drug family which has received the
most recent sensationalistic attention, the psychedelics or
hallucinogens. Among the oldest of these for which we have
records are ololiuqui from the *Rivea corymbosa* plant and
mescaline from the peyote or *Lophophora williamsii*
cactus, both of them used for hundreds of years prior to
the Spanish conquest by the Indians of Mexico and Central
America. Another plant used by the same peoples and for
similar purposes was the so-called magic mushroom or
teonanacatl ("the flesh of God"), *Psilocybe mexicana*. There
are several species of morning glory which contain indole
alkaloids producing "consciousness-expansion." These
prophetically named species are Heavenly Blue, Pearly
Gates, Flying Saucer, Summer Skies, Blue Star, and Wedding Bells, all of them once easily obtainable from seed
racks or catalogues in the United States but now usually
coated with insecticides or otherwise "neutralized." To this
list of naturally occurring "hallucinogens" must be added
the fly agaric used by Siberian peasants, pituri used by
Australian tribesmen, and caapi used by Colombian Indians. More recently has come the Hawaiian woodrose.
Botanists and anthropologists have discovered more than
fifty species of plants that some call *Phantastica,* most of
which contain alkaloids such as atropine (in *Datura stra-
monium* or jimson weed) or scopolamine (hyoscyamine).

However, despite their long history in diverse cultures,
all of these, including the peyote used by American Indian

members of the Native American Church, remained basically esoterica or curiosities until the advent of LSD started the psychedelic preoccupation or aberration.

LSD-25, or d-lysergic acid diethylamide, was first synthesized by the Swiss chemist Hofman (in 1938), who later accidentally discovered its profound mind-altering properties, in 1943.

What happened thereafter can be roughly divided into three phases. The first began with Hofman's discovery (during his twenty-fifth experiment in a series of tests of synthetic substances derived from the ergot fungus) of LSD and extended roughly ten years to the early 1950s. During this time, research focused on the then assumed "psychotomimetic" properties of the drug, seeking to imitate and study the loss of contact with reality, delusions, and hallucinations of schizophrenia. Also during this period research on the biochemistry of the mind and brain occurred utilizing LSD as a tool. In the 1950s came a series of studies on the use of LSD in psychotherapy and other positive uses in creativity, problem solving, and religious exploration. Then in 1963 came the highly publicized separation of Doctors Timothy Leary and Richard Alpert from the Harvard faculty because of their formal and informal psilocybin and LSD experimentation with Harvard students, convicts, and other special groups. The yellow journalism which followed popularized LSD in the same way that Hollywood stars and politicians are "made" through highly selective, exaggerated, and lurid presentations in the mass media. At that time there were already several thousand articles and books, mostly scientific, on LSD and the closely related drugs, such as mescaline and psilocybin, but this had attracted little public interest or concern prior to the sensationalism. With the tremendous publicity came a wave of nonmedical, self-experimental, and generally indiscriminate use of LSD-type drugs, at first overtly, and then later, after ambitious politicians had competed over which would be first to make it a crime, clandestinely. As it was driven underground, it became increasingly difficult to

ascertain what was happening and all that was talked about
were the bad "trips." New similar but less studied substances were synthesized and substituted for LSD, including STP, DMT, and several others.

As many as a million or more people in the United States
have probably tried LSD or the related synthetic or naturally occurring substances, most of them using them only
once or a few times. Medical and scientific use continues
in England, Czechoslovakia (at least up to the time of the
Russian invasion), and Canada, and there is some illicit use
occurring in Europe and England primarily among young
people influenced by the tales from America. The traditional cultural use of the many naturally occurring LSD-
type substances discussed above continues, and should be
seen as an important component of the worldwide picture
in regard to psychedelic use.

CHAPTER 3
Never Send To Ask Who Is the Drug User

> "That humanity at large will ever be able to dispense
> with artificial paradises seems very unlikely." A. HUXLEY

It should by now be clear that when one talks about the
full context of drug usage, essentially everyone is a drug
user even if the discussion is restricted solely to mind-
altering substances. As we now attempt to assess the present dimensions of use and abuse of the major mind-altering
drugs in America, we have the advantage, in the case of the
generally approved and legal drugs, of production and sales
figures, and with all the drugs, recent survey data, but in no
instance do we have anything equivalent to a house-to-
house census of users or abusers. With those drugs that have
been driven underground, reliable data become even more
difficult to obtain, and arrest records and seizures of illicit
drugs are at best only a partial indication of what is happening. Self-serving statements by drug policemen and their
agencies or other government departments, and overblown
accounts of isolated individual or group drug experiences
have contributed greatly to the incorrect impressions existing in our society about drug use and drug problems.

MARIJUANA

Although it ranks well below caffeine, nicotine, and alcohol in the extent of use (and abuse), let us begin with
marijuana, which is receiving the greatest public attention
now as *the* drug problem. Estimates by various writers and
spokesmen on this subject range from one million to 12
million current users. Ordinarily such estimates fail to
distinguish between one who has used it once and one who

has used it repeatedly, and between an individual who has used it in the past and one using it currently. Bearing in mind the deficiencies of the available data, it seems reasonable to estimate the current number of pot users in the United States as between six million and twelve million. The tens of thousands of arrests for illegal marijuana possession or sale in 1967 and 1968, the seizure of tons of marijuana (generally estimated to represent, at most, one tenth of what is smuggled), and, most importantly, the results of scientific surveys of student populations, ghetto youth, and general adult drug use all testify to the reasonableness of such an estimate. Urban high schools from New York to California have reported 30 percent or more of their student bodies as using marijuana; often such reports, however, are very crude estimates by local school administrators or narcotics police rather than the result of carefully designed and administered sociological surveys which are responded to anonymously by a representative statistical sample of the total group.

In the summer of 1968, San Mateo County, California, a suburban area just south of San Francisco, made public a survey of its 19,000 high school students, finding that 32 percent had tried marijuana and more than half of these had used it ten times or more.

In surveys I have personally directed or supervised of almost 9,000 young people in 20 Northern California school districts ranging from the fourth to the twelfth grades, I found in the most complete one, involving an urban heterogeneous population (Berkeley), that 24 percent of *seventh-grade* boys and 22 percent of the girls had had *opportunities to smoke* marijuana, with 18 percent of the boys and 12 percent of the girls having *tried it*. In the *eighth grade* of this school district, 45 percent of the boys and 39 percent of the girls had had the drug available, with 27 percent and 18 percent respectively using it. Skipping on to *tenth grade*, we find that just over 60 percent of both boys and girls had had the opportunity to try the drug, and 38 percent of the boys and 43 percent of the girls went on to use marijuana. By the *twelfth grade*, 64 percent of the boys and 61 percent of the girls had had the chance to use it, and 41 percent of the boys and 43 percent of the girls had done so. At the time of the completion of the survey in the spring of 1968 *ongoing or continuing users* of marijuana (carrying no implication of frequency or excessive dosage) included nine percent of *seventh-grade* boys and six percent of the girls; 25 percent of *eighth-grade* boys and 11 percent of the girls; 29 percent of *tenth-grade* boys and 34 percent of the girls; and 37 percent of *twelfth-grade* boys and 32 percent of the girls. Even by the seventh grade, almost half of the students responding in the survey knew people who smoked marijuana, and by the twelfth grade, more than 75 percent of the respondents knew someone doing so. Usually these were friends their own age, but also commonly they were older friends, with about five percent being parents who themselves "turn on" with "grass." About half of the students saw no differences between those their own age who smoked marijuana and those who did not. Fewer than a third at each of the grade levels responded that they found anything good about marijuana smoking, while roughly half stated in answering another question that they found something bad about such smoking. Disappointingly, and pointing to one of the difficulties this society faces in seeking to reduce drug usage, only a small minority in each of the grades said that there were facts that they would like to learn about marijuana.

In a smaller, more homogeneous middle-class residential community surveyed as part of the same study, we found that five percent of *sixth graders* had had the *opportunity to try* marijuana, increasing up to 56 percent of *twelfth graders*. An *overall* 16 percent of the students had *tried* the drug sometime, and 12 percent were using it regularly. Looking at *twelfth grade* alone, 25 percent had tried it, and 18 percent were using it with some degree of regularity.

Blum of Stanford's Institute for Human Problems, surveying 1,300 students at five colleges, found that roughly 20 percent had used marijuana at least once, half of these using it intermittently—less than five times a year—and most of the rest about once a week or less.

Simon and Gagnon, then at Indiana's Institute for Sex Research, found in a national survey of college youth that 15 percent had used marijuana, five percent of them were using it regularly, and only half as many girls as boys were involved in this use.

A survey by the Family Research Institute's Mannheimer and Mellinger of the general adult population of San Francisco revealed that 13 percent had used marijuana at some time in their lives. All of these studies were done in 1968.

The "numbers game" is often overdone in our society. But in any case, far more significant than the number of millions involved is the fact that marijuana use now pervades all socioeconomic, occupational, and age groups in American society. In addition to Negro and Mexican-American youth, the "hippies," the pop musicians, and the college students, usually thought of as *the* pot smokers, we have businessmen, housewives, doctors, judges, policemen, professors, white- and blue-collar workers, journalists, and socialites all blowing a little pot now and then, and sometimes regularly. Prominent hostesses have been known to serve a little grass to their friends instead of, or in addition to, the usual selection of alcoholic drugs. Some celebrities openly carry a "lid" of marijuana in their cars or on their person to be used in the course of their day's activities. Peace Corps volunteers in Africa, Asia, and Latin America often go along with local customs in occasionally using the plant. Regular use by half or more of the 500,000 American soldiers in Vietnam has been repeatedly reported by returning veterans and outside observers, who also indicate that the plant is easily available both in combat areas and in Saigon markets. Army, Navy, and Air Force personnel are showing increasing interest in the drug, whether stationed in this country or in the foreign lands of our allies.

Knowing that there are some seven million college students, and about six million people in each of the young-adult age groups, 18, 19, 20, etc., if we generalize from the several estimates of one-in-five to one-in-seven college students, my own surveys, and the surveys of others as described above, and the police statistics, one is faced with the unpleasant fact that there are clearly millions of users in spite of, and because of, the drug laws and their enforcers, and the values of the older generations.

Remembering that neither marijuana nor any other drug is harmless, and that any of these drugs sought for pleasure can sometimes have dangerous effects, one is still left with very limited specific evidence or documentation on abuses of marijuana. That some may find this statement startling or difficult to accept reflects the narrow and incomplete context usually used in discussing the subject and the lack of definition of what constitutes an abuse or problem. If, for example, you subjectively or moralistically decide that any use of a given drug, or any illegal use of it, is "abuse," then the words and concepts lose all meaning, and neither understanding nor solution is possible. Thus a psychiatric administrator in New York in his public statements for various governmental and medical-political bodies states without elaboration that marijuana is harmful and dangerous, producing changes in mood, volition, and memory, with occasional outbursts of sudden psychotic behavior in people taking the drug for a long time in large doses. As an afterthought he sometimes adds that the reaction depends also on the mental set of the individual, his expectations, and his basic personality. He may also add under direct questioning, as in a Boston court room in 1967, that "there are no known and demonstrated pathological effects directly due to the action of the drug." Abuses frequently mentioned in such political testimony include psychic dependence, vagabondage, chronic disease, and psychiatric disability. Another New York "expert," an even more regular witness for the prosecution and a bacteriologist by profession, again without laying any basic groundwork for meaningful comparisons, always rushes in to state that marijuana is harmful and dangerous because it causes acute panic reactions, acute intoxication, acute psychosis, deterioration of personality, is entirely unpredictable in its effects, leads some people to the use of more dangerous drugs such as heroin or LSD, distorts time and space perception, causes traffic accidents and leads to proselytizing marijuana use by others. As a final example of this type of thinking, there is a Greek physician who has stated that he can recognize a chronic marijuana user from afar by the way he walks, talks, and acts: slurred speech, lethargy, lowered inhibitions, and loss of morality. Like the others he is not at all inhibited in his statements by never having worked with marijuana or its users.

Some objective criteria are very much needed of what constitutes abuse with any drug, and unless better ones are developed, measurable impairment of social and/or vocational adjustment or damage to one's health must remain the criteria. Whether a given drug-induced phenomenon has been noted to occur spontaneously or has had to be searched for; the frequency of such occurrences as compared to the number of instances of use and the number of users; the number of years during which the drug has been available for observation and recording of possible detrimental effects; the basis for making the judgment, i.e., training and experience of the "judge," types of questions asked, kinds of observations made, and the presence or absence of control groups: With all these things in mind and recognizing the thousands of years of general use of marijuana and the many decades of use in this country by millions of people, the incidence of verifiable, documented abuses is very small, in and of itself, and by comparison with other widely used mind-altering drugs. Usually what is talked about in discussing the dangers of marijuana is what *might be* rather than what is or was, and one hears accounts of (possible) relationships to driving accidents, sexual behavior, crime, and mental illness, all of a highly speculative, and sometimes illogical nature. Whether a particular effect is temporary or permanent is another important dimension, and fortunately, in the case of marijuana, the abuses that have been reported consist of clinical cases of acute "psychotic reactions" numbering fewer than 50, and the experimental induction of such "psychoses" with large doses of synthetic delta-9-tetrahydrocannabinol (the active principle of marijuana) given to 30 former heroin addicts in prison. It would be strange indeed if some such episodes did not occur, since the underlying personality of the user is so important to the mind-altering drug effect, and the amount and purity of the marijuana smoked is never certain. Obviously, in some instances a temporarily or permanently unstable personality will take an excessive dose of the drug, and have an adverse reaction.

As with any inhaled smoke, there is temporary irritation of the throat and bronchial tree, the degree and extent of which will depend on the frequency of smoking, which of course is much less than with tobacco cigarettes.

No deaths, no permanent damage to body organs, and no lasting psychoses have been reported resulting solely from marijuana use. No addiction or physical dependency occurs, but psychological dependency or habituation does occur with a certain number of users as with all the mind-altering drugs and may sometimes be damaging. The possibility of driving or other accidents certainly exists with this or any other potent drug, but there are no authenticated reports of such accidents stemming from marijuana, so those concerned about this should properly devote themselves to the enormous and well-documented problem of drunk driving. Finally, the fact that a given drug doesn't "kill" in no way indicates that it will give pleasure to everybody or is inherently desirable or beneficial.

ALCOHOL

Approximately 80 million Americans are users of the drug alcohol, including three-fourths of all adults of all socioeconomic and occupational groups. As shown by the earlier production figures, even among adults a significant segment

of this involves illegal use of "moonshine," and generally
for those under twenty-one (sometimes eighteen) involves
a willful, deliberate violation of the criminal law.

The aforementioned Blum survey data showed more than
90 percent of college students as users of alcohol. Almost
65 percent of the San Mateo County, California, high school
students (ages 14-19) reported at least one-time usage and
25 percent said that they have used alcoholic beverages
ten or more times. My own Berkeley survey found 67 percent of *seventh-grade* boys and 70 percent of the girls had
tried alcohol, with ten percent of the boys and eight percent
of the girls regularly using it. By the *twelfth grade*, 71 percent of the boys and 87 percent of the girls had tried the
drug and 18 percent of the boys and 24 percent of the girls
were regularly using it. Thus alcohol (and nicotine) ranks
well ahead of pot in popularity and law violation. More
than half of all of these students in each of the grades surveyed were with their parents when they first used alcohol.
The majority responded negatively to the question about
whether they thought there was anything good about
people of their age drinking, and more than half said they
found something wrong in people their age drinking. Only
a small percentage at all grade levels indicated that there
were any facts they would like to learn about alcohol.

Nothing more clearly reveals the overwhelming hypocrisy of American society than the massive, completely
authenticated abuses of alcohol and the relatively scant
public or professional attention given to this problem. At
least six million of our citizens are alcoholics or problem
drinkers, meaning chronic excessive users of alcohol to an
extent damaging to their health, or social and vocational
adjustment. The estimates of alcoholism incidence are
based upon the Jellinek formula, which mathematically
extrapolates from the number of deaths due to cirrhosis of
the liver (caused mainly by alcoholism). California has a
disproportionately high number of the nation's alcoholics
(750,000) and the city of San Francisco a disproportionately
high number of the alcoholic Californians. There are more

alcoholics in metropolitan San Francisco alone than narcotics addicts in the entire United States, an eye-opening
statistic for people who have been lied to since childhood
about narcotics addiction being *the* drug problem. Associated with alcoholism are many millions of man-hours of
absenteeism from work and loss of jobs, which together are
estimated to cost American firms two billion dollars per
year. One-third to one-half of all arrests by police in
America are for chronic drunkenness, usually involving
Skid Row alcoholics (other more affluent alcoholics being
handled quite differently by society). Cirrhosis is the sixth
leading cause of death in this country (fourth in San Francisco); as many as 20 percent of the inmates of state mental
hospitals are there because of chronic psychosis due to
alcoholic brain damage, an *irreversible* condition. A number
of less obvious important social phenomena such as marital
conflict and divorces, sexual indiscretions, welfare dependency, and child neglect are also associated with
chronic alcoholism. Physical dependency (addiction) occurs in those alcoholics who use the drug daily in large and
increasing amounts over a period of weeks or months, and
the withdrawal illness, commonly known as DT's or delirium tremens, is the most severe of all the drug-withdrawal
syndromes with more than half of untreated cases having
either generalized convulsions and/or a toxic psychosis
(delirium), and up to ten percent dying.

More than half of those in our jails and prisons for crimes
against the person or property, including murder, rape,
theft, burglary, and embezzlement, committed these crimes
in association with (excessive) alcohol use. Many suicides
and accidental deaths involve heavy consumption of alcohol, often in combination with a biologically identical drug,
barbiturates. Between 50 percent and 70 percent of the
almost 55,000 deaths and 2.5 million severe injuries each
year from automobile accidents involve or are caused by
alcohol. Habituation is common, and innumerable business,
police, and political decisions are made by those under the
influence of the drug, if not by alcoholics. As a source of

calories, but with no food value, alcohol adds to America's obesity problem (and often malnutrition), and its physiological effects on the stomach and other body organs foster or cause peptic ulcers and other illnesses to develop. Lastly its cost represents for many a significant diversion of income from other, more essential matters.

NICOTINE

It is commonly estimated that about 75 million to 80 million Americans smoke cigarettes, including about two-thirds of adult males and one-third of adult females, again in all socioeconomic and occupational groups. Roughly 3,000 for every man, woman, and child, or eight cigarettes daily per capita are consumed in this country alone or almost 600 billion yearly. College student surveys find that about 75 percent have used tobacco, and the previously cited San Mateo County survey found 56 percent of high school students had smoked tobacco at least once, and most of them ten times or more. My survey of the Berkeley schools revealed that only 30 percent of *seventh-grade* boys and 40 percent of the girls had *never tried* tobacco, and by the *twelfth grade*, only 17 percent of the boys and 18 percent of the girls had not tried. The students usually began smoking with someone their own age, but not uncommonly they were with older users or with their own parents. Some 12 percent of seventh-grade boys and eight percent of the girls *smoked regularly*, escalating to 35 percent of the boys and 22 percent of the girls in twelfth grade. Only about one-quarter of both boys and girls in the seventh grade found anything good about smoking, and about four-fifths felt that there was something bad about it. One third of twelfth graders saw something good about smoking, and about four-fifths, something bad. Only 20 percent of the seventh graders and ten percent of the twelfth graders expressed a desire for more facts about tobacco. In another school district I found a significant minority of fourth graders already smoking and on the road to premature death.

Historically, concern about abuses of nicotine and coal tars, the two major components of tobacco cigarettes (which also contain small amounts of arsenic, cyanide, carbon monoxide, and other noxious substances), began with spontaneous observation of the high frequency of lung cancer among smokers. The first definitive study confirming the causal relationship was published in 1954 and by 1968 some 12,000 books and articles on the social and health hazards of cigarette smoking had been published. No other form of drug abuse has been so extensively studied and measured. It has been found, for example, that Americans who smoke cigarettes experience in their lifetimes millions more episodes of chronic illness than comparable numbers of nonsmokers, including a million more cases of chronic bronchitis or emphysema, two million extra cases of sinusitis, and one million more cases of peptic ulcer. Smokers spend three million more days on restricted activity each year than nonsmokers, including almost a million more days in bed due to illness. More than 50,000 people a year die from lung cancer, the major cause of which is tobacco-cigarette smoking. The rate of occurrence (and death) of lung cancer has increased ten times in the past 30 years. It is now estimated that, if present trends continue, about one million children now in school will die of lung cancer before the age of seventy. Those smoking two or more packs of cigarettes per day have a 20 times greater chance of dying from lung cancer than nonsmokers, and regular smokers in general have an annual lung-cancer death rate seven times as high as nonsmokers.

About 60,000 men die prematurely in the United States each year from heart attacks associated with the smoking of cigarettes, and another 10,000 die prematurely from other diseases in addition to the already mentioned lung cancer. Death rates from heart attacks are much higher among smokers than among nonsmokers. Thus, it can be said that cigarette smoking is directly responsible for the premature deaths of more than 125,000 Americans each year, and the overall cigarette-related mortality figure is

300,000, according to the U.S. Public Health Service. Even minimal or occasional smoking temporarily impairs the normal functioning of the breathing apparatus and larynx; constricts blood vessels (aggravating arteriosclerosis); sets off an allergic response in those sensitive to tobacco; interferes with gastrointestinal functioning; pollutes the air space of other human beings in schools, homes, restaurants, and airplanes, producing not only unpleasantness and discomfort but actual physiological harm; and kills and injures many thousands each year from home and forest fires plus destruction of property. The distraction involved in lighting and smoking a cigarette probably is a significant factor in many traffic (and other) accidents. Large sums of money are spent on the drug, and psychological dependence is usual, with many people finding it more difficult to overcome than the heroin (or other narcotics) habit.

SEDATIVES, STIMULANTS, AND TRANQUILIZERS

Three members of these families of mind-altering drugs, alcohol (sedative), nicotine (stimulant), and marijuana (sedative-stimulant) have been discussed separately.

Caffeine, in concentrated therapeutic doses used medically, is a potent central-nervous-system stimulant, but must be considered mild in the doses found with ordinary beverage consumption. Mainly because of its ready availability and low cost, along with the absence of significant side effects, caffeine appears to be the most widely used of all mind-altering drugs in America, in the form of cola drinks, cocoa, coffee, and tea consumed by the vast majority of people of all ages beyond infancy. Abuses such as overstimulation may occur in both children and adults, with insomnia, restlessness, irritability, and cardiac irregularity. Both increased gastric secretion and increased blood pressure occur, so the drug can aggravate peptic ulcers and hypertension. Psychic dependency on caffeine is very common, but seems not to be a form of drug abuse since there is no impairment of functioning and in fact such functioning may often be improved.

The use, including legitimate medical use, and abuse of cocaine, the most potent stimulant drug, is negligible in the United States and does not merit extensive discussion here. It is usually sniffed or snorted as a white flaky powder known as "snow." As tolerance develops the user shifts to intravenous (IV) injections sometimes combined with heroin as a "speedball." With prolonged sniffing, perforations of the nasal septum occur. The potential abuses are similar to those described below for amphetamines, but more likely to occur. The cost of the drug is high and sources of supply are few compared with other illegal drugs.

The approved sedative-stimulant-tranquilizer drugs available to physicians for prescribing number more than 300, including tablets, capsules, syrups, Spansules, suppositories, and elixirs. Additionally, there are a multitude of over-the-counter (nonprescription) compounds variously promoted as pain-killers, relaxants, energizers, tension relievers, "sedatives," "tranquilizers," or fatigue relievers. These substances contain a combination of homeopathic or less than therapeutic doses of an antihistaminic, aspirin, and belladonna. If they ever have more than a placebo effect, it depends on unpredictable and inconsistent side effects of the active ingredients, such as drowsiness from the antihistamines. The total number of users is unknown, but judging from the sales and profit figures available, it must range into the millions. Diversion of income, psychological dependency, and the sometime use of the belladonna for hallucinatory purposes are all possible "problems."

The number of users of prescribed sedatives (some of them falsely advertised as tranquilizers), mainly barbiturates and meprobamate (Miltown, Equanil); stimulants, mainly amphetamines; and tranquilizers, mainly phenothiazines (Thorazine, Compazine, Stelazine) and Chlordiazepoxide (Librium), probably is somewhere between 20 million and 25 million, bearing in mind the production and prescribing figures previously cited. One study of patients admitted to the general medical and surgical wards of a large hospital found that almost 20 percent were users of one or more of these drugs. More than a hundred single-dosage pills or capsules for every man, woman, and child in America could be made from the total quantity produced each year, as much as half of which is said by federal authorities to pass into black-market distribution. In general, doctors over-prescribe these substances, patients overrequest them, sometimes from several doctors. Almost everyone coming to physicians, including psychiatrists, for treatment of psychotic, neurotic, psychosomatic, or just nonspecific symptoms is placed on tranquilizers or other psychotropic drugs for an indefinite period.

The college survey found that about 30 percent of students had used sedatives at least once, 25 percent, amphetamines, and almost 20 percent, tranquilizers. In the Berkeley schools that I surveyed, five percent of the boys and four percent of the girls in the *seventh grade* had tried sleeping pills or tranquilizers without a prescription and without parental approval; 13 percent of each in the *tenth grade;* and 10 percent of the boys and 15 percent of the girls in *twelfth grade*. As for amphetamines, about five percent of both sexes in *seventh grade* have tried them; 12 percent of *tenth graders;* and 15 percent of *twelfth graders*. The findings were similar in other districts I surveyed.

A considerable amount of the overall use of these drugs can be considered misuse — nonspecific, excessive in amount or the duration of time used, serving to obscure real causes while treating symptoms, or not being beneficial.

Because it often goes unrecognized even by physicians; is often untreated, particularly in the instance of illicit use; and since other diagnoses are frequently given for insurance purposes, figures of abuse are difficult to come by, but it is likely that about 500,000 of the millions of users can be considered abusers. With true tranquilizers, it is particularly difficult to define abuse because of the involuntary nature of the phenomenon (the drug being urged on the patient by the physician) and the individual's disturbed mental state. There is also the complex question of differentiating toxic side effects from abuse. We know that a significant minority of those taking tranquilizing drugs will have physical or mental reactions including skin rash, light sensitivity, rigidity of the muscles, hepatitis, and a kind of robotization or blunting of emotion and activity.

The most serious abuse of the sedative drugs—also known as hypnotics or sleeping pills, including barbiturates, meprobamate, chloral hydrate, and glutethimide (Doriden)—is accidental death or suicide from an overdose, occurring in more than 10,000 Americans each year, particularly women, with a much greater number being temporarily disabled when the amount ingested is less than lethal. Physical dependency (addiction) is not uncommon with the sedatives, and the withdrawal illness is severe and generally comparable to that of alcohol withdrawal. Drowsiness, morning hangovers, diversion of time and money, and psychic dependency would be other more common occurrences with prolonged use.

With regular daily excessive use of the amphetamines, tolerance, in addition to psychological dependence, develops, often accompanied by restlessness, irritability, insomnia, and loss of appetite and weight. If nothing occurs to interrupt the sequence of events, this will progress to an amphetamine psychosis characterized by delusions of persecution and hallucinations. This is becoming more common in association with indiscriminate use of "speed," (methedrine or methamphetamine) in our large cities. Inability to work, diversion of money and energy, and possible accidents would also enter into the picture.

NARCOTICS

Narcotics—including opium, morphine, codeine, Demerol, methadone, and others—are used on a short-term basis by millions of Americans each year to relieve severe pain and treat other medical conditions. A large number of these users become addicted legally in connection with incurable cancer and other protracted conditions. Illicit use and addiction involves mainly heroin and various cough syrups containing significant amounts of one of these substances. Official estimates of the extent of illicit addiction vary widely. The Federal Bureau of Narcotics (since mid-1968 part of the Bureau of Narcotics and Dangerous Drugs) each year convinces Congress it has been effective by carefully underestimating the number of addicts while at the same time attempting to show that it remains a big enough menace to justify the "dope fiend" mythology which has always been the mainstay of its existence. Excluding the pleasure-seeking use of cough syrups by at least hundreds of thousands, the number of illicit narcotic addicts is probably around 100,000, with 50 percent of them in New York City and 15,000 in California, three-quarters in the Los Angeles metropolitan area. There are additional numbers of intermittent users of heroin or other licit and illicit narcotics, but most regular users must expect physical dependency to develop and eventually the focusing of their life energies and all available funds on obtaining supplies of the drug. About one percent of college students surveyed have used narcotics and in the largest metropolitan school district I surveyed three percent of both boys and girls in seventh, eighth, and tenth grades had tried (not become addicted to) heroin, while five percent of the boys and eight percent of the girls in twelfth grade had done so. Other than its high potential for inducing physical dependency (along with psychological dependency) and its capability for inducing death from an overdose, like any other depressant drug, there is little specific abuse that can be directly attributed to heroin or morphine. Most of the phenomena ordinarily associated with heroin addiction and thought of as "the problem" are effects of our social and legal policies rather than of the drug itself, i.e., the drug being obtainable only on the black market and at extremely high prices (leading to crimes against property to get money), and the handling of users as criminals, thereby preventing rehabilitation. Some estimate that about 100 deaths per year occur in New

York City from (mostly) accidental overdoses due to the person's not knowing the purity or concentration of what he is taking. Increasing thousands of cases of hepatitis are occurring among both heroin users and the even more common injectors of "speed," both due to the use of un-sterile needles and temporary physical deterioration. These and skin abscesses must be listed as complications of heroin addiction, but fortunately—and paradoxically, in terms of most people's conception of this form of drug abuse—there are no permanent effects on body organs. Addicted pregnant women inadvertently transfer their cellular dependency on the drug through the placenta so that some hundreds of newborn infants are born each year with a physical dependency which can prove fatal if un-reported or unrecognized.

LSD-TYPE DRUGS

In addition to continuing and for the most part legal use of peyote by the Indians of the Native American Church and very limited scientific use, there are probably several hundred thousand occasional users of LSD, mescaline, STP, DMT, and psilocybin and tens of thousands of regu-lar users. About six percent of college students sampled in two separate surveys had used "hallucinogens," with less than one percent of them regular users. The San Mateo study found that ten percent of their high-school students had tried LSD, with no indication as to regularity. In the two school districts with the largest student populations which I surveyed, Berkeley, a heterogeneous urban dis-trict, revealed (combining boys and girls) five percent of *seventh graders* had used LSD-type drugs, and about the same number were currently using them from time to time. About ten percent of *tenth graders* had used them with seven percent using them from time to time. By *twelfth grade,* nearly 40 percent had had an opportunity to use, 13 percent had used, and six percent were continuing to use one or another of these substances. About one-third of

seventh graders knew someone who used these drugs, and
about 75 percent of twelfth graders knew someone using
them, generally friends their own age or somewhat older,
but also including about one to two percent of parents.
About one-seventh of seventh graders indicated that there
was something good about such use, while almost three-
quarters said that there was something bad about it. One-
third of twelfth graders thought it was good, and, again,
about three-quarters, that there were bad aspects to it.
At all four grade levels only 17 percent overall said that
there were any facts they would like to know about these
drugs, although the girls of the upper grades showed almost
double this interest.

The second sample of students in grades six through
twelve of a medium-sized homogeneous suburban community revealed four percent overall use of LSD, with 22
percent having acquaintances using it, and nine percent
saying that most of their friends use it. Of the twelfth
graders, 32 percent had had a chance to try these drugs,
13 percent did try them, and nine percent continued to use
them. About 86 percent of this youth population stated
they would not try this family of drugs even if given the
opportunity.

Projecting or extrapolating from these figures, my
estimates of current and past use are probably conservative,
and it is clear that a considerable amount of experimentation and occasional use of LSD and the many others
available is occurring despite the criminal laws and hysteri-
cal polemics issued from the American Establishment. The
main changes have been a switching from one drug to
another, often one with greater risks; more hidden or "cool"
(and unsupervised) use, which, just as with prostitution,
seems to make many people happy as long as they don't see
it; more rejection by doctors and clinics; and greater
unwillingness to seek out professional guidance and treatment in connection with the use of these drugs for fear of
being reported to the police.

With scare stories dominating the public impression

about (ab)uses of LSD-type drugs, it is helpful in gaining perspective to go back to a less emotional time. Firstly, with the use for centuries of the naturally occurring psychedelics, or hallucinogens, spontaneous or even solicited reports of "problems" are rare. A survey by Cohen in 1960 gathered information on 5,000 people who had had a total of 25,000 LSD or mescaline sessions with average or large doses. There were no significant physical complications. "Psychotic" reactions lasting longer than two days occurred in less than two-tenths of one percent, and attempted suicides in one-tenth of one percent. Stafford and Golightly point out that, when the 5,000 are divided into mentally sound volunteers for experiments and mentally ill patients receiving treatment, one finds only one serious psychological complication in the "healthy," but among the "ill" given the drugs, prolonged psychoses occurred in one out of every 550 patients. Probably adverse reactions in connection with ordinary everyday nondrug psychotherapy are more common, particularly when one considers that at least some of the experimenters surveyed were attempting to induce a psychotic reaction in order to study the processes of schizophrenia. Less scientific and presumably less discriminate use is likely to increase the incidence of complications.

In the post-Leary period, reports from hospital emergency rooms, psychiatric wards, and drug-police agencies became dominant and still prevail, so that the forest in which the problem trees are growing is invisible or, more correctly, is kept hidden.

The real incidence of objective and verifiable abuses is very uncertain, not only for the already mentioned reasons, but also because the same phenomena occurring in one individual may be interpreted by him and by an outside pathologically oriented observer as a "bad trip," while another individual experiencing this same reaction may welcome it, or at least adapt to the changes in thinking and perception without difficulty. The underlying personality and character structure is most important with LSD-type drugs, as a determinant of the "effect"; and dosage, purity, preparation for the experience, setting or environment, and proper guidance are additional important variables. As a working hypothesis based on the literature and the reports made to me by many users, the incidence of the less serious, short-lived complications may be about one in 1,000 "trips," and the most serious or longer-lasting ones, one in 10,000 or fewer. Even when no noteworthy problem occurs, the intense, pervasive, and lengthy nature of an LSD experience can be most unpleasant and not in any way pleasant or beneficial. Much of the drug experience with any mind-altering drug is learned behavior, and a large proportion of the users fail to get what they anticipate, particularly with the first few experiences.

The most common abuse or side effect with the LSD family of drugs, especially with indiscriminate use ignoring dosage, purity, screening, and guidance, is an acute anxiety or panic reaction which is usually of short duration and without sequelae. This may include auditory and visual hallucinations, depression, with suicidal thoughts, confusion, and paranoid reactions. Some authorities on adverse reactions to LSD, such as J. Thomas Ungerleider believe that these bad trips are totally unpredictable, even with stable people who are properly prepared, while others who have worked with the drug in normative settings believe that careful selection of subjects and attention to all the variables will eliminate trouble.

The other, less common abuses associated with the LSD family of drugs include, in order of seriousness, recurrences of drug-induced perceptual phenomena at some future time, prolonged psychotic reactions, and accidental deaths or suicide. In regard to the first, there are those who actively seek a "consciousness-expanding experience" and therefore welcome the recurrence, which is generally of short duration. Where such an experience is unwelcome or unexpected, it can naturally be frightening and even disrupting or dangerous. Troublesome phenomena of this nature seem to be rare, but, like every other fact about drugs, people should be informed of the possibility so that they can voluntarily avoid such an occurrence. All of the persistent psychotic reactions appear to involve the intensification or precipitation of an already existing schizophrenia, which should not minimize its seriousness but rather should reemphasize the significance of the underlying mental state of the user. Again, the incidence or frequency is unknown, but most certainly there have been at least a couple of hundred such instances. Accidental death and suicide that seem to have some association with LSD-type drug use have, unlike the vastly more frequent violent episodes with alcohol and barbiturates, received great national attention, even though the total number involved in such incidents is no more than ten. In fact, considering the distortions and disturbances of perception, judgment, and thinking occurring during the hours the drug is exerting its effects on the person, it is surprising that dangerous behavior has not been more common. It becomes a popular practice for some individuals engaged in antisocial behavior to claim they are under the influence of certain drugs, thereby attempting to escape punishment, and it is also common for (mis)leading questions to be asked by policemen and some doctors, such as "You took LSD, didn't you?" when they first talk with the person under emergency circumstances. The deaths that do occur come from such things as misjudgment of distances or heights; perceptual distortions of the environment: for example, while standing on a cliff or driving across a bridge, believing that the ocean is a luxuriant carpet which one should roll in; and magical or delusional thinking, such as believing that an oncoming car will stop as one steps in front of it.

What is sometimes described as "dropping out," changing value systems, amotivation, or altered interpersonal relationships is considered by some as one of the LSD abuses, but this is the most difficult of all to assess, because it rests upon so many subjective value judgments. In the main, those whose life style is drastically altered in association with the use of LSD or other drugs are not as commonly believed fully satisfied, productive, happy people who suddenly, upon taking the drug, experience an immediate and profound "conversion" and drop out. Rather they are those who have been inclined toward something different or better than what they see around them presently and in the future, so that LSD or another drug may simply accelerate the process.

Headlines about LSD-induced blindness titillated the public on several occasions, fortunately leading to an investigation which revealed that a high government official in Pennsylvania had deliberately falsified the medical records of several former college students to make it seem as though blindness had resulted from LSD, when it was clearly due to other, "natural" causes. This not only blatantly exemplifies bureaucratic lying (more often observed with the State Department) and the irresponsibility of the mass media, but it clearly demonstrates how even perhaps well-intended distortions can backfire and lead to disbelief of all information about dangers, including those which are true. One *can* "cry wolf" too often.

Then we have the overblown charges that LSD produces birth defects in human infants. At a later point I will discuss the more complex questions involved in evaluating this (and the dropping-out allegation), but suffice it to say now that the "finding" that LSD produces breakage in human chromosomes (it was never found that it produced actual birth defects) remains inconclusive and ambiguous. Several studies report finding increased chromosomal breakage in human white blood cells (leucocytes) exposed to varying concentrations of LSD in test tubes, or coming from LSD users. *An equal number of studies, for the most part better done scientifically, have found no such increase*. Animal studies, usually of pregnant rats injected with LSD during the early part of the pregnancy, are similarly inconclusive. Failure to use control groups, subjective bias, technical difficulties, and other factors appear to enter into these diverse findings. Many, if not most, of the experimental subjects had used a variety of other potent mind-altering drugs which are either potentially or definitely capable of producing chromosomal breakage, and more. Although infants born of LSD-using mothers when examined show no birth defects, one case has been described of a baby with a deformed leg born to a woman who had apparently taken LSD on the twenty-fifth and forty-fifth days after her last menstrual period, and two additional times later. The safest course, the most scientifically valid, and the most humane, would be to advise all pregnant women (knowing that the fetus is most sensitive during the first three months of pregnancy) that if they are otherwise inclined to use, or expose themselves to, chemicals, radiation, viral conditions, aspirin and mind-altering drugs, including not only LSD, but alcohol, tranquilizers, nicotine, and caffeine, they should certainly avoid doing so during this period.

MISCELLANEOUS SUBSTANCES

The total number of users of an enormous variety of additional miscellaneous mind-altering substances must be in the millions when added together. This includes the inhalation of fumes from glue, gasoline, cleaning solvents, amyl nitrite ampoules, Asthmador inhalers, nitrous oxide from aerosol cans and other inhalants; nutmeg and other spices; plants and plant seeds; antihistaminics; atropine or scopolamine; carbon dioxide; and other "turn ons." Some six percent of college students surveyed had used these miscellaneous mind-altering substances. As an intimation of the future if we do not rapidly change our present approach, my junior and senior high school surveys found that 15 percent of the boys and seven percent of the girls in *seventh grade* had tried glue or gasoline sniffing; 11 percent of the boys and six percent of the girls in *tenth grade;* and eight percent of the boys and 11 percent of the girls in *twelfth grade*.

Not all of the drug use described above should be seen as addictive. Most people move from one drug to another, sometimes progressing or regressing, as the case may be, to more harmful substances; sometimes using several drugs at different times; and sometimes substituting a less (objectively) dangerous drug for a more dangerous drug, even though by the accepted standards of law and mythology they might seem to be doing the reverse.

CHAPTER 4
The Traveling Salesman: Drug Traffic

> "He had the wrong dreams. All, all, wrong. He never knew who he was. Nobody dast blame this man. You don't understand: Willy was a salesman."
>
> ARTHUR MILLER
>
> "What's good for General Motors is good for the country."
>
> CHARLES WILSON

In societies where the salesman is king and the sales manager emperor, where creating an artificial demand for a nonessential product designed to wear out rapidly is considered both good business and good morality, drugs, illicit as well as licit, have become just one more commodity to be merchandised. The chains of distribution for both regular and black-market drugs are organized along similar lines, including growers or manufacturers, chemists, wholesalers and other middlemen, retail distributors, neighborhood stores, and owner-supervisors of the overall operations. The split comes in how we conceptualize and react to the two different forms of the drug trade, speaking of one in respectable, high-status terms, and of the other in terms of moral opprobrium and calumny, e.g., "dope peddler," "drug pusher," "connection," "dealer." Sometimes at least the official designations of a society have to be changed almost overnight, as in the case of alcohol, when after the repeal of Prohibition in 1933 bootleggers became restaurant or club owners, and moonshiners became successful manufacterers and lobbyists.

From a rational and moral standpoint, all of the mind-altering drugs can be lumped together, and those involved in any phase of their production and distribution can be considered drug pushers or peddlers, whether the product

53

be tobacco or marijuana, alcohol or heroin, amphetamines or LSD. From at least one standpoint, all those encouraging or promoting social, nonmedical, or nonessential use of drugs are in the same bag, although most Americans will continue to single out only a few of the drugs and their purveyors for concern, while ignoring others.

ALCOHOL AND TOBACCO

Most traffic in alcohol and tobacco cigarettes is straightforward, well organized, and massive as it leads from manufacturing plant to warehouse to retail outlet. The amounts involved have already been cited. Although generally legal and culturally accepted there is a coexisting supplementary network of illegality with these drugs, including illicit production and smuggling to avoid tax payment, illegal sale and transfer of licenses, bribery of regulatory agents and vice police, sale to minors or to intoxicated persons, staying open after hours, watering of drinks, and drunk driving (or flying), all of which together involve millions of instances and people. Those states or districts maintaining official prohibition of alcohol until recently (some still have local option for counties or some form of partial prohibition) regularly saw massive violation of these laws by their citizens, although Will Rogers once said dryly that "Oklahoma will remain dry as long as the voters can stagger to the polls."

Although no reliable national figures are available, occasional newspaper accounts, including those in *The New York Times*, suggest that there is a multimillion-dollar yearly illicit traffic in cartons of cigarettes, which are smuggled from low-tax states such as North Carolina to high-tax states such as New York. This results in large losses of tax revenue for the states whose highly taxed local cigarettes are undersold because of the availability of the cheaper ones.

The 1961 book *The Purveyor* states that the highly organized manufacture and sale of illicit tax-free alcohol, known

as the Business, costs federal and state governments 1.5
billion dollars a year in lost tax revenue and provides
organized crime with financial returns second only to illegal
gambling. The penalties for this are described as so mild
that the Business is referred to as the "pension deal."
Rarely do any but the lower echelon of workers get arrested,
only about 20 percent of those arrested are sent to prison,
the average sentence is less than a year, and the average
fine is less than a few hundred dollars. At the same time, the
public, which generally frowns on such crimes as murder,
rape, and narcotics peddling, cheers as 75 million gallons of
illegal spirits are produced each year with a 400-percent
markup. The $10.52-per-gallon federal tax is evaded, and,
as Starr describes it, the millions of dollars in profits are used
to finance murder, extortion, arson, and illegal narcotics.

PILLS

The legal traffic in "pills," i.e., sedatives, stimulants,
and tranquilizers, includes production of the basic chemical ingredients, sale of these through a variety of pharmaceutical manufacturers who prepare and package the drugs,
distribution to wholesalers who then transmit them to
physicians, drugstores, government agencies, hospitals,
veterinarians, dentists, and researchers, and finally, via
prescription to the individual user.

At any point in this sequence, diversions into the illicit
traffic can occur. The basic raw materials can be obtained
by using false names or phony companies, the drugs can be
synthesized in illegal laboratories, or they can be smuggled
from other countries. Some supplies are stolen, either in
bulk or in the quantities found in burglarizing retail
pharmacies. Sometimes the drugs are sold directly to illegal
distributors by manufacturers, salesmen, pharmacists, and
physicians. There are numerous manufacturers of counter-
feit drugs which appear to duplicate the real thing but
frequently have less than pure ingredients. Some supplies
are transshipped by manufacturers to countries such as

Mexico and then back to the United States, thus avoiding
some of the ordinary controls on distribution. There are
those who receive the drugs legitimately and then transfer
them to acquaintances, friends, and family members; and
of course there are the black market street "pushers." Although such estimates are crude, the U.S. Food and Drug
Administration as well as other enforcement agencies have
estimated that half or more of the thousands of pounds and
billions of pills and capsules manufactured each year pass
into the underground traffic. Amateurs as well as semiprofessionals and organized criminals are involved in this
profit-making venture.

Both channels of distribution—the legal as well as the
illegal—are heavily involved in the widespread use and
abuse of what the law calls "dangerous drugs." To concentrate on one channel while ignoring the other may be
convenient and politic for certain individuals and agencies,
but clearly has perpetuated and increased the problems.

The cost per unit, dose, drink, cigarette, or pill may be
no greater and is sometimes less in the illegal market as
compared to the legal. The legal traffic can be classified as
overavailability, and the illegal as fairly ready availability.
In both cases, the commodities are priced in such a way that
they can be afforded by the vast majority of Americans
without much difficulty except with large daily doses.

LSD AND LSD-TYPE DRUGS

The LSD family of drugs since being driven underground
by federal and state legislation in 1966 has been mainly
distributed by individual amateurs and semiprofessionals,
often on a friend-to-friend basis. The naturally occurring
plant substances such as the peyote cactus are often grown
at home or ordered by mail, or purchased from seed companies as in the case of morning glories. Inorganic and
organic chemicals are easily and inexpensively purchased
and turned into active "psychedelic-hallucinogens" by

those with a moderate knowledge of chemistry. Those synthetic substances, with similar properties, unlike LSD, did not have a prior period of animal and human testing and clinical evaluation. These substances, many of them chemical modifications of amphetamine, include STP, MDA, MMDA, DMT, DET, DPT, sounding almost like a list of federal bureaus (for a time there was one named FDA in mock honor of the enforcement agency). As LSD moved from the laboratory and couch, at first legally made pure supplies left over or diverted from scientific use were used, with a little bit going a long way because of the infinitesimal dosage required (150 micrograms as compared to an ordinary aspirin tablet of 300,000 micrograms). Later, this was supplemented by limited amounts of Sandoz (the name of the Swiss company which originally produced it) LSD from England, Canada, and Switzerland, along with some manufactured in Italy and Czechoslovakia. During the last few years, so-called Owsley acid and other supplies synthesized by unlicensed, and since 1966 criminal, labs have predominated. In some instances, such individuals and their main distributors have reaped large profits, while others have done it mostly as a "public service." Sugar cubes, capsules, crackers, pills, and powders constitute the most popularly used forms of supply, but since LSD is odorless, colorless, tasteless, and usually in liquid form to start with, it can be conveyed in innumerable ways impossible to detect. An effective dose not only for one but for many people can be coated on the back of a postage stamp, put on the tip of a handkerchief or on a shirt tail, mixed with water or any other substances, and used conveniently at any time in the future.

Pure mescaline, the active principle of peyote, has been obtainable from various chemical supply houses and is sold illicitly as a water-soluble powder, often in capsule form. Speaking about this group of drugs in general, a "trip" is usually obtainable for between one dollar and five dollars on the black market.

MARIJUANA

With marijuana, we have a wholly illicit traffic, dating back more than 30 years, involving a small proportion of home-grown crops; significant amounts brought in or shipped in from such countries as Morocco, Nepal (where it is a major source of revenue to the government) and South Vietnam; and probably 90 percent overall imported from Mexico into California and other southwestern states and from there diffused to the rest of the country. The cultivation and sale in Mexico are entirely illegal, but have flourished for decades and are growing bigger by the year, often with the active involvement of government officials who profit from them far more than the peasant farmers who receive a pittance for their cannabis crops.

The chopped-up components of the plant, usually put in the form of bricks, move from Mexico into the United States, mainly at the border junction between Tijuana and San Diego, concealed in the clothing, luggage, and automobiles which cross that and other border points by the tens of millions each year. Annually there are well-publicized and well-photographed public burnings of entire marijuana fields to convince the few Congressmen and others who might complain, that the problem is being dealt with, but the export crop to the United States is estimated at one to three *tons* per week, while our State Department and its inimitable leaders characteristically do nothing and the Federal Bureau of Narcotics (which has had agents stationed in Mexico for years) files its annual progress reports for Congress and the Executive.

When the traffic or market mainly involved left-outs in American society concentrated in the urban ghettos, such as Negros and Mexican Americans, a large amount of the distribution was carried out by organized crime, commonly referred to as the Mafia. Over the past five years, this pattern has been almost completely transformed. Now regularly thousands of people either walk, drive or fly into Mexico and get their own small or large supplies, sometimes selling only enough to maintain their own supply free, and the professional or big businessman is almost non-existent. Marijuana mostly moves "with a little help from friends."

As with legal drug distributors, marijuana disseminators are often convinced of the social utility of their act, feel that the drug's use is beneficial, and scorn the attempted controls.

The cost is modest, often less than for a comparable dose of alcohol. A "lid," or tobacco tin, of marijuana containing an ounce sells for about 15 to 25 dollars and is sufficient for up to a hundred cigarettes, or more, depending on how firmly they are packed by the user. Larger quantities are correspondingly less expensive (from 100 to 125 dollars per kilo, or 2.2 pounds) and purchases made in Mexico or close to it are less expensive than those made hundreds or thousands of miles away.

The gross revenue of the marijuana traffic must certainly be in the hundreds of millions of dollars, but no one person seems to be making his fortune from this. Like that of diamonds, the value comes from artificial demands and inflated prices having been created, but with marijuana, LSD, or heroin, the value assigned to various quantities seized is usually tremendously exaggerated by drug policemen in their press releases. The weight of the actual substances seized (including branches or other inert material) is ordinarily multiplied two- or threefold and then this is valued at the highest possible retail price, perhaps a hundred or a thousand times the actual value. Thus, a pound of marijuana purchased in Mexico for as little as ten dollars, and in the United States for as little as 50 dollars, has been assigned values ranging from 500 dollars to 7,000 dollars a pound in different police seizures. Despite hard work on the part of some sellers who also take considerable risks, the profits are low, in part because of the bulky nature of marijuana as compared to other drugs circulated in the black market. The main economic profit as far as marijuana is concerned devolves to prosecuting and defense lawyers and the drug policemen, including salary and fringe bene-

fits, legal and illegal. The myth of the aggressive drug
pusher hanging around school playgrounds to subvert
otherwise wholly innocent American youth constitutes an
obviously successful political ploy by Anslinger and his
Federal Bureau of Narcotics, but to strain language and
logic slightly, it is even less true now than in the 1930s. The
supply is so plentiful and comes from so many sources that
the price usually remains stable or continues to decrease
even when large seizures are made.

Motives of dealers, small-scale or large-scale, in addition
to those already mentioned, include status-seeking among
their peers, excitement, unconventionality, and protest
against "the system."

Sometimes fraud is involved in marijuana or other illegal
drug transactions, as when oregano or tea or some other
substance is sold to someone as marijuana (a "burn") or
when very inferior-quality stuff ("bad shit") is distributed,
including a recent innovation of dipping it in molasses to
add weight.

Since 1967 a practical formula for synthesizing the active
principle of cannabis, tetrahydrocannabinol, has been
developed, published, and used to produce quantities of
an odorless, colorless liquid available on the black market.
The distribution and use of this synthetic have so far been
insignificant as compared to crude marijuana, but they are
likely to increase as the chemical techniques become more
refined and practical, since they bypass the problems of
bulk, characteristic odor, and smuggling from Mexico involved in the present pattern of distribution.

HEROIN

Heroin distribution is the most complicated illicit drug
business, geographically and politically involving three
main routes: the Southeast Asian, the Middle Eastern, and
the Mexican.

The world's biggest illegal opium-producing area centers
in northern Thailand and also includes portions of Burma,

Laos, and the People's Republic of China (Yunnan Province). Perhaps with mixed motives of patriotism and obscurantism, the Federal Bureau of Narcotics has always attributed the traffic to "the enemy": the Japanese during World War II and, presently, the Communist Chinese. Witness the testimony in 1967 of Giordano, successor to Anslinger as chief of the Bureau: "The majority of the drug in Southeast Asia is coming out of Yunnan Province. The United Nations estimates that about a thousand tons of opium is pouring out of that area." This was in response to a Congressional question as to whether the Communists were using opium as a weapon in their subversive activities. Then, in response to further questioning on whether the flow of narcotics out of Red China had the sanction and participation of the government rather than being exclusively an illicit operation, Giordano said, "There were reports several years ago which indicated that this had the sanction of the government. Several years back such information was furnished by individuals who had been in China and were then in Taiwan. There was a recent article by the *Pravda* correspondent in Hong Kong in which he definitely put the finger on the government of Communist China as being responsible for the opium coming out of that country, and in this case I would say that that is a responsible source."

The facts are, and have been, easily available to anyone who really cares to probe beneath the surface. Several United Nations- and World Health Organization-sponsored studies, including my own investigations for these bodies, have shown that hundreds of tons of opium are being produced each year in the tens of thousands of acres under cultivation in Thailand by hill tribes, including the Meo, the Yao, and others. The opium-growing area is one of mountains, valleys and jungles isolated from the rest of the country and contiguous to similar but smaller opium-growing areas in the other three countries mentioned. For the tribesmen, opium is the main cash crop, but brings them only a subsistence standard of living. The opium grown in the lands adjacent to Thailand is transported between border towns such as Takheelek in Burma and MaiSai in Thailand, and, as either raw opium, morphine, or heroin, moves through the northern Thai cities of Chiengrai and Chiengmai, joining with the larger locally produced supplies and moving on to Bangkok for internal use and for distribution to the rest of Asia and to the United States. The opium is purchased from the farmer by Chinese Nationalists and Thai traders, and is moved southward by jungle trail, road, and river using human carriers, pack animals, Land Rovers, boats, buses, and trains. Along the more dangerous part of this journey, the opium products are guarded by Chinese Nationalist troops who settled in the area following Chiang Kai-shek's expulsion from the mainland and who have subsequently maintained themselves with illicit narcotics profits and, according to some reports, with additional subsidies from the American Central Intelligence Agency as a "bulwark against Communism."

This large and successful traffic requires extensive collusion with Thai officials and considerable corruption, including bribery and profiteering by officials, high and low, in the government including the police and army. All of this despite the long, continued presence of two American agents of the Federal Bureau of Narcotics in Bangkok whose obligation under the law is to expose and cut off the traffic in narcotics. Also involved in the Asian opium traffic are French criminals (mostly Corsicans) operating in Laos and South Vietnam; pilots operating in airlines flying between several Laotian cities and the Gulf of Siam, where it is picked up by boats from Malaysia (the airline is colloquially referred to as "Air Opium"), and according to reports quickly suppressed, Vice-President Ky and other high officials of South Vietnam. The layer upon layer of intrigue, duplicity, and corruption which profitably maintain this opium traffic is rarely surpassed in modern spy novels. In effect, the United States is covering up and sometimes subsidizing the opium traffic which it purports to be eradicating.

The second and most important segment of illicit traffic in terms of supplying American addicts centers in Turkey, which in addition to legally producing opium for medical purposes (mostly codeine cough syrups) manages to divert 50 to 100 tons per year into the black market. Although this amount is far less than the probable 1,000 tons produced in the four-country Asian area, the latter supply is predominantly used locally. As in Asia, tens of thousands of poor farmers in isolated mountainous areas cultivate the Turkish opium as their main cash crop. The crop is purchased by smugglers who move it to Iran for use there and, usually after converting it to morphine, to Lebanon. Mainly Kurds and Bedouins, with almost lifelong experience as smugglers, transport it across the desert inside and on camels, on their person, and hidden among other more acceptable commodities. Because of its location, its banking facilities, and the relationships developed between its underworld and that of France in past years, Beirut has become the main center of the Middle Eastern opiate trade (it is also the main center for transmitting the concentrated Cannabis resin, hashish, to Egypt). As in Asia, the trade in morphine and heroin flourishes with the active participation of politicians and army and police officials. It is merchandised and superintended mainly by French Corsicans, who arrange for its removal via ship, plane, and automobile to Genoa, Marseilles, and Paris. There, the final processing to pure heroin is taken care of and it is then shipped to New York and the rest of America, often via Canada and Mexico.

United States distribution, according to all accounts, is controlled and efficiently organized by the Italian-American Cosa Nostra or Mafia. Whether reaching here by South American diplomatic pouch, Chinese seamen, or otherwise, the bulk heroin moves to various wholesalers in the larger urban centers, particularly New York City, and then, much like ordinary products, is parceled out to various middlemen distributors until it finally reaches the neighborhood pusher. By this time it has been cut, or diluted, repeatedly with either milk, sugar, quinine, or even less pure ingredients, and rather than being say 75 to 100 percent pure, it becomes five to 15 percent pure as the contents of a five-dollar "bag" bought by an addict for his next fix. The profits are huge for the people at the upper echelons in that 20 pounds, which brings a farmer somewhat more than 300 dollars in Turkey, can, depending on how much it is diluted, bring a gross retail income of perhaps 250,000 dollars.

The third center of illicit narcotics production is in Mexico, involving a number of states, particularly Sinaloa and the Sierra Madre Occidental mountain area. In its 1962 hearings, the United States Senate Subcommittee on Juvenile Delinquency was told by a former U.S. Customs Officer that "whenever Mexican officials destroyed opium poppies, it was either a small field that had been planted for that purpose, or large fields after the opium had been extracted." Again, the opium is grown by impoverished farmers, mostly Indian, who sell it to survive. The organizers and profiteers from the Mexican opiate traffic are wealthy businessmen and government officials acting in cooperation with some army and police officers. The raw opium, or *goma*, is converted to heroin in chemical plants near to its place of cultivation and moves into the United States via small planes, automobiles with specially built hidden compartments, and pedestrians. Because of its proximity to the United States, many small-scale addicts and distributors are able to obtain supplies in addition to that handled in the more organized fashion. Regularly praised by Giordano and his associates for the progress they are making, the Mexican government and our State Department are actually retrogressing by all indications, with as much or more heroin being exported to the United States than ever before. As might be expected, the House of Representatives Committee on Appropriations in its annual budget hearings for the Federal Bureau of Narcotics hears no independent testimony and accepts these self-serving reports with high praise and recommendations of increased amounts of money for the Bureau.

There may well be other local and federal governmental agencies that have been as "successfully" ineffective and harmful in their assigned mission as the Federal Bureau of Narcotics, but none for which there are so many objective criteria available to measure their failure. The situation with marijuana has already been discussed. With heroin, the Bureau estimates that some 3,300 pounds are smuggled into the United States each year, based upon their figures on the number of addicts. Having nearly 500 employees and an annual budget in excess of six and a half million dollars, the facilities of the Bureau of Customs and thousands of local and state narcotics agents, they seize less than one-tenth of this amount (which is a gross underestimation of the traffic anyway). This is the analysis made in the Narcotics and Drug Abuse Task Force Report of the President's Commission on Law Enforcement and Administration of Justice in 1967. This official document also points out that the Bureau of Narcotics maintains 19 agents abroad who in 1965 assisted local police in only 82 investigations, resulting in the seizure of 888 kilograms of raw opium, 128 kilograms of morphine, and 84 kilograms of heroin. Using realistic figures of heroin use and addiction, and of the opium traffic as recounted above, the results are much less than the proverbial drop in the bucket, and a McNamara-type cost-benefit ratio would likely result in the use of red ink.

There is the further fact that most seizures result from tips from informers rather than the independent "intelligence" activities of the narcotics policemen.

The Bureau of Customs actually accounts for the largest portion of illicit narcotics seized despite its highly diversified responsibilities, involving detection of all types of contraband being smuggled. In 1965, less than 3,500 men in this department were expected to handle 180,000,000 persons, 53,000,000 cars and trains, 99,000 ships, and 210,000 airplanes arriving in the United States. Considering not only this amount of traffic but the thousands of miles of border of the United States, it hardly seems credible that as much as ten percent of illicit drugs are seized by enforcement officers. One to five percent would seem much more reasonable. Customs' effectiveness was further reduced by some successful political infighting of the Federal Bureau of Narcotics in 1963-64, when they forced out of the anti-drug smuggling business experienced United States Customs agents working abroad, succeeding in having the sole responsibility for this assigned to the Bureau of Narcotics.

CHAPTER 5
But It's Against the Law

> "All laws which can be violated without doing anyone
> any injury are laughed at. Nay, so far are they from doing
> anything to control the desires and passions of men that,
> on the contrary, they direct and incite men's thoughts the
> more towards those very objects; for we always strive
> toward what is forbidden and desire the things we are
> not allowed to have. And men of leisure are never de-
> ficient in the ingenuity needed to enable them to outwit
> laws framed to regulate things which cannot be entirely
> forbidden. He who tries to determine everything by law
> will foment crime rather than lessen it." —SPINOZA

NARCOTICS LAWS

As our historical review demonstrated, attempts have
been made for hundreds of years, if not longer, to stop the
use of drugs ranging from coffee to peyote by legal prohibitions and severe criminal penalties. Due to the efforts of
our politicians, two-thirds of whom are unfortunately
lawyers, the belief has become deeply inculcated in the
American mentality that the solution to problems lies with
passing a law ("There ought to be a law against it") and then
forgetting about it. The assumption of such legislation is
that it will stop or deter the particular activity, e.g., drug
use, and, if it fails to do so, will punish the individual and/
or protect society from such antisocial behavior by im-
prisoning the offender. With increasing secularization and
weakening of moral values, perhaps formal law has come to
seem even more important. Pure food and drug laws in the
early 1900s were the first of many laws enacted in this
century to control various drug phenomena perceived as
problems. With increased opium smoking and the as-

sociation of this smoking with "the underworld," and with extensive use of tonics containing opium, there came the first specific federal narcotics legislation, the Harrison Act of 1914. As Eldridge has stated, this "totally new approach to the narcotics problem can best be described as an effort which set out to control the nonmedical use of narcotics and evolved into the prohibition of nonmedical uses and the control of medical uses as the populace was informed that dope fiends threatened to permeate our entire society." Also involved in the passage of the Harrison Act was the United States' joining in the Hague Convention of 1912, which obligated countries to control domestic sale, use, and transfer of opium and coca products. The Harrison Act is a tax statute administered by the Bureau of Narcotics placing a tax on the manufacture, importation, or transfer of narcotic drugs. Unauthorized possession, sale, or purchase is a criminal offense.

ALCOHOL LAWS

The next major American drug law, and one also with far-reaching effects, was the Volstead Act, which implemented the Eighteenth Amendment to the Constitution prohibiting alcohol manufacture and sale. The wartime prohibition was followed by the January 1920 onset of the provisions of the Volstead Act which specifically restricted beverage alcohol to medical and religious use, vinegar, and cider. The user-buyer-possessor was excluded from the criminal provisions and the penalties for bootleggers were a fine of up to 1,000 dollars and six months in jail for a first offense, and a fine of up to 10,000 dollars and five years in jail for a second offense. Business establishments selling illegal alcohol could be closed by court order for one year. Andrew Sinclair, in his encyclopedic work on prohibition, describes the success of the Anti-Saloon League in passing the law as rooted in "rural mythology, the psychology of excess, the exploited fears of the mass of the people, the findings of science and medicine, the temper of reform, the efficiency of the dry pressure groups, their mastery of propaganda, the stupidity and self-interest of the brewers and distillers, and the weakness of the politicians." Most of the states passed laws to supplement the federal act, some much stricter and including penalties against the possession of liquor. Graft, corruption, injustice, inconsistency, hypocrisy, violation of constitutional rights, and the creation of a new criminal class developed rapidly and accelerated until finally public pressure brought the demise of the act with the Twenty-first Amendment to the Constitution, which became law in 1933. Almost 45,000 people had received jail sentences for alcohol offenses in 1932 alone. In the first 11 years of the Prohibition Bureau, 17,972 people were appointed to the agency, 11,982 were terminated "without prejudice," and 1,604 were dismissed for bribery, extortion, theft, falsification of records, conspiracy, forgery, and perjury.

MARIJUANA LAWS

Although laws regulating the import and export of narcotic drugs and prohibiting the manufacture of heroin were passed in the 1920s, the next major drug law was the Marijuana Tax Act of 1937. The Federal Bureau of Narcotics had been started in 1930 to enforce the provisions of the Harrison Act, and a number of its employees, including its then deservedly obscure commissioner, Harry Anslinger, were former alcohol prohibition agents.

With very little to do since the dope-fiend menace was quiescent for the moment, and with the F.B.I. getting all of the attention among federal enforcement agencies due to Hoover's public relations skills, marijuana must have seemed ideal as a vehicle for a quick rise from obscurity. It was used mainly by outcasts of society carrying no political muscle (clout in 1969 argot), some intellectuals, jazz musicians, Negroes, and Mexican Americans, who had first introduced it to the U.S. around 1910 in the Southwest. In a manner that became the model for future drug hearings and laws, Anslinger and company issued press releases describing marijuana as the cause of crime, violence, assassination,

insanity, and other evils. Newspaper stories headlining the
Bureau's press statements were then submitted to Congressional committees as "evidence," supplemented by
frightening anecdotes in Anslinger's direct testimony
stressing mental deterioration, release of inhibitions of an
antisocial nature, rape, and other lurid tales. Another
Treasury Department official began his testimony by stating that "marijuana is being used extensively by high
school children in cigarettes with deadly effect" and gave
as evidence that of an editorial from a Washington newspaper supposedly quoting the American Medical Association. A Doctor Woodward, present as legislative counsel
for the A.M.A., pointed out that the statement in question
was actually one made by Mr. Anslinger which had only
been quoted in the *A.M.A. Journal.* No medical, scientific,
or sociological testimony was sought or heard by the committee and no alternative ways for dealing with the "problem" were discussed and Doctor Woodward courageously
criticized the Congressmen for proposing a law which
would interfere with future medical use of cannabis and
pointed out that no real evidence had been presented to
substantiate the charges. Specifically, he wondered why no
one from the Bureau of Prisons had been produced to show
the number of prisoners addicted to marijuana or anyone
from the Children's Bureau or Office of Education to discuss the nature and extent of the habit among children, or
someone from the Public Health Service to give "direct
and primary evidence" rather than indirect and hearsay
evidence. Saying that he assumed it was true that a certain
amount of "narcotic addiction" existed since "the newspapers have called attention to it so prominently," he
concluded that this type of statute was neither necessary
nor desirable. Totally ignoring the content of this testimony,
the members of the committee attacked the doctor's character, qualifications, experience, and relationship to the
A.M.A., all of which were impeccable. He was forced to
admit that he could not say with certainty that no problem
existed and finally he was told, "You are not cooperative
in this. If you want to advise us on legislation you ought to

come here with some constructive proposals rather than criticism, rather than trying to throw obstacles in the way of something that the Federal Government is trying to do." After providing for exemptions for the oil seed, bird seed, and paint industries, which needed the hemp plant, the bill was easily passed by the House and soon agreed to by the Senate, which held similar but shorter hearings in which they were provided with verbal "documented evidence" of marijuana-induced insanity.

ESCALATING DRUG LAWS

As had alcohol, both marijuana and heroin were predictably driven underground, becoming increasingly profitable to criminal vendors and more attractive in some ways to potential users. Use and addiction (to heroin) pyramided, the problem as it had been defined increased, in a self-fulfilling prophecy, and since they never bothered to think through cause-and-effect relationships, the application of criminal sanctions continued to be the only approach to the problem conceived of by society's "leaders." Steadily bringing marijuana and heroin more closely together in mythology and policy the Federal Bureau of Narcotics managed to get new legislation in 1951, the Boggs Bill, to increase the indeterminate sentence up to a maximum of ten years provided by the Harrison Act. Under these provisions, the first offense conviction for possession brought not less than two years or more than five years, with probation permitted; the second offense, a mandatory five- to ten-year sentence without possibility of probation or suspended sentence; and third and subsequent offenses, a mandatory ten- to 20-year sentence without possibility of probation or suspended sentence. Not satisfied even with this, and despite the already obvious failure of this approach, still harsher penalties were sought and obtained in the Narcotic Drug Control Act of 1956, which punished first possession offenses with two to ten years, with probation and parole permitted; mandatory five- to 20-year sentences, without probation or parole, for a second possession or first selling conviction; mandatory ten to 40 years, without probation or parole for a third possession or second selling conviction and subsequent offenses; and ten years to life, without probation or parole, or the death penalty if recommended by a jury, for selling heroin to an individual under eighteen. Contrary to the American ideal of individualized justice and to what is done with practically all other criminal offenses except first-degree murder, judicial (and parole-board) discretion was taken away in dealing with so-called narcotics offenses. Among other things, this made meaningful or effective rehabilitation impossible for those imprisoned and further dehumanized the possessor of forbidden drugs.

A Uniform Narcotics Law prepared by the Federal Bureau was recommended to, and obediently adopted by, a majority of state legislatures after 1932, and many of them outdid the Federal Bureau in imposing even more extreme penalties for the same and other drugs and other facets of the cycle of drug use. As penalties were increased in the federal law in 1951 and 1956, most states soon followed suit.

Doctors were repeatedly harassed and persecuted for attempting to treat narcotics addicts despite a 1925 ruling in the Linder case by the United States Supreme Court that addiction is a disease which can be treated by physicians, a position later affirmed in the 1962 Robinson case. There has been a notable increase in the percentage of the state and federal prison population serving sentences for narcotics and marijuana offenses. In federal institutions alone, the President's Commission found there were almost 4,000 drug-law violators confined at the close of fiscal year 1965, representing 18 percent of all persons confined. Comparable figures for states such as California show about 25 percent incarcerated on drug charges. The average sentence being served in 1965 in the federal institutions by drug law violators was 87.6 months, with three-fourths of them ineligible for parole under the mandatory provisions. Not only what drug policemen call the "do-gooders," but judges and prison officials have repeatedly objected to the inflexibility and harmful consequences of this type of approach.

STATE LAWS

A typical present-day state law, that of California, severely limits the treatment of addicts, requiring the reporting by the physician of any habitual user to whom he furnishes a narcotic and limiting administration of narcotics to 30 days in a closed institution; making it almost impossible to obtain marijuana for research purposes; includes peyote under the narcotic felony penalties (while LSD, with similar properties, is under the dangerous-drug misdemeanor penalties); and provides for between 90 days and one year in jail for being *under the influence* of any "narcotic," including marijuana. Individuals on probation, parole, or suspended sentence for any of the narcotics-law violations are required to submit to nalorphine (Nalline) antinarcotic testing even though their offenses may not have involved narcotic drugs; the Nalline does not detect use of amphetamines, marijuana, or numerous other drugs; and the program brings them into regular contact with heroin addicts and sources of supply.

A particularly absurd provision of the law in California and many other states and probably the most unconstitutional of all makes it a misdemeanor, with up to one year in jail, to be in any room or place where marijuana is present even if not known to you. With the present widespread pattern of use, this could include almost any building or location and makes criminals out of additional hundreds of thousands of people. First-offense possession of marijuana in California has been getting one to ten years in prison, with no parole possible for at least a year, but in 1968 the law was reformed to allow judges to impose either a misdemeanor or a felony penalty on the first offense; second offense, two to 20 years, with no parole for two years; and a third or subsequent offense, five years to life, with no parole for five years. A first conviction for sale brings five

years to life, with no parole for three years; a second offense, five years to life, with no parole for five years; and a
third offense, ten years to life with no parole for ten years.
Selling, *giving away,* or furnishing marijuana to anyone
under twenty-one gets ten years to life in prison, with no
possibility of parole for five years on the first offense; ten
years to life, with no parole for ten years on the second
offense; and 15 years to life, with no parole for 15 years on
the third offense. This would be true even if one 19-year-
old gave some to a 20.5-year-old roommate. In Louisiana a
minor transmitting some to another minor is subject to 5
to 15 years, and in Missouri he may receive the death penalty. In Colorado even a first-offense sale by minor or adult
to anyone under 25 can bring life imprisonment. A Dallas,
Texas, court as might be expected recently sentenced a
shoeshine-stand operator, undoubtedly a Negro, to 50 years
for selling a matchbox of weed to an undercover cop. Such
Draconian penalties are rare even with armed robbery or
second-degree murder.

For "any narcotic other than marijuana," California
provides not less than two or more than ten years in prison
for first-offense possession, and not less than five or more
than 20 years for a second-offense conviction. Sale brings
five years to life, with no parole possible until at least three
years have been served on the first offense, and ten years to
life, with no parole for at least ten years for a second conviction. Anyone convicted of any of these offenses is required to register as a "drug addict" and report any change
of address after leaving the institution; any vehicle used to
transport any of these drugs is subject to confiscation; and
possession of any paraphernalia (syringe, pipe, etc.) used
for taking narcotics also brings a jail sentence.

Civil commitment procedures have been established in
California and New York, and in the federal law, allowing
for the setting aside of certain criminal violations of the
narcotics laws if an individual is an addict or in imminent
danger of becoming one, and sending them under civil
procedures to a specialized institution for "rehabilitation."
The individual is incarcerated in the prison hospital for

a year or more, kept on parole supervision for years thereafter, and returned to the institution at any time or tried on
the original criminal charge if there are signs of relapse or
non-cooperation.

The "narcotics" laws covering actual narcotics such as
heroin and opium, as well as non-narcotic substances such
as cocaine and marijuana, carry with them felony penalties,
meaning usually a year or more in prison. Another category
of drug law is the "dangerous drug" laws, applying to
sedatives, stimulants, and, more recently, "hallucinogens," having misdemeanor penalties, meaning less than a
year in a jail (rather than prison but this may not be better)
for first-offense possession convictions. In addition to the
length and place of sentence, a felony conviction is significantly different and worse in that it results in the loss of
the basic constitutional right to vote, the right to a passport,
and the right to serve in the armed forces (an attraction for
some opposed to the Vietnam war). Additionally, it ordinarily bars the individual from many occupations and
educational opportunities.

In the instance of the dangerous-drug laws, the states
preceded the federal government in evolving such legislation. In its rather representative legislation, California
provides for a fine of up to 1,000 dollars and/or imprisonment in the county jail for not more than one year for
illegal possession of a restricted dangerous drug. A second
conviction is punishable by either one to five years in
prison or not more than one year in the county jail. Sale is
punished with the same one to five years in prison or not
more than one year in the county jail for the first offense and
two to ten years in prison for the second offense. Many
states have separate provisions with heavier penalties for
what is called "possession for sale" or "possession with
intent to sell." There are also laws, which are strangely
much milder in their penalty provisions, forbidding driving
under the influence of alcohol, dangerous drugs, or narcotics, and imposing more severe penalties for causing
bodily injury while under such influence.

With the passage of the Drug Abuse Control Amend-

ments in 1965, the federal government moved to play a
stronger role in the control of sedatives, stimulants, and
tranquilizer drugs. The most important aspect of this law
was its break with tradition in excluding possession for
one's own use from the criminal penalties (as did the federal anti-alcohol laws) and instead concentrating on illegal
manufacture and sale. The amendments, which came into
effect in 1966, provide for more controls on distribution by
manufacturers; limit physicians' prescription renewals of
these drugs to five in any six-month period and, since 1967,
bring LSD and related drugs under the same provisions of
control as the barbiturates and amphetamines (or drugs with
like properties). Illegal sale or manufacture can bring one
year in prison and/or a 1,000-dollar fine on the first offense;
and three years in prison and/or a 10,000-dollar fine for a
second offense. In keeping with the recent politically
inspired law and order and anti-(some) drug fever, President Johnson as part of the "Great Society" proposed increased federal penalties against LSD, and in 1968 the
House and Senate passed for the first time a federal law
making simple *possession* of these "dangerous drugs"
(LSD, amphetamines, barbiturates) a crime and increasing
penalties for sale. The misdemeanor penalty of up to a year
in jail for a first offense stipulates that the judge can exer-
cise discretion and impose probation and psychotherapy.

The law is indeed as Dickens said "an ass," with innumerable irrationalities, injustices, and incongruities. It
almost totally neglects the enormous and well-documented
abuses of alcohol and tobacco; treats amphetamines and
LSD more leniently than marijuana, which has far less
potential for abuse; puts drugs with similar chemistry and
pharmacology in entirely different penalty categories;
primarily attacks and criminalizes user-possessors; and
ignores civil penalties in favor of criminal ones. The harsh-
penalty philosophy has led to 31 states having a minimum
of two years in prison as a penalty for a first marijuana-
possession conviction, while 44 states have maximum
penalties ranging from five years to life for the same offense.
Playboy has pointed out that North Dakota provides 99

years at hard labor for simple possession of pot while in adjacent South Dakota a person may get only 90 days. All, except Alaska, which moved into the twentieth century in 1968 by moving it into the "dangerous drug" misdemeanor category, put marijuana under the narcotics laws.

Looking at the full panorama of current drug laws, one must question the quality of civilization, mental health, and democracy in America. Almost without exception they were passed in artificially created climates of hysteria, on the basis of fear and ignorance, proposed and lobbied by drug police and their cohorts, and with only token opposition by legislative bodies eager to climb on the "drug problem" bandwagon. Equally striking is the default of leadership and participation by professional individuals and organization. Groups, such as the American Medical Association, which have consistently opposed any governmental interference in health matters which they consider economically important, quietly allowed the physicians' role in treating drug abuse to be restricted almost completely, and lent the pages of their prestigious journals to the most fanatical and deceptive drug policemen. Neither psychologists, social workers, sociologists, professors in general, nor even the professional liberals were there to question these actions and provide more humane and constructive alternatives. Even now these organizations ally themselves with the forces of extremism issuing statements (as in the case of the A.M.A.'s Committee on Drug Dependence and the National Research Council Drug Committee) furthering one-dimensional viewpoints and preserving the present policy of criminalizing all users. Many of the books and articles written in recent years emanate from this type of medical-political perspective and serve mainly to maintain their authors as acceptable organization men. Narcotics police have repeatedly been invited to both open and closed sessions of these supposedly scientific and professional bodies to deliver diatribes against such rehabilitative efforts as the methadone maintenance program or against efforts to reform the drug laws. It is little wonder that the medical profession has

shown a steady deterioration in its public image or that the
older generation is increasingly despised by young people.

DANGEROUS DRUG LAWS

After passage of the 1965 Drug Abuse Control Amendments, a Bureau of Drug Abuse Control was established in
the Food and Drug Administration. In 1968 by Presidential
order this bureau of several hundred agents was shifted to
the Department of Justice and combined with the Federal
Bureau of Narcotics, which was shifted out of the Treasury
Department. The reorganization is intended to improve the
efficiency of enforcement, and may have the benefit of
providing some degree of supervision over the traditional
excesses of the Bureau of Narcotics, which had operated as
a law unto itself in the Department of Treasury. However,
there may be negative implications for the Bureau of Drug
Abuse Control, which had at least officially emphasized
education, research, and getting the major distributors of
illegal drugs. A new director, John Ingersoll, was named
to head the combined Bureau of Narcotics and Dangerous
Drugs with its more than 800 agents, thus dropping both
Giordano of Narcotics and Finlator of Drug Abuse down a
notch in the hierarchy. In early 1969 Giordano was ousted
in an internal power struggle, thereby completing the face-
lifting and ending the Anslinger-Giordano era.

INTERNATIONAL LAW

Almost directly paralleling the evolution of domestic
drug laws has been a system of international so-called
controls resting upon a series of treaties. First was the
Shanghai Opium Conference in 1909, which urged governments gradually to suppress opium smoking, restrict
morphine to medical uses, and impose national controls on
opium derivatives. This conference led to the Hague Convention of 1912, the first international opium convention
and the first to impose international law on the control of
narcotics. With the establishment of the post-World War I

League of Nations, this body under its articles was given "general supervision of the execution of agreements with regard to the traffic in opium and other dangerous drugs."

A Geneva Convention was signed in 1925 establishing the present system of record-keeping and reporting on the implementation of narcotics treaties. A Permanent Central Opium Board was set up to carry out this function.

The next major international development was the 1931 Convention for limiting the manufacture and regulating the distribution of narcotic drugs. Its aim was to limit world manufacture of narcotic drugs to medical and scientific needs and to restrict the quantities of drugs available in each country. Still another agency was created, the Drug Supervisory Body, which became part of the ongoing bureaucratic apparatus of the League and later of the United Nations.

Then, in 1936 came the Convention for the Suppression of Illicit Traffic in dangerous drugs, which called for punishment of illicit traffickers and sought measures to prevent such individuals from escaping prosecution.

During World War II, token activities continued on the part of the Permanent Central Opium Board and Drug Supervisory Committee, although the League of Nations had dissolved. In 1946, with the formation of the United Nations, its Economic and Social Council created the Commission on Narcotic Drugs to carry on the functions of the former League of Nations committee. The United States Representative to this commission since its inception and its most influential (because of personal forcefulness and the U.S. contribution of 50 percent of the UN Budget) member has been Harry Anslinger, now retired as Commissioner of the Federal Bureau of Narcotics, but continuing his traditional activities in an international forum.

The next piece of international "legislation" was the Paris Protocol of 1948, which brought under international control newer synthetic narcotics which the World Health Organization finds to be addiction-producing.

Then came the 1953 Protocol for limiting and regulating the cultivation of the poppy plant; and the production of,

trade in and use of opium (seeking to limit this to medical
and scientific needs with legal production only by seven
countries, Bulgaria, Greece, India, Iran, Turkey, the
U.S.S.R., and Yugoslavia).

The most recent and most encompassing of the treaties is
the 1961 Single Convention on Narcotic Drugs, designed to
pull together, simplify, and revise the content of the previous nine treaties and to close various gaps, such as tight-
ening controls on nonmedical use of opium, cannabin and
coca leaf. This Single Convention begins with a rather self-
righteous and ambitious preamble:

> Concerned with the health and welfare of mankind,
> recognizing that the medical and scientific use of nar-
> cotic drugs continues to be indispensable for the relief
> of pain and suffering, and that adequate provision must
> be made to insure the availability of narcotic drugs for
> such purposes, recognizing that addiction to narcotic
> drugs constitutes a serious evil for the individual,
> and is fraught with social and economic dangers to
> mankind, conscious of their duty to prevent and com-
> bat this evil, considering that effective measures
> against abuse of narcotic drugs require co-ordinated
> and universal action, understanding that such univer-
> sal action calls for international co-operation guided by
> the same principles and aimed at common objectives,
> acknowledging the competence of the United Nations
> in the field of narcotics control and desirous that the
> international organs concerned should be within the
> framework of that organization, desiring to conclude a
> generally acceptable international convention replac-
> ing existing treaties on narcotics drugs, limiting such
> drugs to medical and scientific use, and providing for
> continuing international co-operation and control for
> the achievement of such aims and objectives.

The treaty or convention established a new International
Narcotics-Control Board to take over the previous functions
of the Permanent Central Opium Board and Drug Supervisory Body, and to work collaboratively with the Division

of Narcotic Drugs of the United Nations. For a number of years, Anslinger managed to keep this treaty from going before the United States Senate, because he felt that it weakened the international controls. However, as the movement to reform and revise the country's marijuana laws came to prominence, he rushed it before the Senate, which then acted without any hearings or any attempt to seek knowledgeable information on the subject and rubber-stamped it with an 84-to-nothing vote in early 1968. The subsequent statements made by various drug-police agencies show quite clearly their motivation, in that they now say that our country's agreeing to the Single Convention makes it impossible to change the marijuana laws in any way. Leaving aside the simple fact that many nations have ignored treaties when the politicians in power felt it was in their interest to do so, the current claims on the implications of the convention are totally false on several counts. Firstly, marijuana per se is not even included, since cannabis for the purposes of the treaty is defined as the flowering tops of the cannabis plant, excluding the seeds and leaves when not accompanied by the tops. Secondly, a 25-year period is provided for a country to eliminate gradually use of the forms of cannabis which are prohibited. Thirdly, the treaty explicitly states that it is not binding if it conflicts with any constitutional provisions of a given country. This would mean that if the United States Supreme Court were to find the marijuana laws or the drug laws in general to be unconstitutional in certain respects, the American law as interpreted by the court would prevail. Finally, even though the treaty and its predecessors call for stopping the traffic in drugs defined as dangerous and for penalties against traffickers, penalties, whether light or severe, are not demanded or required against users and, in fact, specific penalties are not prescribed for traffickers.

The activities of Anslinger and company have not stopped with the international activities described above. They also have exerted major influence on the hiring policies of the United Nations and World Health Organization departments dealing with drugs; strongly influenced the topics

taken up by the Secretariat and by the Commission itself
and the policy statements or articles issued to the press
or published in the *U.N. Bulletin on Narcotics*.

Although Anslinger succeeded in imposing a *lex Ameri-
cana* in terms of these drug treaties, the international
results have been as unsuccessful and harmful as in this
country. The banning of the traditional and widespread
opium smoking in Iran, Hong Kong, Thailand, and other
countries has resulted in replacing a nuisance with a massive criminal, addiction, and youth problem, since heroin
use by injection and inhalation predominantly by young
people has replaced usually moderate opium smoking by
the older segments of the population. There has been notable breeding of internal corruption in these countries.

THE DRUG POLICE

Thousands of drug policemen work in the often overlap-
ping and competing city, county, state, and federal agencies of the U.S. which purportedly seek to stop drug abuse.
Since the people focused on are what sociologists call
"status criminals," or practitioners of a crime without victims, meaning they are engaged in private behavior that is
not antisocial, the police receive no complaints or direct reports and depend upon the use of informers and special
methods. These informers may be drug abusers themselves
who are bribed or blackmailed, rewarded or threatened, to
provide information. If they do, they are often permitted
to continue their illicit drug use, and sometimes are even
provided with supplies by the narcotics or vice-squad officers. If they fail to "cooperate," they will be charged with
the most serious offense possible, and a recommendation
be made that they receive the maximum penalty. Often
moral if not legal entrapment is involved, in which informers or undercover agents who may have infiltrated into
high school or college groups, hippie communities, etc.,
will "turn on" with their pretended friends and later turn
them in after gathering evidence against them and trapping

them in a situation in which they can be "caught with the goods."

Very rarely are major distributors or sellers apprehended, let alone imprisoned, but instead we have almost constantly and widely publicized arrests of possessors or small-time distributors. The entire system involves basically un-American and totalitarian or communist-type secret-police practices which are corruptive of the society and of those individuals involved in them. Each year a significant number of local or federal drug policemen are found to be involved in overtly illegal activities, sometimes making the newspapers and other times being covered up and quietly disposed of. Within the past year, the entire New York City Narcotics Squad was investigated, restructured, and re-staffed, because of widespread corruption; state and local agents in various parts of the country have been suspended or dismissed; and more than 30 agents of the Federal Bureau of Narcotics were dismissed, suspended, and indicted on charges including the sale of narcotics, and bribery. Since the days of Prohibition the corrupting influence of this type of work (and of sex police work) has been so well known in police departments that men on these assignments are usually transferred every few years.

One reason for the popularity of harsh penalties, mandatory minimum penalties, and penalties against user-possessors is that it gives additional leverage to the drug policeman in forcing the individual apprehended to inform on others and lead them to further arrests. Regular harassment, particularly of narcotics addicts, has been a constant practice, the police arresting them on sight and making it almost impossible for them to develop a normal adjustment in this society. Wiretapping and electronic eavesdropping are not unknown, and the false incrimination of certain individuals by planting drugs on them, as happened to Lenny Bruce in one of his arrests, also occurs. In fact, slipped through virtually without debate in the 1968 Omnibus Crime Control Bill is a provision providing for wiretapping in suspected marijuana cases as well as national security ones, thus opening endless vistas of power for already ambitious agents.

The average drug policeman has only a high school education, and his special "training" on drugs consists of memorizing decades-old mythological chapters in police manuals written by Anslinger. False stereotypes about the drug user ("dope fiend") are also taught to the rookie by the more senior cop in their daily interactions. Many are underpaid and undersupervised, which, along with the corrosion of moral values inherent in their work, makes them more susceptible to improper practices, such as taking bribes or selling confiscated drug supplies or other merchandise themselves.

Substantial efforts are devoted to "educating" the public about the correctness of the police biases regarding certain drugs and the need to maintain the system of criminalization; preventing clinical and research use of the drugs by scientists; and slandering and attacking any who dare to criticize their activities or propose reforms in our policies. The first academic victim of this law and order response was the prominent sociologist Alfred Lindesmith of Indiana University, who for years courageously stood alone in public opposition to the Federal Bureau of Narcotics. He has written about the Bureau's sending a man to see him and the university trustees in order to force a change in his stand that drug addicts should be treated as medical rather than criminal problems. Additionally, in 1949, Anslinger got the U.S. State Department and the Canadian government to ban the showing in the United States of the film *The Drug Addict* because it favored a medical approach. Doctor Karl Bowman, a collaborator in the La Guardia Report on marijuana, was also attacked and repeatedly misquoted by Anslinger in a letter printed in the *Journal of the American Medical Association*, of all places. When an attempt failed to stop publication by the Indiana University Press of the Joint Report of the American Bar Association and American Medical Association on the treatment of the drug addict, a compendium of attacks on this report was simultaneously published by Anslinger and with the same title, in order to confuse readers and convey a picture opposite to the real version. More and more, however, in recent years, these individuals and agencies have operated behind the scenes to seek to discredit their opponents; see that they are not invited to important professional or public gatherings; and try to have them dismissed from whatever positions they hold.

DRUG LAW EFFECTS

Although William Eldridge, in his 1962 study for the American Bar Foundation, conclusively demonstrated "that the available evidence does not prove the claims made on behalf of the effectiveness of the American system of narcotics control," we continue to use and intensify this approach and there is still no attempt at the systematic collection of national data which could demonstrate even to poorly informed legislators how bad the current system really is.

Arrest figures continue their astronomical rise, this being a function both of increased use of certain drugs and of increased police activity. What is happening nationally in terms of drug arrests, leaving aside the already described situation with drunk offenders and drunk drivers, is best reflected in the reports of the Bureau of Criminal Statistics of California's Department of Justice. Their review of trends between 1960 and 1967 shows dramatic changes with far-reaching implications. Among adults arrested, only 11 percent in 1960 had no prior arrests on record, whereas by 1967, 28 percent had no histories of arrest or, to put it more bluntly, appeared to be in no way involved in criminal activity except by being labeled and handled as such by the drug laws. In studying the new drug arrests, it was found that one of seven marijuana offenders and one out of eleven dangerous-drug offenders were arrested on subsequent heroin charges within five years, suggesting, that the legislative policies themselves, and the traditional belief in progression to heroin, may have come from the drug offenders having originated from a criminal group to start with. In 1960, the median age of drug offenders was twenty-seven years, while in 1967 it was nineteen years and continuing downward. Adult drug arrests were up more than 200 percent over the seven-year period studied, but juvenile drug arrests were up more than 900 percent. There was a 1967 total of 47,032 adult drug arrests, and 14,760 juvenile drug arrests. Adult marijuana offenses were up 87 percent over 1966, and adult heroin (narcotics) offenses up 29 percent. The total number of people involved in these arrests was 29,627, including 28,655 who had never before been arrested on drug charges. The overall juvenile drug arrests amounted to a 100-percent increase over 1966, and with the marijuana arrests, which jumped from 4,034 to 10,987 juveniles, represented an increase of 172 percent. Those over eighteen arrested on marijuana charges alone increased by 525 percent between 1960 and 1967. In this same period, dangerous-drug arrests increased 171 percent, and heroin offenses, 30 percent.

The response of the drug police to this national epidemic is to ask for still more laws and blame it on excessive leniency by judges, the statements of "do-gooders" that marijuana is not so dangerous as the police have claimed, overpermissiveness, lawlessness, and insufficient personnel.

Actually, the total picture since the American system of drug control was instituted is even more appalling than looking at the changes of recent years. One of the most popular of drug statistics regularly quoted by the drug police and their "scientific" advisers in government is that in 1914, when these laws began, one in 400 Americans was an "addict" and now due to the "effectiveness" of the laws and their enforcement, only one in 4,000 Americans is an "addict." The facts not surprisingly are quite different. There are and were no statistics on the extent of opiate addiction in 1914, and heroin was not even being used then, but rather many Americans (no one knows how many) were using tonics or elixirs containing combinations of opium and alcohol. There was not even a generally accepted definition of addiction that could have been used to establish that figure for 1914. But in any case, it is one of the most shocking and absurd aspects of the drug scene that people are seeking credit for, and taking comfort from, the actual massive increases that have occurred in American drug use in the more than half century since the time of that phony statistic. Today there are somewhere between 100,000 and 250,000 heroin addicts and users as compared to none or very few in 1914, six million alcoholics (and 80 million users of the drug), 500,000 abusers of sedatives and stimulants, many millions of regular users of cough syrups (as with the pre-1914 tonics containing some combination of narcotics and alcohol), and millions killing themselves with tobacco. More drugs and more dangerous ones are being used by ever-increasing numbers of people, and new criminals by statute are being created by the tens of thousands while many grow rich or powerful through the black-market traffic and profits. How indeed can one cite a figure of one in 4,000 now and claim that progress has been made in alleviating the problem, even the problem as defined by drug policemen and politicians. It would seem that even self-delusion and wishful thinking should have some limits.

In addition to the criminalization of so many otherwise normal and socially acceptable people, there are other implications of present policies that require discussion and evaluation. First, in human terms, as has been mentioned, an arrest record in itself often greatly interferes with or prevents a normal life adjustment in the future, and if in addition the individual is sent to jail or prison, say for marijuana possession, he may well be taught how to use heroin, how to commit real crimes, and have homosexuality forced upon him. The costs of maintaining the present basic agencies dealing with just one state's, California's, crime problem is now more than 630 million dollars per year, not including the costs of federal agencies dealing with crime in that state. A significant and growing segment of the costs of police, district attorneys, public defenders, courts, jails, prisons, and probation and parole departments involves drug offenses. Using the projections of California's Bureau of Criminal Statistics, by 1973 the felony-arrest figures for both adults and juveniles will reach 300,000, including

100,000 drug offenses if no changes are made in present
laws, arrests, and prosecution practices. This is a grim and
expensive picture, in terms of both ruined lives and the
tax burden. It will take more than name-calling, scapegoating, law-and-order slogans, and political demagoguery
to solve this problem, but surely it can be accepted on the
basis of currently available evidence that the present approach has been a terrible failure and that we are long
overdue for change.

CONFERENCES AND COMMISSIONS

A White House Conference and two Presidential commissions have been convened since 1962 to examine drug
abuse and crime in general. In 1963, the President's Advisory Commission on Narcotic and Drug Abuse issued its
final report, which cautiously called for a complete attack
on the illegal drug traffic; rehabilitation of the individual
abuser rather than retributive punishment; abolishing the
Federal Bureau of Narcotics and dividing its responsibilities between the Department of Justice and the Department
of Health, Education, and Welfare; increased research and
education; greater flexibility in punishment and in rehabilitation programs; and allowing physicians more latitude in
dispensing narcotics for treating addicts.

The 1967 Task Force Report on Narcotics and Drug
Abuse of the Commission on Law Enforcement and Administration of Justice recommended increased enforcement staffs for the Bureau of Narcotics as well as for the
Bureau of Customs, but stressed that the former should use
the added personnel to design and execute a long-range
intelligence effort aimed at the upper echelons of the illicit
drug traffic. States were urged to adopt model drug-abuse-
control acts similar to the federal Drug Abuse Control
Amendments of 1965, and modification of both state and
federal drug laws was urged to give discretion to the courts
and prison officials so that they could deal flexibly with
violators. Many traditional assumptions about the marijuana
problem were questioned, and the commission recom-

mended that the National Institute of Mental Health carry out a wide-ranging program of research on this drug, and also develop a drug-education program. This 1967 report also characterized narcotics and drug abuse as a "growing problem," but despite this went on to make basically the same kinds of recommendations. Four members of the commission expressed dissatisfaction that the commission had been unable to confront a number of basic questions in the drug area, but, "for reasons not justifiable, it assumes that the laws and the traditional methods of enforcement which have continued for over fifty years are the only proper ways in which to meet the problem."

Both groups at least indirectly questioned the validity of the Federal Bureau of Narcotics' theory that severe penalties act as a strong deterrent and favored some increase in emphasis on treatment and rehabilitation.

DETERRENCE?

A 1968 study by the California State Assembly Committee on Criminal Procedure, geared to study one of the key assumptions of drug and other criminal laws, made some far-reaching recommendations in its report, "Crime and Penalties in California." They found in their comprehensive study that there was no evidence that severe penalties effectively deterred crime and that the prime deterrents to crime are fear of quick apprehension, certain conviction, and any length of imprisonment. There was no evidence that prisons rehabilitate most offenders but there was evidence that larger numbers of offenders can be effectively supervised in the community with little risk and major tax savings. It was emphasized that the timing of parole release for minor offenders is determined by arbitrary and unscientific criteria that do not serve the ends of justice, economy, or public safety. They further cite the American Bar Association's recommendation that "no confinement is preferable to partial or total confinement with the absence of affirmative reasons to the contrary" and the recommendation of the President's Commission on Law Enforcement that there be greatly increased use of extramural probation and parole supervision. As a result of this, it was recommended that the California Legislature direct the release to parole of all offenders at the expiration of statutory minimum parole-eligible periods with the exception of those convicted of crimes of violence. It was urged that the resulting savings in annual prison costs and further capital outlay be used to subsidize local supervision of offenders and make improvements in local and statewide crime control.

There are some further indications of change to be summarized later, but basically there remains a great gap between the findings of social scientists and these special commissions on the one hand and public policy on the other. The explanation for this gap lies mainly with our bureaucratic-political process — that is, who influences legislative and administrative policy and who doesn't; who administers or supervises. One recent indication of how deeply entrenched the severe-penalty and drug-as-totally-evil concept have become is a 1968 poll by *Good Housekeeping* magazine. In response to the question "Should marijuana laws be changed?", one woman wrote, "I feel that marijuana poses a threat to our young people, and I favor tight controls and strict enforcement of the law with no exceptions. Marijuana is just a stepping-stone to barbiturates, amphetamines, LSD, and heroin. It is another contributing factor to the moral decay of this country." Several readers declared that a jail term or a criminal record was a small price for a young person to pay if this punishment saved him from a lifetime of drug-induced misery. Most readers wanted strong penalties in order to deter use and prevent escalation on the part of young users to even more dangerous drugs, and without strict laws they foresaw a chaos of mass experimentation and wholesale seduction of the young into drug usage.

Individual narcotics officers, district attorneys, and their professional associations, as well as some members of the medical profession, continued to espouse similar views before courts, legislative bodies, and the general public, and with the help of the mass media, they have obviously had great success in their propagandizing.

Psychologist Richard Blum in 1964 interviewed 50 California state legislators who were members of committees processing drug legislation. The study concluded that drug abuse is considered a major social threat by the majority of California legislators. Those holding key positions of power re drug issues try to influence human conduct through enacting laws of punishment and confinement, measures thought to contain rather than solve the problem. Treatment is considered, but for the most part is limited to within-institution programs. Many lawmakers felt even then that the present approach is inadequate, and a few thought it inhumane. Only a minority of legislators were interested in new approaches because they believed the public to be strongly in favor of punishment and confinement. In their own eyes, many legislators were more "liberal" than their assessment of the electorate. Positions on legislative alternatives in the handling of drugs and users varied according to the drug under discussion. About LSD, many had no current convictions and were quite open to informed proposals. A hard-core one-third stood by the present tight control laws. With marijuana, a far milder drug than LSD, but one about which public opinion is strong (and incorrect), punitive positions were firm out of both conviction and political self-interest, and most legislators opposed any effort to make marijuana use legal (other possible law changes were not inquired about). Most lawmakers were ready to remove the drunk from police purview (although five years later they still haven't done so) provided they are convinced that a treatment program would work and not be too costly. For those considering possible new approaches, the choice of sources for information was found to be a matter of real importance. The legislators turned to organized medicine (not to individual experts or social scientists) and to law-enforcement associations and bureaus for testimony on drugs. About half, however, expressed respect for the potential value of research into human behavior. Those lawmakers rated as "liberal" on drug issues — seeking information, willing to change, interested in rehabilitation as well as punishment — were also "liberal" in voting on other social issues while "conservatives" in the drug area were "conservative" in their other votes. Most of the conservatives were Republicans while all of the liberals in this California sample were Democrats. Anti-treatment forces were seen to be stronger than rehabilitation-oriented groups (which makes one think, on the basis of national public opinion polls showing up to three-fourths of Americans favoring treatment, that it is the anti-treatment *lobbies* which are stronger). As long as there were pressure groups on both sides, legislators felt they had a freer hand. A number of the lawmakers used or exploited the "narcotics" issue for political advantage. Newspapers and law-enforcement lobbies were seen as capable of whipping up a troublesome storm over "lenient" measures. There are a number of exceptions nationally, with marijuana law reform being called for by conservatives as well as liberals, Republicans as well as Democrats.

In 1968, despite all of the above and despite the general political climate of the country, two states, Alaska and California, instituted significant reforms of their marijuana laws. As previously mentioned, the President consolidated the two main federal drug enforcement agencies and Congress customarily moved backward in enacting increased penalties for "dangerous drug" offenses. The then commissioner of the Food and Drug Administration, Doctor James Goddard, publicly questioned the accuracy of the marijuana demonology and the efficacy of the severe penalties system, and also made comparisons unfavorable to alcohol. Expectedly he was attacked by the alcoholic-beverage industry, the Federal Bureau of Narcotics, and representatives of the pharmaceutical industry, each for different reasons. Several congressional servants of these lobbies condemned Goddard and a few months later he resigned. The landmark change in the State of Alaska's drug laws removing marijuana from the narcotics category and penalties came about due to the initiative and concern for justice on the part of the then Alaska Attorney General, Edgar Boyko and, in turn, the willingness of the relatively young and progressive legislative leaders to look at the broader context and recognize the failures and dangers of the policy which prevailed there, and still prevails else- where in America. In testifying as an invited expert witness this writer had a stimulating and productive fact-finding session with the members of the House and Senate com- mittees holding the formal hearings on the drug laws which led to the reform. Since then local and federal drug police have been going all out to change the law back even be- fore it can be assessed.

The more modest change in California was guided by Assemblyman Craig Biddle, chairman of the Assembly Criminal Procedure Committee, which had held a series of hearings on different aspects of the drug question be- tween 1966 and 1968 before which a number of expert wit- nesses, including the author, testified as to the real prob- lems and the advisability of drug-law reform. The bill finally passed as somewhat of a compromise in that while authorizing possible misdemeanor penalties for a first marijuana possession conviction, it increased the penalties for LSD and "dangerous drug" possession.

At the time of this writing, the most far-ranging attempt to reform marijuana laws and hopefully the overall drug laws is now taking place in the courts. Constitutional challenges are now moving slowly through the processes of the "ad- ministration of justice" in Oregon, California, Michigan, Iowa, Washington, D.C., Florida, New York, and Massa- chusetts. Additionally, there is the appeal (to be ruled on in 1969) before the United States Supreme Court of the con- viction of Doctor Timothy Leary by a federal district judge in Texas and upheld by the United States District Court of Appeals in New Orleans for the transfer (possession) of one- half ounce of marijuana with a maximum sentence of 30 years in jail and a 30,000-dollar fine. The original legal arguments in this case stressed the religious-freedom issue, but also argued before the Supreme Court was the issue of self-incrimination based upon the 1968 Gambling Tax

decision that an individual cannot be required to register
and pay a tax on something that will subsequently make
him subject to arrest. If the court rules similarly in regard
to the Marijuana Tax Act, it would be invalidated, but of
course the state laws under which most people are prose-
cuted and criminalized would remain. Before Congress in
1969 will be an Omnibus Drug Control Bill seeking to perpetuate and intensify the hard line and increase the power
and status of the Bureau of Narcotic and Drug Abuse.

By far the most thorough and complete hearing, legislative, judicial or otherwise, on marijuana occurred in conjunction with what has come to be called the Boston Trial
(actually *Massachusetts* v. *Leis and Weiss)* in the fall of
1967. The properties of marijuana; its pattern of use and
abuse; comparisons with alcohol, nicotine and other drugs;
basic definitions; and varying kinds of social policy were
exhaustively illuminated through the direct examinations
conducted by Attorney Joseph Oteri of a series of expert
witnesses including the author, Professor Howard Becker
of Northwestern University, Professor Herbert Blumer of
the University of California at Berkeley, and others. The
constitutional questions propounded by Mr. Oteri and opposed by the special prosecutor and his own series of American and foreign witnesses included: the lack of sufficient
legislative basis for enacting the present laws; the denial
of equal protection of the laws as required by the Fourteenth Amendment to the Constitution (involving comparisons of marijuana with other drugs such as alcohol and
other potentially dangerous phenomena); the wrongful
categorization of marijuana as a narcotic; invasion of privacy; infringement of the right of pursuit of happiness; and
the advantages of regulation over prohibition. As expected,
the lower state court in Massachusetts upheld the present
statute, but the more than 1,000 pages of testimony from the
two-week hearing should reach the U.S. Supreme Court
in 1969 following a decision by the Massachusetts Supreme Court. The Florida Supreme Court is also reviewing
the same testimony and issues since a lower Florida court

agreed to accept the Boston transcript in lieu of live testimony.

The other constitutional challenges involve one or several of the same issues raised in the Boston trial, and, after moving up through the appropriate state courts, they may be joined together at the level of the U.S. Supreme Court. An additional benefit of all of these court challenges is the public education which has gone along with them via the mass media, which helped to dispel some of the mythology and hysteria. Also, now a matter of public record are numerous misstatements, contradictions, and inconsistencies elicited by Mr. Oteri in cross-examining the prosecution witnesses, who were predominantly government or A.M.A. affiliated. One such statement includes an admission perhaps with a hint of irony by a prominent physician, when asked why he had decided to testify for the prosecution, that "I can be bought."

A final comment is in order concerning the ramifications of our present drug laws. Real crime: murder, rape, theft, burglary, and embezzlement, is increasing at a staggering pace in America, sometimes more than 30 percent per year in our large cities, while police and politicians talk about so-called crime-in-the-streets and drugs as the problems. The President's Commission on Law Enforcement and the Administration of Justice found that some 50 million major crimes are committed each year in this country, with only about half of them reported, and less than half of those resulting in arrest (and many fewer in conviction or imprisonment). Obviously, there are limitations in what even the best police forces can do, and if our limited resources continue to be deployed as they are in detecting and arresting certain types of illegal drug users (while ignoring others), fewer policemen are available to deal with the far more serious problems of crimes against people and property. Furthermore, disrespect for law and police by youth and some elders is also increased by this obsession with drugs. Prosecutors, courts, prisons are devoting so much time and money to drug cases that major criminal violators remain at liberty for years or are never tried. Thus crime is really helped because of hypocrisy and irrationality.

CHAPTER 6

Once Upon a Time: Hard Drugs; Crime and Violence

> "Then the Emperor walked along in the procession under the gorgeous canopy, and everybody in the streets and at the windows exclaimed, 'How beautiful the Emperor's new clothes are! What a splendid train! And they fit to perfection!' Nobody would let it appear that he could see nothing, for then he would not be fit for his post, or else he was a fool. None of the Emperor's clothes had been so successful. 'But he has got nothing on,' said a little child. 'Oh, listen to the innocent,' said its father. And one person whispered to the other what the child had said. 'He has nothing on—a child says he has nothing on! But he has nothing on!' at last cried all the people. The Emperor writhed, for he knew it was true. But he thought, 'The procession must go on now.' So he held himself stiffer than ever, and the chamberlains held up the invisible train." —HANS CHRISTIAN ANDERSEN

Among the many concerns engendered in the public mind, usually in a kind of amorphous combination of horror-inducing fantasies about risks, dangers, or harmful effects from certain drugs, are sexual excesses, crime, violence, assassination, insanity, accidents, brain damage, birth defects, and dropping out. In the minds of some people, a type of paranoid ideation has developed in which the word "drug" joins with other sources of fear and anxiety to produce an almost instinctive overreaction and condemnation.

These fears have been cleverly played upon by many politicians and bureaucrats who have profited from them. Few of the concepts have been analyzed or adequately dissected to separate fact from opinion or reality from fiction. The best place to begin the journey toward reason is with an analysis of the concept of "hard drugs," disseminated by the drug police in recent decades in association with heroin and heroin users ("dope fiends"). Never has the concept of "hardness" really been spelled out, but it has been most successful in triggering these fear reactions and in leading to our ineffective social policies. It would seem to mean, as customarily and vaguely used, some destructive physical or mental effects on the individual and/or on society, effects which presumably don't occur with "soft drugs," whatever those might be.

Stating it once more since it is so misunderstood, no mind-altering drug and, for that matter, no drug of any kind can be said to be completely harmless, and none of them can be said to be always or totally harmful. Any of them can involve risks or dangers, and to evaluate these risks meaningfully people must have some basis of comparison and understand the basic concepts and dimensions of drug use and abuse as I have described them in an earlier chapter.

Small, moderate, and large doses; short-term and long-term effects; physical and mental changes; liability for inducing physical dependency or for abuse in general; and numerous other dimensions must be considered. Basic also to such understanding is, again, the concept of mind-altering drug effects, that is, that the prime ingredient is the underlying personality and character structure of the person taking the drug, whether one is talking about possible effects on sexual behavior, criminality, or anything else.

THE "HARD STUFF"

"Hardness" itself really includes many subcategories involving many drugs. Starting with the best-documented, most extensive, and most serious instances of hardness, one might expect that even extremists ranging from the Progressive Labor party and Communist Party to the John Birch Society and the Minute Men would agree that death from using a drug is hard indeed. Thus, without minimizing in any way possible serious consequences associated with other drugs, the highest priority would be given to alcohol and the hundreds of thousands who die every year from cirrhosis of the liver, drunk driving, and overdoses. Running a close second in this dimension of hardness would be nicotine and tobacco, with 300,000 U.S. deaths yearly from lung and vascular disorders, and from cigarette-induced fires. Barbiturates and other sedatives come into the picture with the tens of thousands of accidental deaths and suicides from overdoses, often in combination with alcohol. Damage to the body and chronic disability short of death from each of these and other drugs would be another dimension of hardness.

Still another major component of hardness is the production of psychosis, most commonly from alcoholic brain damage (permanent) or delerium tremens (temporary) and then with decreasing frequency from such other drug abuses as amphetamines, LSD and, rarely, marijuana.

Another facet of hardness and the one that is usually talked about in isolation as the core of the demonology is physical dependence (addiction), and here heroin or other opiates rank highest in risk followed by alcohol and barbiturates (sedatives). However, heroin is "soft" in another dimension in that it produces no permanent damage to the body even with decades of heavy use (in marked contrast to alcohol which also is responsible for far more individual addicts than heroin). Hardest of all are the consequences of our drug policies: arrest, expulsion, imprisonment and their sequelae.

Most people are likely to continue to find certain forms of drug use a nuisance, objectionable, unpleasant, evil, and immoral, but, to go beyond that to define real problems and what to do about them they should have some *hard* facts.

THE STEPPING-STONE THEORY

This brings us to the stepping-stone or progression theory, which in effect says that even though drug X may not really be as bad as the public is told, it remains necessary to make criminals out of everyone having anything to do with it in order to keep them from stepping up, or moving on, to the hard stuff, usually referring to heroin and more recently also LSD. More pithily the belief is that anyone using marijuana will inevitably end up using heroin. Such statements have no validity once the concept of hardness is correctly defined as in the preceding sections and when patterns of drug use are understood. People may move up and down or back and forth from "soft" to "hard" and "hard" to "soft" depending on the dimension of hardness used as a baseline; people may use a potentially hard drug in such a way that it never produces any hard effects on them; and people may use concurrently several drugs with varying properties. Probably the most common progression is from caffeine to alcohol and (tobacco) cigarettes, with most people continuing the basically hard pattern of drug use represented by the tobacco and alcohol, while a minority moves to, or substitutes, generally softer, sometimes illegal drugs. Clearly, the legal categories or implications of what is hard and soft, bad and good, harmful and harmless have little relationship to reality.

The origins of the stepping-stone mythology, like the domino theory in foreign policy, rest with attempts to support or justify through fear techniques otherwise unjustifiable policies. In 1937, during the Congressional hearings leading to the passage of the Marijuana Tax Act, in a context in which every conceivable lie was being offered as justification for the new law, Anslinger stated on the record, in response to a Congressman's question, that there was no relationship between marijuana and heroin and that they were completely separate drugs. The limited association that subsequently developed between the two seems clearly to have been an effect of the laws and their enforcement rather than having anything to do with the intrinsic properties of marijuana. As one of the many criminogenic effects of such laws, the drug and the user are driven underground as the substance is made attractive and profitable to purveyors of "vice." In large urban centers in the 1940s and 1950s, particularly in the ghettos, the source of supply for these and other illicit drugs soon came to overlap so that people seeking one soon learned about the other and would often be subjected to dares, taunts, or other pressures to try it. Thus, it came about that in later years heroin addicts in prisons and prison hospitals indicated, when asked just the one question, that 50 to 70 percent of them had used marijuana before becoming heroin addicts. It is unclear as to how many used marijuana before any *use* of heroin rather than addiction or how many moved to heroin addiction as a direct or indirect consequence of being sent to jail for marijuana and forced into close association with heroin addicts and pushers.

More to the immediate point, if the people framing such questions would ask about the full context of mind-altering drug use, they would find that 95 to 100 percent of the addicts used as their first potent mind-altering drugs alcohol and nicotine, both of them *illegally* in their early teens, with some of them later taking up marijuana and some who took up marijuana turning to heroin. Hume and other philosopher-logicians have repeatedly pointed out that, simply because events occur in sequence, it does not show causality, or, as some have put it, all heroin users drank milk as infants, so obviously the milk must have caused their heroin addiction. To be consistent in our *post hoc, ergo propter hoc* logic and policies, we would aggressively seek out and imprison all users of alcohol and tobacco in order to be sure that no one "steps up" to marijuana and heroin. A study of a national sample of 2,213 narcotics addicts in-stitutionalized at the Lexington, Kentucky, Federal (Prison) Hospital found a positive association between marijuana and opiate use in only 18 states or territories and either insufficient data, or no evidence of prior marijuana use in the other states. A coexisting background and environment of delinquency, and differential association with a drug-taking group are pointed out as being key factors. It should also be mentioned that both drugs become objects of curiosity and foci of rebellion as a result of the way they are handled by society.

Those sincerely worried about this stepping-stone concept can be comforted from the fact that, as marijuana use has increased by the millions and the sources of supply have changed, heroin addiction has decreased proportional to the population, so that whatever relationship exists can be said to be inverse. In countries such as India where millions regularly use cannabis derivatives, heroin use is unknown, and obviously even in the United States, there are large numbers of addicts who did not previously use marijuana and the majority of marijuana users would never think of using heroin. There is nothing in the pharmacological or psychological effects of cannabis preparations that could possibly cause a person to take up heroin or any other specific drug. Finally, even if a particular drug did lead to some other drug neither user should be treated as a criminal.

VIOLENCE

As to drugs and violence, most such tales have centered on heroin, marijuana, and LSD. In a series of studies done for the President's Commission on Law Enforcement and the Administration of Justice it was discovered, in analytically reviewing all existing articles and books on the subject, that the only drug which could be causally related to accidents and violence was alcohol. The Commission report states, "There is no evidence that opiates are the cause of crime in the sense they inevitably lead to criminality, but there is no doubt that among addicts with a delinquent life style, drug use is part and parcel of their other activities, crime included. There appears to be no solid ground for extreme anxiety or outrage over the current dangers posed to the community by opiate use." Actually, the immediate effect of opiates is generally a quieting one and the crimes which occur as a result of illicit addiction, namely crimes against property, or prostitution, are other effects of our laws, representing efforts by the addicts to obtain sufficient money to purchase their regular fixes on the black market. No evidence was found implicating barbiturates, amphetamines, tranquilizers, LSD, or marijuana as causes of crime.

ALCOHOL

The already mentioned fact that more than half of the people in jails and prisons committed their crimes after (excessive) drinking represents the most extensive association of any drug with criminal behavior, including violence (also demonstrated in the many civil disorders or riots when liquor stores are quickly ordered closed), but even there does not mean that an otherwise noncriminal, socially conforming person committed his criminal act solely because of ingesting the drug alcohol. Normal, mature, well-integrated individuals taking average or even heavy doses of mind-altering drugs will not engage in behavior foreign to them or commit acts that they would never do if not under the influence of a drug. Immature, neurotic, or emotionally unstable individuals may incur some loss of control or inhibition as the result of the interaction of the physical properties of the drug with their personality and the setting, and this may make it more likely for them to engage in self-destructive or antisocial behavior which they would already be inclined to engage in. This would be true whether the drug was alcohol or marijuana. Possible negative effects on judgment and coordination certainly influence behavior, particularly in regard to accidents. In regard to alcohol and violence some cultural anthropologists have postulated that Americans use the drug to allow themselves to more acceptably express aggression otherwise frowned upon.

MARIJUANA

The most deeply embedded, demonic, and perhaps least truthful of the tales linking illegal drugs to crime and

violence is the one linking marijuana with assassinations.
As Anslinger told it in 1937:

> In the year 1090, there was founded in Persia the
> religious and military order of the Assassins, whose
> history is one of cruelty, barbarity, and murder, and
> for good reason. The members were confirmed users of
> hashish, or marijuana, and it is from the Arabic *Hash-*
> *shashin* that we have the English word "assassin."

Several popular magazines and medical publications as
far back as 1912 published accounts, often differing in such
things as whether hashish came before or after the murders.
Marco Polo, whom everybody quotes (or misquotes),
actually told the tale as follows:

> In a valley between two mountains, the Old Man had
> made the largest and finest garden that ever was seen.
> In it there were all the good fruits in the world, the
> fairest houses and the most beautiful palaces covered
> with gilding and adorned with pictures of all the
> beautiful things of the earth and conduits through
> which flowed wine, milk, honey, and water. There
> were also ladies and damsels there, the fairest on
> earth, who could play on all kinds of instruments and
> sang and danced better than other women. And the
> Old Man made his people believe that this garden was
> Paradise. Into that garden no man ever entered except
> those he wished to make Assassins. The Old Man
> kept with him at his court all the young men of the
> district from twelve to twenty years of age. He used
> to have these youths put in his garden in the following
> way: He had a potion given them as a result of which
> they strayed away, fell asleep; then he had them taken
> up and put into the garden, and then awakened. When
> they awoke they so believed that they were really in
> Paradise. And the young ladies and damsels remained
> with them all day and the young men had their
> pleasure of them. So these youths had all they could
> desire, and would never have left the place of their

own free will. When the Old Man wanted to send any of his men anywhere to kill some person, he would order the potion to be given to a certain number of them, and once they were asleep, he would have them taken up and brought into his palace. When the youths awoke, they would be greatly amazed and by no means pleased. They would now go into the presence of the Old Man, believing that they were in the presence of a great Prophet. The old man would then ask them whence they came, and they would answer they came from Paradise. The other youths, who had not been there and were present at the narrative, would then be consumed by the desire to go to the Paradise, feeling ready to die in order to be able to do so, and longing for the day when it would come about.

Mandel, who thoroughly researched the history of the Assassins, points out that it was not those who tasted of the supposed hashish paradise who killed, but rather those who had not been there and, further, that several editions of Marco Polo's writing indicate that the potion was opium, meaning that the two mind-altering drugs available were alcohol in the wine and the opium, with hashish nowhere mentioned. Some current historians specializing in the Arab countries consider Marco Polo's tale a romantic fable, pointing out that the word "assassin" may derive from the name of their leader, Hassan (the Old Man), and that they were a group of religious fanatics seeking to free themselves from oppressive Crusaders. There may have been some use of hashish to help them temporarily experience "Paradise," which included, most prominently, the beautiful women, but no one was under the direct influence of either a drug or a woman as they killed, and probably not even the most fanatical would want to imprison all beautiful women even though they may indeed be dangerous sometimes. By no means, however, has the historical research resulted in corrected versions from drug policemen. Witness a late 1967 legal affidavit by a supervising narcotics agent in San Francisco, saying,

Marijuana is a substance that has been smoked, chewed, eaten, drunk and consumed in every conceivable fashion down through the centuries. It dates back to the Crusades when Mohammedan troops capitalized by using the drug to produce a violent, aggressive influence which gave them the feared reputation of maniacal murderers. These troops ferociously killed other combatants with an almost insane frenzy, and this gave historical note to the term "hashish," which in Arabic means assassin or killer. Undoubtedly their hysteria was a combination of herd psychosis potentiated by the drug effect, but that does not nullify the potential danger involved, nor can it be viewed harmless if only consumed in a favorable, relaxed, gay atmosphere.

It is doubtful in any case that effects attributable to large doses of the concentrated cannabis resin would be any more accurate indicators of what to expect from the moderate use of marijuana as is characteristic in the United States than if we were to use violent killings such as those of Richard Speck following consumption of large amounts of concentrated alcohol, to draw conclusions about the ordinary social beer drinker. Strangest of all is how a vague eleventh-century mixture of fantasy and fact as recounted by a series of drug policemen without any relevant expertise is accepted as a legitimate basis for far-reaching twentieth-century legislation. The story seems to have been effective in the same way that more recent creations, such as "Marijuana is more dangerous than the hydrogen bomb," aroused Congressmen from their alcohol-induced stupors even though they have never been particularly concerned about the hydrogen bomb itself.

If our newspapers were to feature prominently every instance of crime and violence in which those involved had been drinking, not a couple of times a week, as with the present distorted accounts about marijuana or LSD, but several times a day, we would see such headlines as:

"Alcohol-Crazed Man Kills Wife and Children," "Drunk Woman Kills Three on Freeway," "Intoxicated Man Attacks Policeman," "Boy Drugged with Alcohol Falls Out of Window," etc. The metaphorical man from Mars seeing such headlines and hearing politician's speeches would naturally conclude that the particular drug mentioned in the media was our most important problem, more important than the many things getting far less attention—racism, poverty, disease, education, and war.

Best of all for those who find security and status by contracting and distorting awareness, no one is thereby troubled by reflections on emotional instability, disturbed family life, incompetent leadership, and a sick society, all of which are much more involved in crime and violence than the mind-altering drugs.

CRIME

Since the image that has been deliberately created, albeit "through a glass darkly," emerges in the public mind as a close interrelatedness of the concepts "drug," "crime," and "violence," we must look at the fuller dimensions of crime and violence, just as we have done with drugs. Most Americans appear to think of themselves as law-abiding citizens, with "crime" the province or vice of a small group of antisocial lawbreakers in the streets, ghettos, or campuses. Actually, the studies of the President's Commission in 1967 found that: one out of every six boys is now being referred to the juvenile court; more than two million Americans per year are sent to prisons, jails, and juvenile "schools," or placed on probation; 40 percent of all male children now living in America will be arrested for non-traffic offenses sometime during their lives; and, most striking of all, more than 90 percent of Americans have at some time during their life committed acts for which they could have been sent to jail or prison. There are some 3,000 federal crimes and perhaps 6,000 state crimes listed in penal codes at least in the more urbanized, highly populated states. Some of these involve bodily harm, some property crimes, some public "morals," and some the regulation of the economy or of the environment. Some are white-collar, some blue-collar, and some no-collar crimes; some occur in the streets, some in homes, and some in offices or factories. Violence against the person is probably the area of greatest concern to the greatest number of people, and this would include not only those crimes annually reported by the Federal Bureau of Investigation in its incomplete Uniform Crime Reports (willful homicide, forcible rape, aggravated assault, and robbery), but also such serious acts of violence as arson, kidnapping, child molesting, and "simple" assaults. About 70 percent of willful killings, 66 percent of aggravated assaults, and a high percentage of forcible rapes are perpetrated by the victim's family members, friends, or acquaintances. Robbery, which usually doesn't involve any prior victim-offender relationship, occurs about half the time on the streets, and the same proportion involves the use of weapons. The overall figures of the President's Commission indicate a probability of one in 550 for any American being attacked in a given year, with the risk of such an attack being twice as great from family members or friends as from strangers, and with the risk for slum dwellers being much greater than for other Americans. The overall risk of incurring an injury serious enough to require any hospitalization is about one in 3,000 (less for most Americans), but this does not include the arson, kidnapping, child-molesting, and simple-assault offenses.

In 1967, guns were used in over 125,000 assaults, rapes, and robberies (one such crime every four minutes); 7,700 murders (more than 20 a day); and 10,000 suicides (nearly 30 a day). Some American is killed or injured every two minutes by a gun, and since 1900 about 800,000 have been killed by guns, more than were killed in all of our wars from the Revolution to Vietnam. The estimates of the number of guns in private hands in America vary from 100 million to 200 million, or one gun for every one or two men, women, and children. Over the past few years, assaults with a gun have increased by more than 35 percent and President Kennedy, Reverend King, Senator Kennedy and thousands of others rich and poor, famous and unknown, were killed with guns or rifles made easily available to the killers without questions or required registrations. It is estimated that every single day 10,000 guns are purchased by private individuals, including mail-order purchases, which increased by 50 percent last year. Despite this enormous panorama of violence, under federal law and practically all state laws there are still no significant controls on the distribution of hand guns, rifles, or shotguns to either convicted criminals or noncriminals. Although, according to reliable polls, four-fifths of American adults favor strong federal gun-control laws (including two-thirds of those who themselves own guns), the combination of merchants of death (weapon and munitions manufacturers and the National Rifle Association); the inadequacies of the mass media; and gutless, ignorant legislators have been successful in blocking such control. Many of these people including pseudo-patriotic legislators can therefore fairly be designated as "soft on crime and violence," although they profess, particularly in election campaigns, to be strong on "law and order." The motives and rationality of legislators who condone and encourage such monstrous violence while eagerly criminalizing anyone involved in the basically private use of a few drugs, are not only questionable, but highly deserving of condemnation and defeat at the polls.

Other components of the crime and violence picture are the more than 50,000 deaths and several million per year injuries from automobiles each year (more than half alcohol induced); the more than 30,000 American deaths and hundreds of thousands of severe injuries in the Vietnam war; the more than 40,000 Americans killed in home accidents each year, one-third of these from poisoning; the 20,000-plus suicides yearly (more than half from drugs); and the hundreds of thousands of deaths and serious injuries from falls, drowning, and fires.

The property crimes of burglary, auto theft, and larceny (tabulated only for amounts over 50 dollars) make up about 87 percent of the F.B.I.'s index of crimes, as compared to 13 percent for the most common crimes of violence. Fraud, embezzlement, and other white-collar crimes, actually more significant in terms of money involved, are strangely not counted in this index. The estimated number of index offenses for 1965 (all significantly increasing each year since) were: 9,850 murders and (non-negligent) man-slaughters; 22,467 forcible rapes; 118,916 robberies; 206,661 aggravated assaults; 1,173,201 burglaries; 762,352 larcenies (50 dollars and over); and 486,568 auto thefts. These figures came from 800 police agencies which cover about 92 percent of the total population. All of this is a very incomplete measure of the volume of crime, since it fails to include white-collar crime; millions of unreported property or even person crimes; the vast majority of such crimes without victims as acts of prostitution, liquor and other drug-law violations, and gambling; and is based upon arrest statistics rather than offense statistics. Arrest statistics reflect the number of arrests, of course, rather than the number of law violators or criminals, since many are arrested repeatedly. Present figures also give little measure of organized crime as opposed to semiorganized or unorganized. Surveys done by the President's Commission found far more crime than is ever reported. Burglaries appear to occur three times more often than they are reported to police; aggravated assaults and larcenies over 50 dollars, twice as often as reported; and robberies 50 percent more than are reported. In some areas surveyed, only one-tenth of the total number of some crimes were reported to police. Apparently most commercial firms do not report theft committed by their employees and often do not report the thefts of shoplifters (150,000 each week amounting to 2 billion dollars yearly), simply passing on the loss to consumers through higher prices.

Although trends in criminality are even more difficult to measure than the amounts, and adequate comparison figures do not date back very far, the F.B.I. reports cover less than 70 percent of the population, and the population is rapidly growing. Still, the evidence indicates that the number of violent crimes, property crimes, and crimes without victims has been steadily increasing. About 45 percent of all arrests are for the victimless crimes, with drunkenness alone accounting for a third of all arrests. The latter would be even more significant had not New York City and other cities decided in recent years not to arrest people for public drunkenness (also demonstrating the importance of police activity in measures of certain crimes or certain neighborhoods).

Not only are the total figures disturbing, but also the pervasiveness geographically, socioeconomically, and in terms of age, with young people committing a disproportionate share of crime, and this segment of our society growing at a faster rate than the overall population. The fifteen- to seventeen-year-old age group represents about five percent of the population, but accounts for 13 percent of all arrests, the highest arrest rate for any age group. Since about 23 percent of our present population is ten or under, we can anticipate further increases in the proportion of arrests represented by the adolescent or teenager.

The economic costs of crimes, while not on a level with the human costs, are nevertheless enormous. The taxpayers nationally are expending 4.5 billion dollars per year for police, jails, prisons, and courts dealing with or, more correctly, attempting to deal with crime. Measured by the loss of future earnings, the financial impact of crimes causing death, including homicide, highway accidents, and illegal abortions, totalled 1.5 billion dollars in 1965. Property crimes are estimated to cost nearly four billion dollars per year; other crimes, such as driving under the influence of alcohol, tax fraud, and abortion, about two billion dollars per year; illegal goods and services ("narcotics"), alcohol, loan-sharking, prostitution, and gambling, about eight billion dollars a year; and the private costs of preventive services and equipment, insurance, and legal expenses come to almost two billion dollars a year. These must be seen as relatively rough and incomplete estimates, since only a small proportion of some offenses become known, and there are many civil as well as criminal violations which except for a technicality involve the same factors and similar costs.

Also highly important in assessing the crime picture is the impact of both criminals and police on personal freedom, privacy, the pursuit of happiness, and the general quality of American life. Large and increasing numbers of the population fear to leave their homes at night, do not speak to strangers, lack confidence in the ability of police to protect them, and significantly alter their life style because of both real and exaggerated problems.

We are clearly both a crime-ridden and violence-ridden society, with drugs playing a very minor role in the total picture, and alcohol being the chief "villain" to the extent that drugs are involved.

ALCOHOL

There are two million arrests each year in the United States for the criminal offense of public drunkenness or intoxication. Such arrests are variously made under charges of "drunk in a public place" (usually without a legal or scientific definition of drunkenness), "breach of the peace," or "disorderly conduct." The last charge is used against inebriates in Chicago and some other cities even when no disorderly conduct has occurred. The total picture involves not only the most commonly arrested chronic skid-row drunk offender, but also many intermittent or occasional drinkers and carousing high school or college boys. A greatly disproportionate number of these arrests involve poor people living in urban slum ghettos, as there is differential enforcement of these statutes, with the satisfactorily dressed white person in "respectable" neighborhoods generally being overlooked when "high" on alcohol or sometimes being driven home by the police rather than arrested. Those who are arrested go through a revolving-door cycle involving punishment without treatment, rejection, and further alienation. Many arrests for vagrancy or trespassing also involve, or are really based upon, alcohol intoxication which the policemen decide requires an arrest.

A more clear-cut and significant involvement of alcohol in criminality was found in a study of 588 victims and 621 offenders of homicides in which either or both had been drinking immediately prior to the slaying in two-thirds of the cases. And in a study of 882 people who were picked up immediately after committing felonies, it was found, upon prompt urine examination for alcohol content, that physical violence, including knife wounds and other assaults, was roughly ten times more frequently committed by those intoxicated. The relationship to highway accidents-crimes has already been commented upon, as has the association of problem drinking with about half of the institutionalized felons in the United States. It has also been found that there is greater likelihood of recidivism, that is, of a continuing criminal career, when a particular criminal offense involves intoxication. All together, about 55 percent of all arrests involve alcohol-related offenses including drunkenness, liquor-law violations, and drunk driving.

NARCOTICS

As to opiates or narcotics, addiction itself, although conceived of and reacted to as a crime by police and politicians, since 1962 has not been a crime although absurdly everything involved in being an addict is still a crime. In *Robinson* v. *California,* the U. S. Supreme Court struck down the state laws which had permitted arresting people for being addicted, a medical diagnosis made by drug policemen, usually on the basis of fresh or old needle marks or a history of having been a user. After the decision, certain passages of California and other state laws were rewritten so that the word "prisoner" was replaced with the word "patient" in connection with addicts, "prison" by "hospi-

tal," and criminal proceedings by so-called civil commitment proceedings. Since an addict by the nature of the
physiological process of physical dependency requires
repeated daily doses of the narcotic, usually heroin (except
for the large number of people legally addicted through
doctors' prescriptions or cough syrups), he is simply arrested
for possession of illegal narcotics or illegal syringes and
needles. If these are not sufficient to perpetuate the handling of the addict as a criminal, various vagrancy statutes
can be invoked or probation or parole regulations forbidding being in a place where there are other addicts or
illicit drugs.

Obviously, in a circular fashion, one can obtain unlimited statistics purporting to show the relationship
between the use of a certain drug and criminality, simply
by defining any possession or sale of that drug as illegal
and arresting as many people as possible who do so. Given
the special concentration on this matter by innumerable
specialized drug- or vice-police agencies; the regular
exposure required in order to continue obtaining the drug;
and the multitude of laws bearing upon the cycle of drug
use, it is easily understandable why there are so many
"drug crimes" reported.

Attempting to separate drug offenses from nondrug offenses that addicts are involved in, there is still great
difficulty in blaming the criminal offenses on the drug.
There is general agreement that acts of violence are rare,
although this continues to be hinted at or even charged by
drug-police agencies and is a vital component of their
catechism. As was the case with alcohol prohibition, one
of the criminogenic effects of the narcotics laws has been to
foster an expensive illicit traffic and drive the heroin user
underground. In order for the addict to maintain his "habit"
at the artificially inflated prices, significant sums of money
are thereby required (usually 15 to 50 dollars a day), and
since most are unemployed and lacking necessary education or vocational skills (again, mainly as an effect of the
system), they must steal in order to obtain funds. Crimes

against property, such as burglary and shoplifting, are the usual means of doing this, supplemented by prostitution among female addicts. Somewhere between three and five times the amount needed for a "buy" must be stolen, since "fences" or other purchasers siphon off part of the profit. Using calculations based upon a 50-dollar-a-day habit, narcotics officers often calculate that 50 percent of all crimes (really meaning property crimes although not specified) in cities such as New York are attributable to heroin addicts, although many significant variables are ignored in these calculations. Actual police statistics (which don't include alcohol) in New York show that between ten and 12 percent of those arrested for crimes against property are admitted drug (mostly heroin) users. Without question, property crimes associated with illicit narcotics addiction are extensive, but they are, for the most part, a direct effect of our drug policies rather than of the drug. A number of chicken-and-egg studies have been done as to whether addicts were criminals before or after becoming addicted. The overall results appear to indicate that most illegal narcotics addicts in the United States have grown up in environments generally conducive to delinquency and crime, and the drug subculture can become for some a part of a broader criminal life style. The question has not been asked and answered in association with illegal alcohol or tobacco use in the teens, nor with heroin *use* as compared with *addiction,* so the oft-reported findings that some 50 percent were criminals before they were addicts is relatively meaningless. In countries where addicts are not criminalized and in special rehabilitative activities in this country, such as the methadone maintenance program, one finds little or no association between the addiction and criminality, either drug offenses or nondrug offenses. As stated by the President's Commission in 1967, "The simple truth is that the extent of the addicts' or drug users' responsibility for all nondrug offenses is unknown. There is no reliable data to assess properly the common assertion that drug users or addicts are responsible for 50 percent of

all crime." In England, where addiction is considered a
medical problem and special clinics are available to provide
addicts with legal narcotics under certain conditions, there
has been no evidence of a relationship between addiction
and crime, and the same was true in this country prior to
the adoption of the present system.

MARIJUANA

Returning to the alleged relationship between marijuana
and crime, the speeches and propaganda releases of the
Federal Bureau of Narcotics and their local "affiliates"
continue to be full of such statements as "The files of the
Bureau of Narcotics are punctuated with murders and
atrocities committed under the influence of marijuana."
Minimal research reveals that the original source of most of
these sweeping statements is a 1953 Anslinger book which
presents them without sufficient information or conceptual
framework to permit even partial verification. Even the
simple understanding of the logical difference between
"some" and "all" would cut through much of the verbiage
on the subject and this should then be supplemented by
some elementary education on the full context of drugs,
cause-effect relationships, statistical inference, multi-
factorial phenomena, and control groups. Then the following typical statements would be recognized as political, not
scientific: "The number of marijuana users among major
criminals is very high," "Not infrequently addiction to
cannabis preparations [in India] was the immediate cause
of sudden crime such as murder," "Criminal behavior will
not necessarily or inevitably result from the use of this
drug," "Violent behavior has long been associated with the
abuse of marijuana," "An individual with a propensity to
crime is relieved of inhibitions and normal self-control,"
"Not only do people commit crimes under the influence of
cannabis, but also a large number of criminals are led to the
use of the drug because without it they cannot operate
effectively." Such statements are very frequently cited in

reports from local or national police agencies, always presenting only one dimension, quoting out of context, citing only references favorable to their point of view, and uniformly neglecting each of the basic concepts or dimensions that are necessary for an understanding of drug use and abuse. One of the more recent of this genre of publication is a pamphlet entitled *Facts About Marijuana*, put out at considerable taxpayers' expense by the Los Angeles Police Department. This states in part:

> In 1966, the L.A. Police Department conducted a *survey* into the relationship between the use of marijuana and criminal behavior. During a one-year period, hundreds of cases were documented in which marijuana was involved as a factor in criminal behavior. Examples of reports utilized in the survey are presented in the following paragraphs. While on patrol, radio car officers observed a vehicle which fit the description of one used in a robbery a short time before. Officers stopped the vehicle, and upon interrogation, the driver admitted he had been involved in a robbery. A search of the vehicle disclosed a partially burnt marijuana cigarette on the floorboard, and a large bag of marijuana under the seat. The suspect stated that he was a marijuana smoker and had smoked two marijuana cigarettes that day.

Another example cited:

> Officers received a radio call that shots had been fired. Investigation disclosed that the suspect had been earlier ejected from *a bar* for disturbance, and that he returned fifteen minutes later to fire several shots from a shotgun in the street outside the bar. As patrons of the bar quickly emptied into the street, the suspect fired in their direction, striking one in the leg. When the suspect was arrested, numerous shotguns, rifles, and pistols were found in his home. In a closet was a large quantity of marijuana and the suspect admitted

smoking marijuana that day and on numerous previous occasions.

Still a third:

> Officers observed a suspect driving a stolen vehicle. When they pulled alongside and identified themselves by showing their badges, the suspect increased his speed and forced the police vehicle into the curb. The officers continued their pursuit, the suspect's vehicle narrowly missed oncoming traffic, and on several occasions, the suspect attempted to force the police vehicle off the roadway. He was eventually stopped when officers shot out his rear tires. When his home was searched, several marijuana cigarettes were found and his wife stated that he had smoked a marijuana cigarette earlier that day.

If the implications of such case histories on our policies were not so tragic, their simplemindedness and fallaciousness would be ludicrous. More specifically, their inadequacies can be detailed by a thorough examination of the main documents used in support of the marijuana and crime myth such as an article by Munch, a pharmacist and long-time associate of, and adviser to, the Federal Bureau of Narcotics. The article reports "details" on 69 case histories described as "authenticated case reports in the files of the Bureau which are typical of the various crimes committed by individuals after using, and while under the influence of, marijuana. This objective evidence supports published statements of the association between the use of marijuana and various types of crime." It is first noteworthy that the cases cited date back to 1921 and thus in the 45 years which had elapsed before the article was published in the 1966 U.N. Bulletin on Narcotics, only 69 "murders and atrocities" were recorded in the supposedly voluminous files of the Bureau. Considering the number of people in America who have used marijuana in that time interval and the number of times they have used it, this would be an insignificant number in any case even if a cause-effect relationship could be shown, but, of course, such a relationship is not demonstrated since, in most of the cases cited, marijuana, if involved at all, was quite peripheral, including eight cases in which it was not even mentioned. In about one-seventh of the cases, alcohol or other drugs are stated to have been involved, and may have been involved in many of the others, since there is no indication that this was inquired into or investigated. Only 19 of the 69 cases are shown to have involved convictions for the crime charged.

Some typical "case histories"-of alleged criminality *from marijuana:* "Threw glass at bartender while smoking marijuana just bought from peddler." "After smoking two marijuana cigarettes, married a waitress, although already married." "Smoked marijuana for years; held up three taxis." "First degree murder, blamed on smoking marijuana." "Murdered in penitentiary by striking on head repeatedly with axe because of argument over who would control marijuana traffic in the penitentiary." "Prostitute stabbed Mrs. O'Shannon for not cooperating in lesbian activities," and "Attempted rape under influence of marijuana and rum." Many of the references cited to "prove" the inevitability of crime after smoking marijuana upon investigation actually contradict this view or don't have any bearing on it. One Nigerian study cited actually points out in its text that it is not easy to establish relationships between crime and cannabis smoking because of the anecdotal nature of the information available; one from Tunisia concludes that the cannabis plant does not influence criminality; and one from South Africa compares dagga (pot) favorably with alcohol. An American study of more than 2,200 convicts finds no correlation between marijuana and their crime, including the statement "No crimes were committed in this group during or immediately after the intoxication." Studies from India state that hemp drugs do not lead to premeditated crime or violence and may actually serve as deterrents by quieting the individual. A (non)-study from Greece purports to show that, among 374 men arrested or sentenced for public use of hashish between

1919 and 1950, violent crimes, dishonesty, vagrancy, and sentences increased following "smoking of marijuana" (which is not used in Greece and was not even said to be involved by the original author). Another Nigerian study stressed that the relationship of cannabin to crime and antisocial behavior was "complex and elusive." A Canadian survey of the psychiatric literature found that cannabis does not induce aggressive or criminal activities, that these are in fact less common with cannabis than with alcohol, and the reduction of work-drive said by some to occur would lead to a negative correlation between marijuana and criminality rather than a positive one. Then there is a Brazilian doctor's finding that there was no relationship between cannabin use and criminality in that country, and an American paper by two authors who take pains to point out about all the major mind-altering drugs including cannabis and alcohol that "they do not cause the addict to indulge in crimes of violence or crimes of sexual nature." The La Guardia report debunked many of the then (1944) and still existing myths associating marijuana with various types of depravity. Pointing to a causal relationship to crime is a chapter in a 1938 book by Walton offering figures by the New Orleans Police Chief to the effect that many of the people in the jails there were marijuana smokers and an entirely anecdotal polemic by Wolff about the menace of marijuana in South America.

A good example of Anslinger-Federal Bureau of Narcotics distortions is their often-published treatment of an early and important article by Allentuck and Bowman which states: "Marijuana, like alcohol, does not alter the basic personality, but by relaxing inhibitions may permit antisocial tendencies formerly suppressed to come forth. Marijuana does not of itself give rise to antisocial behavior." Anslinger turns this into: "Drs. Allentuck and Bowman say definitely that marijuana by relaxing inhibitions may permit antisocial tendencies to come to the fore thus confirming the information in our possession."

Giving some insight into the intensity of the drug-crime tenets of the drug policemen's religion is a survey done by

Blum on a sample of narcotics officers who were asked to rank different groups on a scale of menace to the community. Heroin addicts were ranked as less of a menace than the Communist party, but more of a menace than syndicated crime, burglary rings, and confidence men. Marijuana users were ranked as less of a menace than any of the foregoing, but more of a menace than the Mafia, white supremacists, crooked real-estate operators, etc. LSD users were seen as more of a menace than the John Birch Society. The drug police described a typical heroin user as self-indulgent, greedy, and insatiable, easily exploited by others, and morally degenerate. Marijuana users were described as disrespectful of, or rebellious toward, authority, exploitative of others, self-indulgent, and abusing sources of pleasure. LSD users were seen as disrespectful of, or rebellious toward, authority, self-indulgent, and as professing superior moral ideas. In terms of ideal punishments as they saw them, marijuana users were lumped with prostitutes and income-tax evaders, with recommended sentences of from one day to one year in jail; while LSD users were grouped with drunks, beatniks, homosexuals, adulterers, and speeding drivers, for all of whom probation with no time in jail was recommended.

These responses are in marked contrast to another Blum survey, of academic and professional people, most of whom considered the police unduly punitive in enforcing drug laws, condemned present narcotics legislation, wanted more humane handling with emphasis on treatment, and tended to denigrate the knowledge and humanity of the police as a group.

Wolfgang, a criminologist, has stated that the public fear of violence is greater than the actual amount of violent behavior and that the dominant middle-class society morally denounces violence partly because every established political power needs to uphold nonviolence as a means of discouraging attacks against that power. He outlines a subculture of violence (within the dominant nonviolent culture) which expects or requires the use of violence in many kinds of social relationships and thus helps to bring it about. Others write of violence as a form of achievement, as a danger signal, as a catalyst, a symbol of reality, a regenerative or creative force, and a symbol of masculinity.

Violence is as American as apple or cherry pie, not only as part of (real) crime, but in our perpetual wars, television and motion pictures, magazines and newspapers (regular and underground), and in politics, particularly among extremist nihilistic groups on the far left and right. Even to suggest that the activities of Yippies (mostly a public relations creation); Klansmen, and Hell's Angels; the magnicidal: Oswald, Sirhan, and the killer of King; the Boston Strangler; and student militants are somehow due to the ingestion of certain drugs, not only is totally wrong but is itself likely to fan the flames of violence by ignoring the real sources. In all probability, sometimes mind-altering drugs, whether alcohol or others, will interact with a personality made prone to violence by social and psychological influences to precipitate or intensify violent behavior, while in other instances such a drug may well dampen the fires of violence through depressant actions, and reduce the likelihood of its being expressed antisocially.

CHAPTER 7

Demons and Demagogues: Insanity; Sex; Birth Defects; and Dropping Out

> "Ignorance is strength. War is peace. All animals are equal but some are more equal than others." —ORWELL

INSANITY, PSYCHOSIS, BRAIN DAMAGE

Temperance lecturers in America used to drop a worm in a container of pure alcohol and, as it shriveled up and died, inform the audience that what they were seeing was what would happen to their brains if they drank alcohol. In more recent decades, drug policemen have informed secondary-school children and others that the use of marijuana would destroy their brains. Similar stories are sometimes heard about LSD, amphetamines, and other drugs that have become relatively easy routes to power and publicity.

Actually, none of the mind-altering substances under discussion here have been found to produce brain damage with average doses, or with moderate use. Only one, alcohol, has been found to do so with large doses and/or extended use, usually many years. This damage is permanent, frequent (under those conditions), and disabling, with impairment of memory, judgment, reasoning, and overall intellectual functioning.

Strangely, the overemphasis on brain damage as a criterion of drug risks has been, like the other approaches of the drug police, self-defeating because absence of brain damage resulting from a drug doesn't demonstrate that the drug is harmless. As has been pointed out, the multiplicity of dimensions of action, effects, and "hardness" must always be considered.

Leaving aside philosophical questions about psychosis, except to stress that the concept is often used loosely as a kind of psychiatric name-calling, we must examine the criteria used in asserting that various drugs produce psychosis. "Insanity," although used as a lay appellation for anyone who appears to be behaving strangely or has ideas at variance with the standard, is really a legal rather than a medical-psychiatric concept. Although there is some variation from state to state, the legal determination is based upon an individual's ability to differentiate right from wrong and an awareness of the nature and quality of his acts. Drug use per se, or being under the influence of a drug, whether alcohol or LSD, is not accepted as sufficient basis for insanity defenses in legal proceedings, although it may sometimes be sufficient for a "diminished responsibility" plea.

Broadly speaking, the psychiatric definition of psychosis is based on a loss of contact with "reality" (frequently described as depersonalization or derealization) accompanied by hallucinations and delusions. This description mainly refers to schizophrenia, the most frequently occurring psychosis, but there are also psychotic reactions characterized by depression, paranoia, or organic brain defects. Psychotic reactions can be acute (temporary), ranging from hours to days or weeks, or they can be chronic, lasting for an indefinite period, usually characterized by cycles of relapse and remission (periods free of at least overt symptoms). A chronic or permanent psychosis would obviously be more serious than an acute one.

ALCOHOL

A number of the mind-altering drugs are involved in the occurrence of acute, and sometimes chronic, psychotic reaction, as has already been stated, but alcohol is the drug most frequently involved in such psychotic episodes, and this in several quite different ways. Medical and psychiatric articles and textbooks for decades (and sometimes centuries) have described alcohol-induced psychoses. One such has been called "pathological intoxication," in which people ingesting even small quantities of the drug develop symptoms lasting from a few minutes to many hours, including confusion, disorientation, illusions, hallucinations, and delusions. Impulsive and aggressive behavior, anxiety, and depression have also been described as part of this syndrome. The most widely used textbook of psychiatry, by Noyes, in describing this and other psychoses from alcohol use, says, "Under conditions of anxiety and tension, alcohol may so disorganize discriminating functions that aggressive outbursts are released; the drinking of alcohol tends to be accompanied by release of sexual and aggressive impulses [here explaining alcohol and crime relationships]. In many instances alcohol serves merely to release a reaction that is primarily psychogenic with factors intrinsic in the personality."

Closely related to the psychosis of "pathological intoxication" is the similarly long-described condition of "acute hallucinosis," which is thought to develop out of a background of prolonged heavy use of the drug although precipitated by specific episodes of heavy drinking. This also is thought to be a basically psychogenic reaction, perhaps an underlying schizophrenia, which is manifested through excessive alcohol intake. The major symptoms are auditory hallucinations of a paranoid nature, including threats, accusations, and homosexual charges; delusions and ideas of reference; and an extreme fear which may be accompanied by suicidal attempts. This particular alcohol psychosis is of medium duration, usually lasting about a week to a month, although sometimes continuing as a prolonged schizophrenic-like psychosis. A similar condition, known as "alcoholic paranoia," has been described, thought to be a latent paranoid psychosis hastened in its occurrence by alcohol use.

For a variety of reasons, including neglect by professionals as well as the real difficulties that would be involved, no figures exist as to the incidence or prevalence of the above or other psychotic conditions stemming from alcohol. Presumably, most such incidents are overlooked, since a "normal" frame of reference is applied to alcohol-

induced problems as compared to a "pathological" frame
of reference automatically applied to either the use or the
abuse of various other drugs. With these other substances,
we have, of course, highly publicized anecdotal accounts of
a relatively small number of psychoses associated with
their use, but again have no idea of how often such things
occur in particular individuals using the drug, or how extensive such phenomena are among the general population.
The most solid statistics exist with the chronic, permanent
psychoses brought about by alcohol, since mental hospital
records have long been able to confirm this. Even with the
acute and transitory psychoses, however, one can presume
that they occur far more commonly in association with
alcohol than with all of the other drugs combined mainly
because of the far more extensive, regular, and frequent
use of alcohol.

A quite different and apparently far more frequent (than
pathological intoxication or alcoholic hallucinosis) alcohol
psychosis is delirium tremens, commonly abbreviated as
DT's. Long misunderstood, this condition is now recognized to be the withdrawal illness or abstinence syndrome
occurring in those alcoholics who have been daily heavy
users of the drug for a long enough period (ordinarily requiring many weeks or months at a minimum) for their
body cells to have become physically dependent on the
drug. When the drug is abruptly reduced in amount or
discontinued a massive physiological reaction, DT's,
develops. Only a minority of our estimated six million
alcoholics are thought to be addicted in this manner, but
even if this were only ten percent, it would represent an
enormous number, only the most visible segment of which
is the chronic drunk offender or skid-row habituate (arrested by the police). Since alcohol is biologically equivalent to the sedative drugs such as barbiturates, the
withdrawal illnesses with the two drugs are essentially the
same, are far more serious than the much more publicized
illness of narcotics addiction, and if treated at all (when
recognized) are treated for the most part inadequately or

improperly. It is estimated that about 50 percent of those who fail to receive proper (gradual) substitution and withdrawal treatment will have a combination of either or both a toxic psychosis and generalized epileptic-like convulsions. Visual hallucinations, often of a frightening nature, predominate in this psychosis, but tactile, olfactory, and auditory ones also occur. Additionally, there is irritability, restlessness, tremor, confusion, disorientation, insomnia, and other physical and mental symptoms. If proper treatment is provided, the severe symptoms can be prevented or very quickly aborted, but otherwise the illness will continue for several days.

It is not clear in terms of current research information whether the brain damage incurred from many years of heavy alcohol intake is due to direct, toxic action of the drug on the brain cells or indirect effects of malnutrition and vitamin deficiency, or a combination (which is most likely), but in any case, such damage is irreversible. As with all biological phenomena, there is a continuum with some in the early stages of this process, some in far advanced stages, and most somewhere in between at any given time. With minimal brain damage, there might be no observable impairment of functioning, but as additional numbers of neurons are destroyed, atrophy or shrinking of the brain ensues particularly in the frontal areas concerned with intellect. Memory loss, impaired judgment, confusion, and disorientation develop as consequences. By the time the individual reaches the state psychiatrically diagnosed as chronic brain syndrome due to alcohol (organic psychosis from alcohol), he is incapacitated and generally requires institutionalization. Presently this situation accounts for as many as 20 percent of the patients in the mental hospitals of certain states and a large percentage, if less, in all states. Thus, at a minimum, this type of drug psychosis involves hundreds of thousands of Americans at any given time and, over a period of years, millions. It is the most permanent of the drug-induced psychotic reactions as well as the most frequent. Other common symptoms of this condition include impulsiveness, loss of emotional control, and loss of energy, motivation, and ambition.

PILLS

Barbiturates, chloral hydrate, paraldehyde, meprobamate (Equanil, Miltown), Doriden, and other sedatives with daily heavy use (best defined in terms of present research knowledge as more than 500 milligrams or five ordinary capsules of barbiturates, or the equivalent of the other drugs) produce physical dependence (addiction). Considering the enormous amounts of these drugs being used, despite the fact that the condition is often overlooked or not treated, we can safely assume that there are hundreds of thousands of sedative addicts who, when their drug is not available, or is significantly reduced in quantity, will develop hallucinations and disorientation, i.e., a psychotic reaction. This psychosis is temporary in nature, can be prevented by proper withdrawal treatment, and, if untreated, will run its course within a few days although often with severe complications. Those taking 400 milligrams or less daily would be psychologically dependent (habituated) and will often exhibit drug abuses other than addiction but usually will not develop addiction.

Receiving considerable attention within the past year has been the psychosis stemming from the use of amphetamines such as Methedrine (methamphetamine, speed), Dexedrine, and Benzedrine. A similar phenomenon occurs with excessive use of other stimulants, such as Preludin, or cocaine. Tolerance develops to the drug as it does to alcohol, sedatives, and narcotics (although with stimulants there is no withdrawal or abstinence illness so they are not addicting in the scientific sense) and as the daily amount builds up over a period of weeks or months, restlessness, insomnia, irritability, loss of appetite and weight, and ultimately a psychotic reaction occur. This amphetamine psychosis is characterized by visual hallucinations and delusions of persecution; requires hospitalization; and is temporary in nature, ordinarily ending within a few days when the drug is stopped. It occurs more frequently among middle-class older adults receiving these chemicals on doctors' prescriptions than among the young adults presently labeled as "speed freaks" or "meth heads."

LSD

Psychoses attributed to LSD have received so much attention since 1965 that probably most of the public not only thinks of this as a frequent occurrence, but considers it the only drug psychosis. When bad trips occur with LSD, STP, mescaline, psilocybin, DMT, or the many other naturally occurring or synthetic LSD-type substances, they most commonly involve a response to the drug variously described as acute anxiety, panic, or psychosis. Whether one describes or categorizes this as "psychosis" is not always simple, except for the simpleminded. When confusion, disorientation, and clear-cut visual or other hallucinations are present (as they sometimes are), this can properly be diagnosed as psychosis and fortunately this type of acute condition ordinarily clears as the pharmacological effects of LSD (or the others) wear off (8–12 hours after ingestion of average doses). A small number of authenticated chronic or long-lasting (not necessarily permanent) psychoses have also been reported, these involving, as mentioned above with alcohol, an underlying personality instability or actual schizophrenia which is intensified or precipitated by the LSD. If treatment is provided (as described later) for the acute LSD psychosis, there is usually a quick return to "normality," while the chronic ones respond according to the severity of the underlying psychopathology, most of them within several months.

MARIJUANA

A small number of marijuana-induced psychoses were reported in this country in the 1930s and again in the last several years, involving temporary hallucinations and sometimes panic, and clearing within a matter of hours (or less, with proper treatment). No chronic psychoses from marijuana, even with heavy use, have been authenticated in this country or abroad, although they are talked about in anecdotal, unscientific reports from Morocco, Egypt, Nigeria, and India. The study mentioned earlier where synthetic tetra-hydrocannabinol (THC), an oral extract of crude marijuana, and ordinary smoking marijuana were administered to a small group of narcotics addicts in federal prison found that with low doses of each of the three substances, the subjects experienced the same "high" obtained with social marijuana smoking, while with high doses of the THC or the concentrated crude extract, most of them showed marked perceptual changes or distortions interpreted by the experimenter as "hallucinations" and "psychoses." In addition to confirming an axiom of pharmacology—that is, with increasing doses of any drug, different responses, usually more intense or dangerous, occur—the study has been widely used to maintain the marijuana demonology and harsh penalties for all users or possessors of the drug. All of the responses mentioned were short-lived and the subjects were soon able to resume their ordinary prison routines with the added benefit of earlier release from the institution as a reward for having participated in the experiment, and perhaps for having given the answers suggested by the questions and environment provided by the experimenters. A more recent report by Weil and associates not surprisingly replicated the La Guardia Report, finding pot to be a "mild intoxicant" after giving it to 17 volunteers, only half of whom even got "high." A 1969 University of Washington study found no evidence of driving impairment after ingestion of average doses of marijuana by 36 sophisticated users and as compared to alcohol which did produce impairment.

In addition to wanting to know with marijuana or any other drug the nature of the user's personality and mood, the dosage, the setting, and other variables we also need to differentiate normal perception from perceptual alterations, illusions, hallucinations, and psychosis. Any one, or several, of these might occur while under the influence of a particular drug. An illusion is defined as a misinterpretation of an actual or real sensation while a hallucination is a false perception, arising inside the individual without external stimulation or sensation. In addition to mind-altering substances, other kinds of drugs, meditation, starvation, prolonged sleeplessness (sleep deprivation), hypnosis, and fever, can all cause illusions and hallucinations. Depending on the personality-drug interaction, the subjective interpretation by the user of what he is experiencing, the phraseology of the questions asked by an experimenter seeking to determine what is happening, and the subjective interpretations of the experimenter, widely different "results" can be obtained in any study of drug effects. Whether a person has one hallucination or a series of hallucinations, and whether the hallucination lasts five seconds or many minutes or hours should have bearing on the judgments arrived at. Isolated or short-lived hallucinations, when they do actually occur, using a precise definition, if they do not involve psychological disintegration and loss of contact with reality, cannot properly be referred to as a "psychosis." It was for this reason that early "psychotomimetic" research with LSD had to be abandoned. Although illusions and hallucinations could be produced, the experimental subject was always aware of reality, cognizant of being under the influence of the drug, and able to respond to the external world. Since then, no drug has been considered psychotomimetic, although some are misleadingly labeled "hallucinogen." The setting or environmental component of the drug response requires additional emphasis in several dimensions. The presence or absence of companions, acquaintances, friends, or loved ones is certainly an important determinant. If warmth, reassurance, and knowledgeable guidance are provided, bad experiences, including distortions of perception, are less likely to occur or to be bothersome. If the individual is in a comfortable and familiar environment such as his own living room, he is much less likely to experience drug troubles than if he is placed in a jail or hospital emergency-room atmosphere, both of which have been found to intensify and prolong panic and "hallucinations." Obviously, if the person is at home and at rest, the experience will have a different significance and potential danger than when he is at work or driving.

In mid-1968, ignoring or, more accurately, being unaware of and uninterested in the full picture regarding hallucinations and psychosis, a joint committee (actually mainly one committee serving a dual function) of the American Medical Association and the National Research Council issued a statement that marijuana was a "dangerous drug," basing this on the THC experiment with heroin addicts cited above. Even if these political Committees on Drug Dependence had only added the qualifying word "some" so that the statement would have indicated that marijuana use involved some danger, although a truism, it might have added to public education, particularly if it had been pointed out that all drugs, including aspirin and antibiotics as well as marijuana and alcohol, have some risks or dangers. Digressing for a moment, one wonders if they were just then finding that marijuana was "dangerous," on what basis the fanatical and ineffective laws were justified and acceded to by doctors, legislators, and others. The committee spokesman, a pharmacologist, and a psychiatrist, both of whom move in the unreal and remote worlds of administration and academia, went on to "take a strong stand against the smoking, selling, or legalization of marijuana"; dismissed as "unfounded" the idea that marijuana is less harmful than alcohol; said that when the drug is "used to the point of intoxication, as it usually is, it can cause serious disorders of behavior and interpersonal problems"; and argued that "readier availability, especially of the more potent forms, would inevitably result in greater numbers of users, greater numbers of psychologically dependent users, and even more serious medical and social consequences." In strange contrast to these statements and despite the fact that the committee members serve as advisers to the Federal Bureau of Narcotics, they also expressed support for rehabilitation, research, and education ("with respect to marijuana's hazards"), and "recognized that antimarijuana laws frequently result in harsh and unrealistic punishment of the user."

Paradoxically, the possibility of experiencing perceptual changes or hallucinations actually makes marijuana or other drugs so designated more interesting and attractive to some, just as the drug-police (and marijuana cultists') practice of labeling it as a "mild psychedelic" has added to its popularity. Among the multitude of reasons for drug use, whether of marijuana or others, are dissatisfaction with reality, boredom, desire for new experiences, and curiosity, so that temporary feelings of unreality or perceptual changes may be welcomed, perhaps especially by those reacting against the reality of contemporary politicians and bureaucrats.

A kind of antipsychotic phenomenon is also involved with mind-altering drugs, since psychotic or prepsychotic individuals — depressive, schizophrenic, or otherwise — sometimes use alcohol, marijuana, narcotics, or other mind-altering drugs as a defense against psychotic symptoms, to hide, suppress, or escape from them. When this works, as it does in an unknown proportion of such instances, the person would actually be less psychotic and better able to function as a result of mind-altering drug use even when such use may be abuse by other standards.

Many other mind-altering substances, including glue, nutmeg, amyl nitrite, etc., are capable of causing perceptual changes or distortions that would sometimes include hallucinations and could be called, depending on the criteria used, acute psychoses.

As the sociologist Becker has pointed out, when a person takes a medically prescribed drug, he does so to cure or control a disease and he ignores or considers as unpleasant side effects whatever subjective experiences occur. With nonmedical use of drugs, in a sense the opposite occurs, because people deliberately seek out the subjective effects, wanting to get "high," and disregard the medical effects. With some drugs, then, these people become known as "drug users" and as "lawbreakers," thereby becoming objects of special attention by social scientists, police, politicians, the mass media, and the public.

Not only do the underlying personality and mood of the mind-altering drug user serve to determine the nature of the experience, but each of these substances has a variety of effects, any one of which may be singled out and "experienced" by the user while he ignores others. A good deal of this involves learned behavior, the individual being taught by other users that his subjective experiences with alcohol, nicotine, marijuana, etc., are a direct consequence of the drug and are to be interpreted as "pleasurable." Often with early experiences with any of these drugs, users have negative or neutral experiences and may not even be aware that they are experiencing specific drug effects. The choice of what to pay attention to becomes significant and is greatly influenced by the advice of one's associates as well as the cultural traditions in the society. Many of the sensations commonly experienced with alcohol could, if one used a pathological frame of reference, be described in a frightening, unpleasant, and wholly negative light. Imagine, as an example, *Time* or *Newsweek* reporting that a scientist gave 20 volunteers two ounces of alcohol finding that the drug was a mild intoxicant, half got "high," and some were aggressive, talkative, and disoriented.

Pointing out that the verified reports of drug-induced psychoses (from marijuana or LSD) are quite scarce, Becker also stated that in any society whose culture contains concepts of sanity and insanity, a person finding his subjective state altered, as for example space perception, may interpret this happening as becoming "crazy," "insane," or "nuts," and may fear this irreversible. He proposes a natural history of the "assimilation of the intoxicating drug by society," showing how reports of "marijuana psychosis"

over the last several decades fit this theory, and how the
more recent "LSD psychosis" seems to be falling into a
similar pattern.   Someone in a society discovers or invents
a drug which has the properties described earlier. The
ability of the drug to alter subjective experience in desirable ways becomes known to increasing numbers of
people, and the drug itself becomes simultaneously available, along with information needed to make its use effective. Use increases, but users do not have a sufficient
amount of experience with the drug to form a stable conception of it as an object. They do not know what it can do
to the mind, have no firm idea of the variety of effects it can
produce, and are not sure how permanent or dangerous the
effects are. They do not know if the effects can be controlled
or how. No drug-using culture exists, and there is thus no
authoritative alternative with which to counter the definition, when and if it comes to mind, of the drug experience's madness. "Psychotic" episodes occur frequently.
But individuals accumulate experience with the drug and
communicate their experiences to one another. Consensus
develops about the drug's subjective effects, their duration,
proper doses, predictable dangers, and how they may be
avoided; all these points become matters of common knowledge, validated by their acceptance in a world of users. A
culture exists. When a user experiences bewildering or
frightening effects, he has available to him an authoritative
alternative to the lay notions that he has gone mad. Every
time he uses cultural conceptions to interpret drug experiences and control his response to them, he strengthens
his belief that the culture is indeed a reliable source of
knowledge. "Psychotic episodes" occur less frequently in
proportion to the growth of the culture to cover the range
of possible effects and the spread to a greater proportion of
users. *Novice users*, to whom the effects are most unfamiliar
and who therefore might be expected to suffer most from
drug induced anxiety, learn the culture from older users in
conversation and in more serious teaching sessions and are
thus protected from the dangers of panic, or "flipping out."

The "psychosis" as Becker sees it is a function of the stage of development of the drug-using culture.

SEXUAL "EXCESSES"

In recent years, it has become common for disseminators of one-dimensional misinformation about drugs to speak about sexual excesses as one of the dangers of the use of certain drugs, particularly marijuana. If even a fraction of the statements that are made about marijuana by the drug police were correct, it would be the most remarkable drug ever discovered by man, since in different contexts they claim that it diminishes sexual interest and capacity, and that it provokes sexual excesses; that it leads to aggressive behavior, and to passivity and dropping out; and many similar and equally impossible polarities. The basic concept of mind-altering-drug effects applies to the sexual area as well as the other dimensions already covered and it indicates that the individual's sexual training, beliefs, propensities, and inclinations basically determine the kind of behavior he will engage in, with the drug playing only a secondary role. Thus, no drug can be said to be a specific aphrodisiac, none of them would give consistent, uniform sexual results, and any of them on any given occasion might have no effect on sexuality, "decrease" it, or "increase" it depending really on the person and the social context.

Symbols and potions of love have an ancient history which includes Egyptian pharaohs being buried with spices at their side; searches for philosopher's stones, Holy Grails, or Fountains of Youth; roe mixed in wine (champagne and caviar); pigeons, partridges, and turtle doves; the blood of bats in asses milk; rhinoceros horns; Spanish fly; tiger testicle; calves' brains; amulets worn on the wrist, genitals, or head; the May Pole Dance; the mandrake root; belladonna; special condoms; perfume; oysters; ginseng; yohimbine, and many other objects, chemicals, or superstitions.

At least a twofold definition of aphrodisiac is necessary,

including the concepts both of stimulating or increasing sexual desire, and improving sexual performance. Sex hormones, particularly testosterone, furnish a necessary constitutional foundation for sexuality; in ordinary doses given to people without hormonal deficiency, they have no aphrodisiac effect. Placebo effects are common with all drugs, and all other things being equal, if a person believes and expects that a certain substance will improve his sexual performance, this will sometimes occur, but not as a specific result of the drug. Impotence is usually psychological in origin, as is frigidity, although some patterns of use of some drugs, mind-altering (narcotics *addiction* most notably) and otherwise, can temporarily bring about these conditions.

Alcohol is the mind-altering drug most often used in Western society in connection with sexual behavior, ranging from kissing, necking, and petting to intercourse. It has a long history of being considered an aphrodisiac and in some societies even presently this belief is deeply entrenched. Alcohol or other drugs, such as marijuana, may be used in moderate or average doses to temporarily increase or free sexual desire, lower inhibitions, reduce anxiety, or eliminate guilt. No mind-altering drug, whether alcohol or marijuana, can by itself cause an individual to engage in sexual behavior that would otherwise be alien, uninteresting, or abhorrent to him. Excessive doses of sedative or depressant drugs, such as alcohol, barbiturates, or narcotics, ordinarily diminish sexual performance, thus having an anaphrodisiac or anti-sexual effect. As Shakespeare said of alcohol, it (sometimes) increases desire but diminishes performance. Narcotics addiction, alcoholism, and other types of drug abuse usually are accompanied by greatly diminished sexual interest and performance, impotence, and sometimes sterility, all of these reversible when the drug is discontinued. When sexual relationships involve a great deal of anxiety or tension for a person, tranquilizers, alcohol, or barbiturates are sometimes helpful in improving sexual performance, as with premature ejaculation, but more often some form of counseling or psychotherapy will be necessary.

Aphrodisiac properties have been attributed to a few of the psychoactive drugs, such as heroin, cannabis (hashish), or alcohol, because of their sometimes prolonging the pre-ejaculatory phase of intercourse by diminishing the sensitivity of the penis. In such situations, both dosage and personality variations would greatly alter the result.

Anaphrodisiac (interference with libido or erection) effects have occurred as side effects with several of the tranquilizing drugs: autonomic nervous system drugs; Antabuse (used in the treatment of alcoholism); estrogens given to males (either for treating prostatic cancer, reducing blood cholesterol or feminizing a male transexual); and various others.

Those who have misdirected public attention onto certain drugs by crying sexual "excesses" have been successful by tying together a series of basically unrelated phenomena which concern the public: premarital or extramarital sex, hippies, mental health, crime, drugs, anarchy, over-permissiveness, radicalism, communism, fluoridation, and other preoccupations of a paranoid life style.

Recently claims have been made by Timothy Leary and others that LSD has remarkable aphrodisiac properties. R. E. L. Masters, in his *Playboy* article evaluating such claims about "psychedelic" drugs in general, states that they do not produce or encourage sexual desire and do not excite the sexual organs, but they *can* "profoundly enhance the quality of sexual acts that occur between people who would in any case have had intercourse" and in that sense only can be described as sometimes aphrodisiacs. Strong emotional bonds or positive feelings for each other; changes in time (and other sensory) perception; unusual genital sensations; diminished inhibitions; and symbolic overtones can be part of an LSD experience and will in some circumstances produce a mystical or ecstatic sexual union which may seem endless. Again, such an experience would derive mainly from the underlying characters of the lovers, discriminate and experienced use of the LSD, the setting, and chance factors. Many instances have been reported of lessened sexual interest and involvement while under the influence of an LSD-type drug, and no instances have been authenticated of repetitive male orgasms resulting from taking the drug.

In sum, the reputed causal relationship between drugs and sex is just one more myth, whether utilized by the alcohol and tobacco industries to sell their drugs, by drug police to sell their agencies, or by politicians to get elected. The effects are inconsistent, variable, mixed, and quite secondary to other factors.

BIRTH DEFECTS AND BODY DAMAGE

Various kinds of physical damage at different times have been attributed to several of the mind-altering drugs by professional viewers-with-alarm (who have carefully refrained from implicating alcohol or tobacco). Thus, brain damage, as previously mentioned, is not infrequently brought up as an expected risk, danger, or harm; the specter of blindness has been raised; and human birth defects have been forced upon us as a continuing concern.

BLINDNESS

In January 1968, as was touched on earlier, nationwide front-page stories appeared stating that LSD had blinded six college students. This was supposed to have occurred when the six young men stared fixedly at the sun under the influence of LSD and was presented as established fact at a press conference by the State Commissioner for the Blind and a state legislator who is a former narcotics agent. They refused to reveal the names of the college students or precise details. It was some days later, after the story had been accepted as "fact" by millions of people, that the Governor of Pennsylvania, under pressure from the federal Food and Drug Administration and others who questioned

the accuracy of the report, publicly announced that the
charge had been a deliberate lie ("fabrication"). The
Commissioner, after attending a scare lecture on the dangers
of LSD, had falsified the records of the six students, all of
whom had been blinded for reasons completely unrelated
to LSD. He was suspended and went off to a hospital, according to later installments of the story which appeared
on the back pages of most newspapers, if at all. No instances
of blindness have been shown to result from LSD use, but,
of course, there are millions of blind people and hundreds
of known causes of blindness which the public and press
have shown much less concern about than the propaganda
associating LSD with this severe disability. The propensity
of the mass media uncritically to accept lurid and sensationalistic stories emanating from generally untrustworthy
and uninformed government sources is probably far more
dangerous to our social fabric than LSD. Printers' ink in
one sense is the most dangerous chemical in use.

CHROMOSOMES

The chromosome story has slightly more substance to it,
but only slightly (less with LSD than with many other
drugs). This chapter in our book of fairy tales began when a
then unknown New York State University geneticist at-
tended a medical meeting in San Francisco and, as people
are wont to do, particularly those critical of the hippies,
made an inspection tour of the Haight-Asbury district. As
he later reported in the "scientific" journal, the *Saturday
Evening Post*, he was so impressed during his tour (of about
30 minutes' duration) with the dirt and unkempt appearance of the hippies that he rushed back to Buffalo to prove
that LSD was harmful. Assuming that there is some rational
thread linking dirt, hippies, and LSD, although a dubious
assumption, one still wonders about the scientific standards
of setting out to prove either that something is bad or that
it is good. The true scientist seeks to understand, to learn,
and to conduct experiments no matter how they may turn

out. At any rate, it was already well known in 1967, when this occurred, that there were significant risks in the psychological dimension from indiscriminate use of LSD. Many of us were seeking to reduce use of this and other drugs through education, and criminal penalties had been instituted against possessors and sellers of the drug, so a false birth defect scare wasn't needed. However, using an enormous sample of three people, two "normals" and one paranoid schizophrenic (who had had electroshock and tranquilizer therapy), he took a sample of their white blood cells, and after exposing the cells of the two normals to varying concentrations of LSD in test tubes, he examined all three with an electron microscope and reported finding significant increases in chromosomal breakage *due to* the effects of LSD. This nonarticle was rushed into press by *Science*, the official journal of the American Association for the Advancement of Science, while an article showing the opposite results was delayed for months, and articles about many more important things continued the usual waits for publication. Within 24 hours of the publication in this relatively esoteric journal, there were national headlines to the effect that LSD had been shown to produce *human birth defects*. A new mythology had been created. *The New York Times* stated that it has been "shown that high rates of chromosome damage can be found in about 90 percent of LSD users." The *Washington Post* put out a headline "Worse Deformities Feared in LSD Than Thalidomide." The *Saturday Evening Post*, showing uncaptioned pictures of deformed children, stated, "if you take LSD even once, your children may be born malformed or retarded." Not featured by the media and relatively unnoticed had been cautionary or corrective statements, such as that by the Vice-President for Research at Hoffman-LaRoche, saying, "We're dealing with an entirely new field. No one really knows what it means if you do find broken chromosomes. We know that many drugs and chemicals can affect chromosomes. Caffeine and aspirin, for instance, also break chromosomes." The

Ladies' Home Journal stated: "Moralists who read a lesson for youth into scientific reports tying LSD to chromosome damage must now face up to the fact that science preaches more complex sermons. . . . New research reports that chromosome damage like that *caused by* LSD can be found in patients using pharmacologically useful and important tranquilizing drugs." Later, more carefully done studies by other geneticists and scientists who found results contrary to those of the original investigator went unmentioned by the communications industry or appeared on page 30 without headlines. The most recent and most scientific of these, done by Unger and associates at the country's leading LSD research center, Spring Grove, Maryland, State Hospital, found no evidence whatever of LSD producing increased chromosomal breaks.

Looking at this first study in some detail, we see that the white blood cells were exposed to large concentrations of LSD, about 350 times an average "psychedelic" dose. Neither shock therapy, other drugs, nor any other possible cause for the claimed chromosomal breakage was even considered. A biochemist, engaged in basic research in genetics, in criticizing the above study said:

> There was no consistent effect of dose on frequency of chromosomal breaks despite the author's statement to the contrary. Plotting of the tabulated data reveals the dose response curves to be very irregular, suggesting a high degree of random experimental variability. Several researchers in the biological sciences working in similar fields noted this experimental result and were particularly surprised by the sloppiness of the work. They feel that the range, the design, and the lack of adequate controls scarcely warrant the conclusions drawn by the author. One doctor added, in fact, that it is somewhat strange that this finding was received with such widespread alarm when in fact a new live measles vaccine which produces chromosome breakage at a substantially higher level than found throughout the bulk of this experi-

ment has been approved for many years by the federal government.

Additionally, a single control figure was used rather than simultaneous normal controls for each sample, and the general culture technique and cytogenetic methodology and interpretations were questionable.

In addition to cashing in on the publicity value of LSD, the authors and disseminators of this initial report succeeded in unnecessarily frightening perhaps millions of people throughout the world who had taken LSD for research, clinical, mystical, or other purposes, and in the long run, they decreased awareness or acceptance of LSD dangers by the young as subsequent studies showed that once more, "honorable men" could not be believed.

In the last two years, following upon this study, an increasing number of scientists have been diverted from other research activities. The National Institute of Mental Health and the Food and Drug Administration have poured an increasing segment of their multimillion-dollar research funds into LSD-chromosome studies as compared to objectively far more important matters requiring attention. Confusion and misinformation have been greatly added to with each new story.

At this point in time, prior to the Spring Grove study (out of the context of other chromosome-damaging substances), some 20 studies had been done on human white blood cells, some from LSD users and some exposed to LSD in test tubes, with the overall results evenly divided between increased chromosomal breakage and no increased chromosomal breakage (some chromosomal breakage is found normally). Early animal studies, especially with pregnant rats, revealed that LSD injected into the abdomen early in the pregnancy resulted in an abnormally high proportion of defective litters, and at that point it seemed safe to conclude that pregnant rats should definitely avoid LSD. Later studies, however, found no such increase in abnormal offspring, and again the findings are mixed. The drosophila, or fruit fly, has long been a popular subject for genetic research, and two studies utilizing it with LSD have been evenly divided in terms of possible genetic damage from the drug. One child born with a deformed limb to a mother who used LSD has been attributed to the drug, without ruling out other possible causes, while thousands of normal infants have been born to mothers who were or had been LSD users.

Among the major variables which require consideration in regard to the possible effects of LSD on babies are: the relationship between a finding in white blood cells outside the body to white blood cells in the body; the relationship between this and chromosomal changes in germ plasm (sperm, or egg); chromosomal changes in germ plasm as they might relate to actual genetic changes; and, finally, the relationship of possible genetic changes to actual birth defects. Then there are such factors as the time when LSD was taken, that is, five years before pregnancy, one year before pregnancy, one month before, or after conception; the dosage, 150 micrograms, 500 micrograms, or 1,000 micrograms; significance of male ingestion of the drug as opposed to female; the frequency of use; possible reversibility of the effect; and many other physical, genetic, psychological, and sociological factors. The technique of studying drug effects in terms of chromosomal alterations is only about nine years old and many drugs in common usage have not been evaluated in this dimension at all, so that we do not know whether they produce chromosomal or genetic changes. Possibly other kinds of cells need to be examined and might even differ in findings from those of leucocytes (white blood cells). In the more than 25 years of experimental, clinical, and black-market use of LSD, no indications of genetic changes have become spontaneously known, as they likely would and have with other substances with significant damage. With the even longer history of use of related drugs there have likewise been no spontaneous observations of this nature.

About 250,000 children are born each year in America alone with birth defects (plus an additional 100,000 mentally retarded), most of which cannot be attributed to any specific external cause, and all of which have been ignored by the mass media and the rule makers of the society as compared to the LSD furor.

Moving to the broader context of substances involved in cellular change, there are many drugs, chemicals, and types of radiation known to produce chromosomal breakage and sometimes genetic changes and birth defects. Of the mind-altering drugs, both alcohol and caffeine have been found to be potent radiomimetic agents producing mutations and chromosomal aberrations in plant cells. The concentration of only one-half percent of ethyl alcohol was found to be equivalent in its effect to 20 roentgens per day of gamma radiation or an accumulated dose of 75 roentgens. Thalidomide, a tranquilizer formerly widely used in western Europe, was repeatedly found to produce abnormal infants and there is some evidence that other tranquilizers currently used produce at least chromosomal breakage. Measles, measles vaccine, German measles, and probably other viruses, also produce significant chromosomal breakage and, at least in the case of German measles, birth defects if it is contracted by a woman during the first trimester of pregnancy. Nuclear and X-ray radiation are certainly far more prevalent and serious dangers to chromosomes, genes, and unborn children than any one drug, yet they have received relatively little attention from this standpoint, with no one calling for jail sentences even for those who disseminate radiation against the wishes of the recipients such as the U.S. Atomic Energy Commission or the French and Chinese governments. DDT and other insecticides have been found to affect chromosomes and may have even greater dangers. The massively used artificial sweeteners, cyclamates, found in diet drinks and foods produce broken chromosomes and genetic changes in animals and perhaps man—to such an extent that the *drastic* governmental action of labeling packages is being considered.

There are many other kinds of adverse reactions, sometimes fatal, produced by the physical properties of drugs, including dermatitis, anemia, agranulocytosis, hepatitis, allergy, and shock from either bromides, barbiturates, phenothiazine, tranquilizers, or others.

Much LSD presently being used is impure, mixed with other substances such as amphetamines, and these impurities may damage chromosomes.

The question of drug substitution must also be considered. What is gained if the roots of the problem are ignored and an individual decides not to use LSD because of the chromosome scare but switches to any of 20 or 30 other substances fairly easily obtainable and with potentially more serious psychological and physical effects than LSD? Will the chromosome scare work with males as well as females, has it worked at all, and, if so, will it continue to work? Has use significantly decreased or has it simply gone further underground? If it decreased wasn't it due to increased awareness of the authenticated dangers of LSD, particularly indiscriminate use of unknown doses without preparation or guidance? Won't many who are attracted to LSD use for complex sociological and psychological reasons use it despite, or even because of, the chromosome sensationalism? What about those who don't want or can't have children anyway? No one can say that LSD doesn't or can't damage chromosomes, but they can, and should, display rationality and compassion rather than distortion and fright.

As is often the case, the most important aspect of the situation has been neglected, namely the desirability of a pregnant woman avoiding, at least during the first trimester of pregnancy, all alcohol, tobacco, coffee, tranquilizers, LSD, aspirin, cyclamates, radiation, insecticides, and viruses. It is staggering to think how much good could have been done had the same efforts expended on speculations about LSD been devoted to truthful, complete, and constructive health messages directed to all pregnant or potentially pregnant women.

"DROPPING OUT"

With "dropping out," again we have a vague but success-ful specter raised as a drug danger. Few have even a work-ing definition of the concept, but as currently used in popular mythology, it appears to refer to someone of un-conventional dress or appearance who does not work an ordinary five-day, 40-hour week, or regularly attend school. With continued magical thinking about drug actions, it is popularly believed that normal, satisfied, healthy, con-forming, mature young people smoke one marijuana ciga-rette or swallow an LSD sugar cube and suddenly "drop out," expressing dissatisfaction with family, school, and society and becoming a "hippie." At some schools, and in some families, it is accepted practice for young people to interrupt their formal education for a period of travel, work, or sometimes thought. Clearly, "drop out" is a very sub-jective concept and means both more and less than is usually expressed. At most, a particular drug may accelerate an already existing dissatisfaction and discontent stemming from a fragmented family life, a mind-contracting educa-tional experience, or an imperfect society. Recurrently, we see the attractiveness of attributing a complex phenomenon that may cast critical reflections on us to a drug, thus pro-viding a convenient scapegoat and freeing us from responsi-bility. Certainly, psychological dependence on any of the mind-altering drugs, alcohol, marijuana, etc., can con-tribute to a significant change in life style, loss of ordinary motivation, or other changes in behavior that could be loosely referred to as "dropping out." With most people, however, regular drug use, if not in the abuse category, does not alter their life in this manner, and in a number of instances drug use may be a factor in preventing "dropping out." Rigid puritanical attitudes about work and leisure lead some to the "drop-out" concern. In San Francisco, many "hippies," at least before the successful war waged on them by the local police and health departments, engaged in productive and creative work at their own pace, during "ir-regular" hours and independently. If one were truly to apply this term of opprobrium to everyone not a full-time student or not working a 40-hour week, we would have to include most teachers and professors, ministers, and artists. As to the puritanical concerns, H. L. Mencken expressed it well in defining Puritanism as the "haunting fear that some-one, somewhere may be happy."

Using a broader and more valid conception of "dropping out" to mean noninvolvement or nonparticipation in the world around them, we can see that there are many millions of adult, "respectable" Americans who are bored and dissatisfied with their work, leisure-time pursuits, or marriage, and who, tense and frustrated, "turn on" daily with alcohol, nicotine, and tranquilizers, or marijuana and other drugs. They maintain a shell of existence, but are not meaningfully engaged and are not working toward self-actualization, self-realization, and social betterment. Thus, alcohol would be the drug most involved in the "drop-out" phenomenon, not only in this common situation, but also in the more specific setting of skid row, where nationally there are hundreds of thousands of homeless men and women who have totally dropped out from ordinary, acceptable activities and live a hand-to-mouth existence, often focused around the heavy consumption of booze.

Thus there are many kinds of "drop-outs" involving many drugs, rather than one or two, and, except for clear-cut cases of drug abuse, these are only secondarily a drug phenomenon.

CHAPTER 8
Better Living Through Chemistry?

> "To see a world in a grain of sand,
> And a heaven in a wild flower,
> Hold infinity in the palm of your hand,
> And eternity in an hour."
>
> — WILLIAM BLAKE

Drugs can be classified in many ways, in terms of the system or portion of the human body on which they act, their physical properties or chemical structure, their mechanism of action, their ultimate effects, or their action against particular diseases or symptoms. They are also sometimes classified in terms of crude legal definitions or real or assumed psychological or perceptual experiences. The substances that we are herein concentrating on are generally listed in pharmacological texts as "drugs acting on the central nervous system." Other common categories of drugs are local anesthetics, cardiovascular drugs, drugs affecting renal (kidney) function, gases, locally acting drugs, hormones, vitamins, drugs acting on the blood, and chemotherapeutic drugs.

The action of drugs, as opposed to their effects, is variously expressed or explained in biochemical, neurological, and pharmacological terms, and ultimately as chemical transformations of cellular membranes. Many drugs do not directly affect the brain because of the filtering activities of the blood-brain barrier, but those which do act directly on the central nervous system are acting on some ten billion cells each having up to 10,000 synaptic interconnections and, together, capable of storing an estimated ten quadrillion bits or pieces of information, thoughts, or impressions. Some drugs act on the entire brain at one time, others on different regions of the brain in sequence, and some only on specific limited portions. Genetic and age factors influence the drug action, as, for example, when a "stimulant" drug has a sedative effect on children or a "sedative" drug a stimulant effect on them. The metabolic activities of the brain cells produce hundreds of chemical substances vital to brain functioning, and any changes in the rate or character of this metabolism can drastically alter normal functioning. One group of such substances is designated as chemical transmitters, and it is upon these transmitters that mind-altering drugs—psycho-chemicals, psychotropics, or other names by which they may be designated—exert their action. Electrical activity is generated by the chemical changes and serves to transmit "messages" among the billions of cells that are involved in thought, perception, and behavior. The best-known and most frequently studied chemical message carriers or transmitters are serotonin, norepinephrine (noradrenalin), and acetylcholine. The direct action of some chemical transmitters is to "stimulate" brain activity, and of others to inhibit such activity. A given drug could, by interfering with the action of the stimulating substance, inhibit brain function, while another drug would interfere with an inhibitory substance and would thereby indirectly stimulate brain function. Thus, if a drug has a chemical structure similar to acetylcholine, the cell receptors would be unable to differentiate the two, the drug would "occupy" the site, and the acetylcholine would be unable to exert its ordinary effects. A similar process could occur with noradrenalin or serotonin. Ordinarily, specific enzymes come into action to destroy a transmitting substance after it has acted on the cell, so another action of mind-altering drugs would be to block the enzyme, thereby saving the transmitting substance from destruction and allowing the cell to continue to transmit nerve impulses. If a drug acts directly on a cell to excite it rather than indirectly through a transmitting substance, there is no enzyme system for destroying the outside drug and therefore the range and unpredictability of effects are increased.

The most precise way of classifying central-nervous-system drugs is on the basis of their mechanism of action in terms of synapses and chemical transmitters, but present knowledge is not sufficiently adequate to allow that. Thus, they are usually classified in terms of their major observable effects or the effect which is most therapeutically useful. Some pharmacologists divide what we might call the "brain drugs" into three broad categories: general, non-selective depressants; general, nonselective stimulants; and drugs selectively modifying functions. In this system of classification, the general depressants include anesthetic gases, alcohol, barbiturates, and other sedative-hypnotic drugs. The general stimulants include strychnine, caffeine, and others. The selective modifiers which may produce either excitation or inhibition of the central nervous system include anticonvulsants, some skeletal-muscle relaxants, narcotic analgesics, aspirin, and the heterogeneous group of "psychopharmacological drugs." The level of excitability of the brain represents a continuum between coma at one pole and convulsions at the other. Depressant drug actions range through sedation, hypnosis, general anesthesia and coma, while stimulant drug actions range through hyperexcitability and mild or severe convulsions. With this kind of classification scheme often similar pharmacological properties are ignored, so that drugs sought for similar or identical purposes (such as pleasure) are covered under widely different categories, categories which also do not take into account the psychological or sociological similarities. Conventional textbooks also mix at least partially scientific categories with vague, misleading wastebasket categories, such as "psychotomimetic," "hallocinogen," "addicting drugs," etc. Often the terms used have emotional connotations or legal implications which further becloud the issue.

Wikler in his *Relation of Pharmacology to Psychiatry* pointed out that the conditions under which drugs are administered depend upon the purposes of the investigator, which are in turn related to concepts of normal and abnormal behavior. The ultimate goal of explaining behavior involves developing a model of causal processes, such as one step inevitably leads to another, which can be fully predicted if the conditions are known. Contemporary theories of behavior postulate such things as a psyche, scanning mechanisms, or intervening variables which lie between receptors and effectors and are capable of learning and adaptation. Most theories are either psychological or physiological or a meaningless hyphenation of the two but fail to define what happens in terms of the operation engaged in and fail to take into account the dynamic, constantly shifting nature of the internal and external transactions. At the least, biochemical, neurophysiological, and psychological theories and mechanisms must all be considered, as he sees it.

Recognizing all of these complexities and parameters, I think a more sensible and understandable basis for classification of these drugs would be their mind-altering or consciousness-changing properties. We could call them drugs sought for pleasure or "pleasure-giving drugs" (even though they certainly do not always provide pleasure), in that they are sought out because they are believed to have such properties; or we can simply refer to them as mind-altering drugs (M.A.D.s). These drugs that change the mind or consciousness can then roughly be subdivided into three broad categories—stimulants, depressants, and a mixed or miscellaneous group.

The depressants, then, include alcohol; sedative-hypnotics, such as barbiturates and meprobamate; and narcotics, such as morphine, heroin, and codeine.

The stimulants include caffeine; nicotine; amphetamines such as Dexedrine or methedrine; phenmetrazine (Preludin); methylphenidate (Ritalin); and cocaine.

The mixed or miscellaneous grouping would include such tranquilizers as Librium, reserpine, and the phenothiazines such as Thorazine and Stelazine; cannabis or marijuana (tetrahydrocannabinol); LSD, psilocybin, STP, mescaline; and the antidepressants (in this sense referring to drugs used to alleviate the psychological feelings of

depression or hopelessness as contrasted to the specifically neurological concept of depressant drug).

STIMULANTS

Taking these three broad subdivisions of "pleasure-
giving" or mind-altering drugs in the order of their combined American and worldwide use, we begin with the
stimulants and particularly *caffeine*. To avoid unnecessary
and sometimes redundant detail, we will discuss in detail
only the pharmacological actions of caffeine, the main
active principle of coffee, tea, cocoa, Coca-Cola, and No-
Doz. Theophylline, another active agent in tea; and theo-
bromine in cocoa are other xanthines similar in action to
caffeine.

Pharmacologists consider caffeine a powerful central-
nervous-system stimulant, exciting all parts of the cerebral
cortex as well as the respiratory and vasomotor centers of
the medulla. The average cup of coffee or tea, depending
on how it is prepared, contains 150 milligrams of the drug,
which after ingestion usually increases the flow of thought,
relieves drowsiness and fatigue, and permits more sus-
tained intellectual or motor activity. When the respiratory center has been depressed by drugs such as morphine,
caffeine by injection (not orally) is of therapeutic value in
increasing the rate and depth of respiration. Caffeine and
the other xanthines also have strong effects on the circula-
tory system, including stimulation of the heart and dilation
of the coronary and other arteries, the latter action accounting for the therapeutic value of caffeine in treating some
headaches. There is no consistent effect on blood pressure.
The smooth muscle of the bronchial tree, biliary tract and
gastrointestinal tract is relaxed.

Skeletal muscles are made less susceptible to fatigue,
thereby increasing their capacity for muscular work.
Urine production and the basal metabolic rate are both increased as is the secretion of hydrochloric acid in the
stomach (which helps to develop and maintain peptic ul-

cers). In man, the fatal oral dose of caffeine is estimated to be about 10 grams (10,000 milligrams), but no deaths from the drug are known. Tolerance develops with regular daily use, as does habituation (psychological dependence). With doses of one gram or more (about six cups of coffee), toxic symptoms often occur including insomnia, restlessness, and excitement, which may progress to perceptual distortions, tremors, and accelerated breathing and heart rate. Insomnia is sometimes a complication of caffeine use, and many people with psychological dependence on and tolerance to the drug will develop symptoms of a "withdrawal" nature, including most notably headaches, when they stop using it.

Nicotine, the next stimulant drug to be discussed, is only one of the powerful chemicals in tobacco. Coal tars and other substances present are discussed separately. Nicotine has no therapeutic uses in medicine. It has been used in neurophysiological research as a tool for studying the transmission of nerve impulses in the autonomic nervous system.

Nicotine strongly stimulates the central nervous system, with excessive doses producing tremors, convulsions, and vomiting. It also has an antidiuretic action, inhibiting the formation of urine. The drug brings about increased secretion of epinephrine from the adrenal medulla, thereby accelerating the heart rate and raising blood pressure. In the peripheral nervous system, small dosages stimulate the nerve cells directly and facilitate the transmission of impulses, but larger doses block neuronal transmission. This latter action brings about a paralysis of skeletal muscles, which, among other things, impairs respiration. A series of complicated effects on the sympathetic nervous system produces constriction of blood vessels, rapid heart rate, and elevated blood pressure. In the gastrointestinal tract, working mainly through parasympathetic stimulation, the drug produces increased motor activity of the bowel, and occasionally diarrhea. Nicotine is one of the most toxic drugs known and is usually thought of as a poison, being used as such in insecticide sprays and ranking with cyanide in rapidity of action. Cigarette tobacco contains between 1.5 and three percent nicotine, with each cigarette containing 20 to 30 milligrams of the drug. As little as four milligrams has produced serious symptoms in nonhabituated individuals, although the fatal dose for an adult is about 60 milligrams. The smoke of an ordinary cigar may contain between 15 and 40 milligrams of nicotine. Heavy doses produce nausea, vomiting, diarrhea, headaches, disturbed vision and hearing, confusion, weakness, a sharp drop in blood pressure, convulsions, and ultimately death from paralysis of the respiratory muscles. About 90 percent of the nicotine in inhaled tobacco smoke is absorbed compared to 25-50 percent in smoke expelled after being sucked into the mouth. Several hundred compounds, many of them toxic, have been isolated from tobacco smoke, including carbon monoxide (one percent by volume in cigarette smoke, two percent in pipe smoke, and six percent in cigar smoke), hydrocyanic acid, and sometimes lead and arsenic from sprays used on the tobacco plant. Irritation of the mouth, throat and bronchi result from the heat, nicotine, and the many other constituents of tobacco smoke. The relationship to lung cancer and cancer of the mouth, larynx and esophagus and to chronic bronchitis and emphysema has already been commented on. Hunger contractions of the stomach are eliminated for between 15 and 60 minutes by smoking a cigarette. Both systolic and diastolic blood pressure are raised by cigarette smoking due to the vasoconstricting properties of nicotine, and the drug is considered a major cause of one of the most serious vascular disorders, Buerger's disease (thromboangiitis obliterans). A condition characterized by loss of vision and possible blindness, tobacco amplyopia, is a sometime sequela of tobacco use. Tolerance develops to the drug when taken regularly, as does psychological dependence and usually a "withdrawal"-like syndrome when cigarette smoking is discontinued.

Amphetamine (racemic beta-phenylisopropyl-amine) is closely related in structure to the naturally occurring

epinephrine and, like caffeine and nicotine, is a potent
central-nervous-system stimulant but, unlike them, is conceptualized from the outset as a "drug." Amphetamine
raises both systolic and diastolic blood pressure, has varying
effects on smooth muscles, stimulates the respiratory
center, and has a marked analeptic action on the brain. The
d-isomer (dextroamphetamine) is several times more potent
than the l-isomer. Alertness, wakefulness, lessened fatigue,
euphoria, greater ability to concentrate, and increased
speech and motor activity are produced. Performance in
athletic or mental tasks may be improved. There is some
analgesia, and appetite is suppressed. The usual oral dose is
two and a half to five milligrams two or three times daily.
With continued use, tolerance may develop and daily intakes
of up to 1,700 milligrams have been reported. No full-blown
physical dependence involving a withdrawal illness occurs,
but psychological dependence certainly does. Excessive
doses taken for long periods of time produce restlessness,
dizziness, tremor, irritability, insomnia, confusion, hallucinations, delusions, anxiety, panic, and depression (psychological). Weight loss, cardiovascular and gastrointestinal disturbances, and other physical manifestations also
occur, and, with large single doses (where no tolerance
exists), there have been cases of fatal poisoning with convulsions, coma, and cerebral hemorrhages. The actions of
methamphetamine are quite similar, but it has the advantage that average doses produce the central-nervous-
system stimulation without much peripheral effect. The
amphetamines are put to a variety of valuable therapeutic
uses, including the treatment of obesity, narcolepsy, fatigue
(from work or athletics), Parkinsonism, poisoning by depressant drugs, psychological depression (neurotic), childhood behavior disorders, enuresis, and such gynecological
disorders as premenstrual tension, dysmenorrhea, and the
menopause. Phenmetrazine and several other sympatho-
mimetic drugs are also used for producing anorexia (loss
of appetite) and sometimes for fatigue reduction.

Cocaine (benzoylmethylecgonine), in a manner similar

to that of other stimulants but more strongly, stimulates the central nervous system beginning with the cortex and working downward. It produces increased alertness and mental acuity and a greater capacity for muscular work due to its antifatigue effect. The heart rate is increased, with vasoconstriction and a rise in blood pressure. Body temperature rises, and when brought into direct contact with the specific tissues, it blocks nerve conduction and eye sensation, thus accounting for its sometime medical use as a local anesthetic. Although quite effective when inhaled (as by sniffing) or injected, cocaine, unlike the other stimulants discussed, is ineffective when taken orally because of poor absorption from the gastrointestinal tract. It is a very potent mood-elevator or euphoriant and perhaps the strongest antifatigue agent, but has not been used medically in the United States for these purposes and exact dosage levels of the pure substance are not known except for its use as a surface anesthetic where solutions are employed which range between one and 20 percent, depending on whether the eye or the nose and throat is the target. Serious toxicity has been reported from doses as low as 20 milligrams and the fatal dose is thought to be 1.2 grams. Restlessness, excitement, talkativeness, anxiety, and confusion develop with excessive doses or use over a prolonged period, and these can progress in more serious cases to headaches, rapid pulse, irregular respiration, dilated pupils, nausea, vomiting, hallucinations, delusions, convulsions, and finally unconsciousness and death from cessation of respiration. With nonmedical regular use, psychological dependence and tolerance commonly occur.

DEPRESSANTS

Although mistakenly thought of by many people as a "stimulant," *alcohol*, like general anesthetics, like barbiturates and other sedatives to which it is actually biologically equivalent, and like narcotics, is a primary depressant of the central nervous system and the most widely used one.

It is the simplest in chemical structure (C_2H_5OH) of all the mind-altering drugs and the easiest to prepare either formally or informally. Once thought by alchemists to be the long-hoped-for elixir of life and long used as a remedy for all ailments, alcohol now has few specific and no essential uses in Western medicine. In its direct action on the skin, alcohol has a cooling effect by producing evaporation, and, in concentrations of about 70 percent (by weight), it kills germs. When injected locally, it blocks nerve conduction and hence is sometimes used for the treatment of severe nerve pain. The drug has little effect on the heart or blood vessels and specifically does not dilate coronary arteries as commonly believed (it may cause constriction of these and cerebral blood vessels). Ingestion of alcohol brings about heat loss by the body and a fall in temperature, which means, among other things, that if taken in cold weather with the objective of getting warm, it will actually make the person colder. Salivary and gastric secretions are strongly stimulated, and higher concentrations of the drug in distilled beverages irritate the lining of the stomach, produce inflammation and, if continued, gastritis or ulcer. Alcohol brings about an accumulation of fat in the liver leading over a period of time to impaired liver function, possibly related to the development of the hepatic cirrhosis seen in alcoholism. Urine production is increased. The amount of circulating epinephrine and norepinephrine is increased by even moderate consumption, and this in turn may be responsible for the observed increase in blood sugar, dilation of the pupils, and modest increase in blood pressure observed with ordinary consumption of the drug. The portion of the body that is most affected by alcohol is the central nervous system, particularly the reticular activating system which is responsible for coordinating the complex activities of the different regions of the brain and nervous system. As ethanol (ethyl alcohol) depresses the reticular activating system, it seems secondarily to depress the frontal cortex of the brain, this dual action resulting in disorganization and disruption of ordinary thought and motor activity. Judgment, memory, reasoning, self-control, speech, and mood are all affected. As measured by a variety of tests, efficiency with either mental or physical tasks is decreased with the exception of some situations with certain individuals who have inhibitions which impede optimum performance and which are diminished by alcohol. Since the brain has an unusually extensive blood supply and brain tissue has high affinity for alcohol, the effect even of what appear to be moderate doses can be intense, particularly when the concentration of the drug is rapidly rising as from fast absorption from the gastrointestinal tract, or ingestion of large quantities in a short period of time. As to an objective or invariable definition of "intoxication," in a sense one can say that any amount of alcohol (or any of the other mind-altering drugs) produces some degree of intoxication. The closest thing to an accepted definition is found in various state and national laws regarding drunk driving. Although a number of states, such as California, and many countries do not fix a particular blood-alcohol level as being evidence of intoxication or drunkenness, most do, and utilize the figure of .15 percent (15/100ths of one percent) as the level beyond which one is presumed to be "drunk." Some states and countries set the level at .10 percent and a few at .05 percent. Under such legal definitions, anyone below the legislated figure is presumed to be "sober." Actual tests of driving performance have shown that there is significant impairment of judgment, coordination, reaction time, and night vision beyond a level of .035 percent, a state reached by drinking one ordinary highball, glass of wine, or bottle of beer. Using a 150-pound individual as a rough standard, the relationship of alcohol consumption to blood-alcohol level and expected performance can be explained as follows. Two ordinary mixed drinks or their equivalent in wine or beer will produce in such a person a blood-alcohol level of .05 percent; four such drinks or their equivalent, a level in excess of .10 percent, and five, a level of .15 percent. An ordinary drink refers to one and a half ounces of 90-proof whiskey or its equivalent in vodka or rum. The time factor is a very important variable in this in that the liver is able to metabolize about an ounce of ethanol per hour, and when the drinking is concentrated into shorter periods than that, the blood-alcohol level will rise correspondingly. One study found that people with a blood-alcohol in excess of .15 (also known as 150 milligrams percent) are 33 times more likely to have a driving accident than the individual without alcohol in his body. Pedestrians killed in highway accidents were studied with the finding that about a third were under the influence of alcohol, most of these showing a concentration of between 100 and 250 milligrams percent. As has previously been commented on, there is a strong association with violent deaths apart from highway accidents, with one survey finding alcohol responsible (or contributing) in about 30 percent of such deaths. Concentrations around 400 milligrams percent produce a semicomatose state and, as the amount increases, there is progressive depression of brain function, including the respiratory center, and at about 500 milligrams percent or more, death ensues. Because there is little difference between the amount required to produce anesthesia, as for surgery, and the amount that would paralyze respiration, alcohol is no longer used as an anesthetic. It does have analgesic effects with the pain threshold being raised about one-third following ingestion of 60 milliliters of 95 percent alcohol. Brain waves are slowed as intoxication develops and the drug may sometimes precipitate convulsions, thereby being contraindicated in anyone with epilepsy. Additive or synergistic effects occur when alcohol is mixed with other depressant or tranquilizing drugs so that each of the deleterious effects mentioned is augmented or intensified. Alcohol can be a source of caloric energy for the body but one without proteins, vitamins, and other essential elements, thereby leading to malnutrition, vitamin-deficiency diseases, and cirrhosis. Psychological dependency commonly develops with regular use of the drug and both tolerance and physical dependency (addiction) occur with daily heavy use.

Probably the only specific medicinal use of alcohol presently, and the reason for its being present in the U.S. Pharmacopeia, is as a disinfectant of the skin, but it is also used as a rubbing agent, in antisweating preparations, and as a solvent for a variety of other medicines, including narcotic cough syrups. Far more frequent is self-"prescribed" use by the general public as a sedative or hypnotic (inducer of sleep), "remedy" for colds and fever, digestive stimulant and, most of all, relaxant and euphoriant. *Methyl alcohol* (methanol, wood alcohol) and other members of the alcohol family require mention here only because they are sometimes used as a substitute for ethanol when that is unavailable and they produce highly toxic effects, usually including blindness and death. Because of the overwhelming toxicity the sought-after effects on the mind and brain soon become secondary and incidental.

First in the hearts of prescribers of depressant drugs are the various *barbiturates* which entered medicine in 1903 and spread rapidly after the 1912 introduction of phenobarbital. In the intervening years, some 2,500 barbiturates have been synthesized, about 50 marketed, and 10 or 12 are extensively used. Other sedative hypnotics have many properties in common with the barbiturates and are mainly evaluated in terms of their similarities to, and differences from, various barbiturates. As general depressants, barbiturates act on an extensive continuum of biological functions, including the central nervous system, the skeletal muscles, smooth muscle, and heart muscle. Although most commonly used to bring about sleep, these drugs are capable of producing central-nervous-system depression ranging from slight sedation or quieting to coma and death. They act at all levels of the brain, including the reticular activating system and the frontal lobes, producing (in doses short of hypnotic action) effects on judgment, memory, and emotional control similar to that produced by alcohol. They are not considered to be analgesic drugs and only the ultra-short-acting ones such as thiopental are sometimes used to induce surgical anesthesia. With moderate doses, increased

fast activity is found in the electroencephalogram, signify-
ing activation of neurons accompanying the clouding of
consciousness, and later, slow waves similar to those seen
during sleep appear. All members of this drug family are
capable of anticonvulsant action, but phenobarbital is the
most reliable in this respect and the most utilized in treating epilepsy. Respiration is depressed with ordinary doses,
but there are no significant effects on the heart, blood vessels, kidney, or liver. There is a relaxing effect on the
smooth muscle of the gastrointestinal system. Allergic and
idiosyncratic reactions occur, including such things as
dermatitis, hangover (as with overindulgence of alcohol:
lassitude, nausea, dizziness, headache), stimulation rather
than depression, pain, and others. Ultra-short, short- and
long-acting preparations, mixtures with other drugs (both
depressant and stimulants), capsules, tablets, elixirs, syrups,
quick-release and delayed-release forms all exist. The drugs
are generally taken by mouth but can be injected. The sedative dose of amobarbital (amytal) is 20 to 50 milligrams
several times a day while the hypnotic dose is 100 to 200
milligrams taken prior to bedtime. With pentobarbital, the
sedative dose is 30 to 60 milligrams several times daily and
the hypnotic dose, 100 milligrams. Phenobarbital is given
in doses of 15 to 30 milligrams for sedation and 100 milligrams for hypnosis. Habituation, tolerance, and addiction
are common and often serious with barbiturate use. Energy
for the work of body cells comes from the production of
adenosine triphosphate (ATP) by enzyme systems. Barbiturates seem to act biochemically by interfering with the
production of ATP, acting on the cell membrane and interfering with enzymes necessary for the utilization of oxy-
gen by the cell. In addition to their heavy use for producing
relaxation and sleep and their less frequent use for controlling various kinds of convulsions, the barbiturates are
used to treat the withdrawal symptoms of alcohol addiction;
to potentiate the effects of amphetamines and of narcotics
or other analgesics; and as diagnostic and therapeutic
agents in psychiatry, i.e., narcosynthesis or "truth-serum."

Serious poisoning is likely to occur if more than ten times the usual sleep-inducing dose is taken at one time, with the short- or quick-action barbiturates being more potent than the long-acting ones. Whether or not this proves fatal will depend on how much time elapses before the accidental or suicidal ingestion is discovered and whether proper medical treatment is available and quickly provided.

A quite variegated collection of other chemicals is capable of depressing the central nervous system in the same manner as barbiturates despite marked differences in structure and in general pharmacological properties. Most of these other depressants have become widely used only in the past decade and none of them have been so extensively researched and evaluated as the barbiturates. They have most of the same side effects, disadvantages, and potential dangers as the barbiturates; cannot be shown to be more beneficial; and are much more expensive. All of these drugs are prescribed and used much too freely without adequate regard for toxicity, misuse, and abuse.

The simplest of all these drugs structurally and the oldest (other than alcohol) is *potassium bromide*, which in the latter part of the nineteenth century was used by the ton for treating nervous disorders. Now it is rarely prescribed but is still widely used as a popular ingredient of over-the-counter nerve and headache preparations. An average dose would be between three and five grams daily, but because the drug is slowly excreted by the kidneys, it can easily accumulate in the body and produce chronic intoxication characterized by drowsiness, impairment of thought and memory, emotional lability, and, if it continues, delusions, hallucinations, coma, and death. Dermatitis, loss of appetite, constipation, tremors, and incoordination also occur with progressive use of bromides.

Chloral hydrate, although synthesized early in the nineteenth century, came to be used as a sedative-hypnotic some years after bromides. Like the bromides, chloral hydrate is irritating to the gastrointestinal tract and may produce nausea and vomiting. In ordinary doses, chloral hydrate has little effect on heart action, blood pressure and respiration, but produces the same pattern of effects on the brain and mind as has been described for the other depressant drugs. The usual therapeutic dosage for sleep-induction is 500 milligrams and the usual fatal dose is about ten grams. The drug has also been used in the "Mickey Finn knockout drops" by combining it with an alcoholic drink and producing an additive depressant effect. The same could, of course, be done by combining any depressant drugs. Regular use may result in habituation, the development of tolerance, and full physical dependence. There are scattered reports of confusion, disorientation, and delusions following ordinary ingestion of the drug so that it could be placed in the psychotogenic category along with the many other drugs specifically covered in the preceding chapter.

Placidyl (ethchlorvynol) is a short-acting hypnotic (dosage 500 milligrams) and sedative (dosage 100—200 milligrams) with properties similar to the short-action barbiturates. Psychological dependence, tolerance, and addiction occur with regular use, and death from single doses can be expected if ten grams or more are ingested. When combined with alcohol, particularly serious effects have been reported, including shock and coma.

Paraldehyde, a close "blood-relative" of acetaldehyde, was introduced into medical practice in the late nineteenth century, and despite its strong odor and bad taste, or perhaps because of these, it came to be regarded as a very safe hypnotic drug and was widely administered. There appears to be no scientific basis for the feeling of a number of doctors that paraldehyde offers advantages over barbiturates or other sedative hypnotics. It may be because it has largely been administered in relatively closely supervised institutional circumstances that possible side effects have not been greater. Despite the many years of use, most of its pharmacology and neurochemistry in the human body is unknown. It is a short-acting substance, with the usual oral dosage three to eight milliliters. If injected, it is highly irritating to the skin and may be damaging to surrounding tissues. Its general depressant effect is similar to the other drugs in this family and it has no significant effect on respiration or blood pressure with ordinary dosage. The lethal dose is uncertain but is probably about 20 times the therapeutic dose. With large dosages, serious toxic effects occur on lung tissue, the liver and kidneys, the body's chemical balance (acidosis). Psychological dependence, tolerance, and physical dependence all can occur with regular use of the drug. Medically it is now used mainly in treating the withdrawal symptoms of alcohol addiction, emergency treatment of convulsions, and the control of panic states in various psychiatric disorders.

Still another representative sedative-hypnotic is *Doriden* (glutethimide), introduced into medical practice in 1954. With typical Madison Avenue ingenuity, it was massively advertised "ethically" (meaning just to physicians and allied professions rather than directly to the general public) as an effective nonbarbiturate hypnotic and sedative which was free of such disadvantages of barbiturates as addiction liability. Within a short period of time, it was ranking second to barbiturates in frequency of prescription and the manufacturer was boasting of having sold more than one billion tablets and capsules. It soon became clear, as it has with other drugs similarly introduced as wholly safe and effective, that it was actually a typical general depressant of the central nervous system and that it had the same potential for psychological dependence, tolerance, and addiction as the others. Hundreds of cases of acute intoxication (overdoses) and poisoning have been reported. The drug closely resembles phenobarbital in structure and is also structurally similar to thalidomide, the sedative drug found to be teratogenetic, producing deformed children from use during the first three months of pregnancy. Such has not been reported with glutethimide, but we must remember that this particular type of drug effect has not been looked for with most drugs and the techniques involved in studying chromosomal breakage and genetic changes from drugs are less than ten years old. The usual sedative dos-

age is 250 milligrams and the hypnotic dose, 500 milligrams, with a lethal dose of between ten and twenty grams.
Finally of the major sedative-hypnotic depressants, there
is meprobamate, popularly known as Equanil or Miltown,
originally synthesized as a potential muscle relaxant, and
used in general medical and psychiatric practice since
1963. Touted as a "tranquilizer" and antianxiety agent, it
gained rapid popularity due to a combination of an expensive advertising and public-relations campaign; initial uniformly favorable clinical reports (which failed to use control groups or to make comparisons with other similar
drugs); misplaced concern on the part of physicians about
barbiturates so that any "nonbarbiturate" was readily accepted if thought to do the same thing better; and perhaps
a lesser likelihood of drowsiness from Miltown as compared
to a barbiturate. Its pharmacological actions are now recognized to be essentially the same as those of barbiturates
and the other drugs in the sedative-hypnotic category, and
the U.S. Food and Drug Administration has officially classified meprobamate as being equivalent in its abuse potential to barbiturates (this is being challenged in the courts),
although it continues to be called a "minor tranquilizer"
and used to dispel worry, anxiety, and tension. The sedative dosage is 200 to 400 milligrams and the hypnotic dose,
800 milligrams. It has an intermediate duration of action
and a more selective depressant action on certain reflexes
than barbiturates. The most important possible toxic reactions to the drug include allergic responses, damage to
blood cells including anemia or agranulocytosis, and hypotensive (low blood pressure) reactions. Habituation, tolerance, and addiction occur, and, on the basis of present
evidence, maximum daily consumption should not exceed
1,600 to 2,400 milligrams if physical dependence is to be
prevented. Perhaps because of the widespread publicity
Miltown and Equanil have received, a number of tests
were done that have not been done with most other mind-
altering drugs. For example, using a series of what are
ordinarily considered sensitive psychological tests, it was

found that a dose of 400 milligrams produced no impairment; 800 milligrams produced some impairment in learning; and 1,600 milligrams brought about definite impairment of learning, motor coordination, and reaction time. Most subjects reported the drug effect as pleasant and euphoric, although with some people it produced restlessness. One tablet (400 milligrams) impaired driving although to a lesser extent than 100 milligrams of Secobarbital (Seconal). The EEG (electroencephalogram) was found to be affected in the same way as by barbiturates.

One last point in concluding the discussion of sedative-hypnotic drugs. The concept of "anxiety" is not at all well defined or measured and it is therefore additionally difficult to determine whether or how a given drug is superior or inferior to a placebo, a barbiturate, another substance, or psychotherapy in relieving anxiety.

The last group of specifically depressant drugs to be considered here are the *narcotics*, opiates and opioids, meaning opium, its derivatives and synthetic equivalents. These drugs are used mainly in medicine as analgesics, i.e., pain relievers, but also for several other important medical purposes. Morphine, being the major active principle of opium and the most commonly prescribed narcotic analgesic, can be used as our prototype for discussion. Although opium has, of course, been used for thousands of years for both medical and psychological effects, it was not until the mid-nineteenth century that its use became widespread in medical practice around the world. Chemically it is an alkaloid, and its neurophysiological, biochemical, pharmacological, behavioral, and sociological effects have been more studied than any other drug, mind-altering or otherwise. Varying kinds of effects have been observed on such neurohumoral transmitters as acetylcholine, norephrine, and 5-hydroxytryptamine, but what the exact interrelationships are remains an unknown factor. In addition to what we already know about the complexities of a mind-altering-drug reaction and particularly the importance of the underlying personality and mood, the presence or absence of pain is an additional modifier and determinant. With average doses of morphine used for relieving pain (about ten milligrams), euphoria occurs along with the cessation of the pain, while the same dose given to an individual without pain may produce a lowering of mood and anxiety. Most kinds of pain are relieved without interfering with other sensory modalities, such as sight and hearing, but some "clouding" of consciousness occurs, with drowsiness, loss of energy, nausea, and sometimes loss of appetite. With larger doses sleep is produced and respiratory depression becomes pronounced. This effect on respiration is the most serious potential toxic effect of excessive doses of morphine or its chemical relatives. Unlike barbiturates or general anesthetics, the narcotics do not have anticonvulsant effects and do not produce the impaired coordination seen with alcohol or barbiturates. The brain electrical changes as seen in the EEG after single average doses of morphine are the same as those seen in ordinary sleep or after small doses of barbiturates. Other effects of the drug include a decrease in urine production, a mild decrease in body temperature, constriction of the pupil, suppression of cough, and dilation of the blood vessels of the skin with accompanying sweating and itching. Morphine and the other opiates are absorbed from the gastrointestinal tract but in a manner so variable that they are almost always given by injection, usually subcutaneously. In the United States, heroin (diacetylmorphine) has been barred for medical use because of pressure from the drug police even though there was never any relationship between its use in medical practice and the illicit traffic. Where available for medical prescription, as in England, an average dose is three milligrams and it is injected subcutaneously, with a more rapid onset of action than morphine. Nonmedical black-market use in the United States often begins with sniffing, or "snorting," but as tolerance develops almost always the user shifts to "mainlining" (intravenous injection). Skin rashes, constipation, nausea, vomiting, dizziness, heightened sensitivity to pain after the drug wears off, and rarely, a state of delirium are among the unwanted effects that can occur with the use of morphine. Respiratory ailments, such as asthma, are often worsened by morphine and needless fatalities have occurred as a result. The depressant effects of the opiates are intensified by mixing them with certain tranquilizers and antidepressants. The preparations available for medical use include tincture of opium (laudanum), paregoric, morphine sulphate tablets and injectable solutions, and codeine tablets and cough syrups. The illicit heroin available is usually in paper packets referred to as "papers" or "bags" and consisting of between five and 15 percent heroin (in the United States) mixed with a variety of inert impurities. Roughly 60 milligrams of morphine taken by mouth produces less pain-killing effect than eight milligrams taken by intramuscular injection. Another interesting comparison is that 30 milligrams of codeine gives about the same pain-relieving effect as 600 milligrams of aspirin, and the two drugs together are better than the sum of their individual performances. That is, they give a 2-plus-2-equals-5 or -6 effect, known as synergism. In addition to their use as analgesics, the narcotics play an important role in medicine in treating cough and diarrhea. Although the impression has been created by drug policemen that, following one injection of a narcotic, people become "dope fiends," fortunately only a small minority of those Americans who have taken opiates medically or even "recreationally" continue using them to the point of addiction. Even though direct controlled comparisons have not been made of the different drugs with addiction liability, it is probably true that the opiates are more likely to bring about this state than alcohol or barbiturates. A reasoned concern about such a possibility is certainly desirable for the physician and the public, but the present overreaction because of exaggerated fears has caused the many serious consequences previously mentioned and also results in millions of people receiving insufficient narcotics for the treatment of severe pain because doctors are afraid of being harassed by narcotics agents. Habituation, tolerance, and addiction, however, are not to be minimized with these drugs. Accidental medical overdoses, suicidal overdoses, and accidental or murderous overdoses in illicit addicts all occur with morphine and heroin. The more than a hundred heroin addict deaths from overdoses each year are due mainly to variations in the strength of the black-market supply they obtain and to fluctuations in the extent of their body's tolerance to the narcotic. Lethal doses of morphine are generally in excess of 120 milligrams, although serious toxic effects can occur with a fraction of that amount.

Although many synthetic morphine-like narcotics or opioids have been manufactured and prescribed, often advertised as nonaddicting or even as a treatment for morphine addiction, there is no proof at present that such drugs offer any specific therapeutic benefits or freedom from abuse superior to morphine or heroin. The most widely used of these opioids is meperidine, also known as Demerol or Pethidine. The major actions of meperidine are on the central nervous system and are essentially the same as those of morphine, although there is a somewhat prompter onset and shorter duration of action than with morphine. An average dose is 100 milligrams, and, although absorbed adequately after swallowing, it is twice as effective when given by injection. Essentially the same kinds of undesirable untoward physiological effects occur as with morphine except that pupillary size is not affected and constipation is less frequent. Because of the shorter duration of action of the drug as compared to morphine, tolerance seems to develop more slowly and the abstinence syndrome following the development of addiction may be less severe. On the other hand, as Jaffe has pointed out, "The need to use a drug repeatedly at short intervals can be viewed as a factor favoring the reinforcement of drug-seeking behavior." Therefore, Demerol may have a higher potential for producing psychological dependence and abuse. The drug is mainly used as an analgesic and not for cough or diarrhea.

One other widely used narcotic, *methadone*, or Dolophine, was synthesized during World War II and came into general medical use after 1945. Its general actions and properties are similar to those of morphine, and it has similar side effects. It is more effectively absorbed from the gastrointestinal tract and is thus most commonly given by the oral route in an average dose of ten milligrams. Habituation, tolerance, and addiction can develop with regular use, but seemingly more slowly than with morphine so that its overall abuse potential must be judged as lower. Its major use is in medicine as an analgesic and in the treatment of those addicted to other narcotics, especially heroin. For the latter, methadone is used in two ways, one involving substitution and gradual withdrawal as the treatment of choice for the abstinence syndrome; and the other, involving long-term administration to former heroin addicts and known as the methadone maintenance program.

The effects of morphine-type drugs come about through interference with cellular enzyme systems, thereby preventing normal function, and also by actually substituting within the cell for some enzyme systems.

The prototype for the *tranquilizer* family of mind-altering drugs is chlorpromazine, a phenothiazine drug known in the United States as Thorazine and in Europe as Largactil. The basic chemical structure was synthesized in 1883, and since the 1940s a number of derivatives have been widely used as antihistaminics for treating colds and allergies. Chlorpromazine itself was discovered in 1950 and its use in treating mental illness began in 1952. In the relatively brief period since then, tens of millions of patients throughout the world have been treated with chlorpromazine and its congeners, and many thousands of publications have appeared evaluating its effects, seeming to make it second only to morphine as a filler for innumerable scientific journals. The chemical structure in which two benzene rings are joined by a sulphur and a nitrogen can be substituted in a number of positions to produce other phenothiazine compounds, such as triflupromazine (Vesprin), perphenazine (Trilafon), prochlorperazine

(Compazine), trifluoperazine (Stelazine), and thioridazine (Mellaril). More than 20 such drugs are in common medical use now, about half of them for the treatment of schizophrenia and other severe mental illnesses, and about half in treating nausea, vomiting, and other nonpsychiatric conditions. None of the psychiatric compounds have been found to be any more generally effective than chlorpromazine, but one will often work with patients that are unresponsive to another and there are differences in side effects which can sometimes be important. Psychiatrists biased in favor of electroshock therapy or lobotomy, or psychoanalytically oriented psychotherapists opposed the use of these drugs in the early years perhaps because they made the society more conscious of the need for evaluation and assessment of the treatments which up to that time had usually rested upon subjectivity and intuition. The focus of this book does not permit a full discussion of that point, but at the least readers should be aware that the results of almost all treatment modalities for emotional problems are reported by investigators as one-third cured, one-third improved and one-third unimproved whether the method being studied was psychotherapy, shock therapy, a particular drug, or simply being on the waiting list at a clinic. The use of control groups, double blind studies in which both the experimenter and the subject are kept unaware of which drugs are being administered, objective scales to rate improvement, psychological tests, and other attempts at objectification have come into wide use only in the 1960s. Although various forms of "verbal" therapies, ranging from psychoanalysis to encounter and Synanon groups, are widely used and widely accepted as beneficial (particularly by those administering them), no adequate determinations of either benefits or harmful effects exist, or are even asked for. Not that we should, but if we did look at psychotherapies with the same perspective we have used with certain drugs, we could set up a psychiatric police agency comparable to the drug police, based on such one-dimensional facts as the higher death rate among suicidal patients who receive psychotherapy than among those who do not. Another interesting question raised by chlorpromazine and the other tranquilizers is the social question of why, despite a number of early reports of severe toxic effects on the body including jaundice, tremor, and death from interference with blood-cell production, this was never sensationalized and never impeded the research and clinical use of these drugs. Two obvious distinctions are that pleasure-seeking behavior did not seem to be involved in the use of phenothiazines and no specific agency of government sought them out as a territory for attack or route to power.

The distinctions between sedative-hypnotic drugs and tranquilizing drugs are by no means fully dichotomized and precise, but basically tranquilizers are differentiated by having specific value in treating psychoses, producing effects on the extrapyramidal portion of the nervous system, suppressing conditioned avoidance responses in animals, not having anticonvulsant properties, and producing no drowsiness or addiction liability as compared to depressants.

Like those of the other mind-altering drugs, the major actions of the tranquilizing drugs are on the central nervous system. They include reduction or elimination of hallucinations and delusions, a calming or sedative effect, slowing of motor activity, a decrease of affect or emotion, and intensification of the effects of narcotic or hypnotic drugs given simultaneously. The neurophysiological actions are much more diffuse than with the other psychoactive drugs, reaching all levels of the nervous system, cerebral cortex, thalamus, hypothalamus, and reticular activating system. Some feel the drug has a depressant action and others a stimulant action on the same or different portions of the nervous system. It also has significant effects on the endocrine system, including the blocking of ovulation and menstruation with resulting infertility; the decreasing of testicular weight; and interference with growth of the body in younger animals. It produces a fall in blood pressure and

dilation of blood vessels, including the coronary arteries.
It is well absorbed from the gastrointestinal tract and is
usually administered orally in doses of 100 to 500 milligrams daily, but doses in excess of 5,000 milligrams a day
have been given without obvious ill effects. It can also be
given by injection and, with very disturbed psychiatric
patients, administration is usually begun in that manner
and later switched to the oral route. It is so slowly metabo-
lized and excreted that, many months after the drug is
discontinued, its presence can still be detected in the body.
Psychological dependence or habituation certainly occurs
in part because of the characteristically prolonged period
of daily use, and in part because of the direct and indirect
pleasurable effects of feeling better and calmer even though
the specific euphoria that we think of with some of the
other drugs is not common. Tolerance occurs to some
specialized properties of chlorpromazine, such as the
sedative effect, but not to the general effects of the drug
and there is no physical dependency or withdrawal illness
when the drug is stopped. Significant side effects seem to
occur in about five to ten percent of the patients receiving
the phenothiazines, including faintness, dry mouth, dermatitis, discoloration of the skin, Parkinsonism (slowing of
motor activity, masklike face, tremor, rigidity), hypotension,
allergic jaundice, grand mal seizures, and blood dyscra-
sias (particularly affecting white blood cells and sometimes
including the possibly fatal condition of agranulocytosis).
The total number of fatalities from the drug is probably
somewhere between 50 and 100, quite small considering
the tons that have been consumed by millions of people.

The major therapeutic use of the phenothiazines is
clearly with severe mental illness, specifically in terms of
reducing or eliminating such common symptoms as hallucinations, delusions, and hyperactivity. The quieting
effect generally occurs without clouding of consciousness
and makes possible the application of social and psychological rehabilitative measures, although these are rarely
available in state mental hospitals and available only to a

limited extent in so-called community mental-health programs. With many psychotic patients, the phenothiazines
have made hospitalization unnecessary or, when it is necessary, have made it much shorter than was the case prior to
the mid-1950's. The drugs are in no sense curative, since
the patients continue to have residual impairments of
thought and emotion. These (and other mind-altering
drugs) are also, of course, indirectly beneficial to physicians and other professionals in giving them something
specific that they can do for people with conditions that
they might otherwise feel hopeless or pessimistic about.
Some patients are maintained indefinitely on phenothiazines just as a diabetic is maintained on insulin while
others are taken off the drug after long periods on it, some
without apparent difficulty and others with a recurrence of
symptoms, usually within several weeks. These drugs are
also widely used in the treatment of neuroses, including
anxiety and tension states, but their relative effectiveness
as compared to the sedative-hypnotics, Librium, or psychotherapy is unknown. Although recommended by their
manufacturers as beneficial in treating the withdrawal
illness of alcohol or narcotics addictions, these drugs are
not specifically valuable for these syndromes but may reduce agitation while being given concurrently with proper
substitution and gradual withdrawal therapy, i.e., methadone for narcotic withdrawal and pentobarbital for alcohol
or sedative withdrawal. In addition to the treatment of
nausea and vomiting which has already been mentioned,
they are also used for controlling intractable hiccoughing.

The first drug with which the term "tranquilizer" was
associated was *rauwolfia* in 1954, the active principle of
which is reserpine. This received widespread publicity
and was used for both severe mental illness and high blood
pressure. Since by a quirk of fate the phenothiazines developed at about the same time and were found to be more
beneficial and easier to administer than the rauwolfia
compounds, the latter have come to be used mainly for
people who have allergic or idiosyncratic reactions to the

phenothiazines or with people suffering from hypertension. Rauwolfia comes from a plant root which has a very
ancient history going back thousands of years, when it
came to be used in Hindu Ayurvedic medicine for a wide
range of things, including mental illness and high blood
pressure. Its therapeutic benefits were written up in a
medical journal in the early 1930s, but despite this it remained neglected by Western medicine until relatively
recently. Its general effects on the central nervous system
are quite similar to those already described for phenothiazines. A number of investigations indicate that reserpine exerts its action through the release of norepinephrine
while others claim that its effects are due to reducing levels
of naturally occurring 5-hydroxytryptamine. Rauwolfia itself
is usually taken by mouth in an average dose of 200 to 400
milligrams per day while reserpine is taken about one
milligram daily for hypertension and five milligrams daily
for psychosis, also mainly orally. Excessive hypotension,
drowsiness, salivation, nausea, diarrhea, nasal congestion,
Parkinsonism, depression of fertility and of potency, and,
most serious of all, severe depression (sometimes with
suicide) are the most common toxic side effects. Not nearly
so many objective, controlled scientific studies of the effectiveness of reserpine in psychoses have been done as
have been done with the phenothiazines, but the consensus
is that the drug is far less effective than the phenothiazines,
and a number of studies have found it to be no more beneficial than a placebo.

Originally synthesized in 1933 but only introduced in
1961 as an antianxiety agent and tranquilizer, is chlordiazepoxide, better known as *Librium*. This drug and
another closely related benzodiazepine compound, diaze-
pam (Valium), are widely used as sedative-tranquilizers, or
sometimes referred to as minor tranquilizers, and some
writers feel that they should be classified with such drugs
as the barbiturates and meprobamate, but on the basis of
the available evidence, there are many significant differences between Librium and these other substances and,

legally, the Food and Drug Administration has not ruled
that these drugs have properties like the barbiturates or
require similar kinds of legal controls. On a number of
tests, such as those involving measurement of impaired
performance, chlordiazepoxide produces results different
from the sedative group and also different from the phenothiazines although sharing some aspects of the effects of
each. Whatever the similarities or differences might be,
Librium is presently being used mainly for the treatment
of neurosis, psychosomatic disorders such as peptic ulcers,
chronic anxiety, alcoholism, and sometimes psychoses. I
have also found it to be additionally useful in the treatment
of chronic cigarette smokers who are seeking to overcome
their dependency on nicotine and the ritual of smoking.

Still another special group of mind-altering drugs are the
antidepression chemicals or *antidepressants*. The termi-
nology is somewhat confusing since, as has been mentioned, one of the major types of effects of certain drugs on
the central nervous system is a "depressant" one, but in
this instance we are referring to the psychological state of
depression as opposed to any specific changes in the nervous system. Various nonspecific drugs have long been
used by self-prescription for depression, most notably
alcohol ("to drown one's sorrows") as well as other sedative-hypnotics. When something more formal has been
required, probably the two most common treatments
utilized have been some form of counseling or psychotherapy from a doctor, whether general practitioner or
psychiatrist, minister, astrologer, or hairdresser; and in the
drug category, amphetamines, such as Benzedrine or
Dexedrine, because of their sometimes euphoriant properties in stimulating the central nervous system. For more
severe depressions, often called "psychotic depressions" as
opposed to "neurotic depressions," although psychotherapy (including psychoanalysis) has been used extensively,
probably electroshock (electroconvulsive) therapy was
the treatment of choice until the specific antidepressant
drugs were discovered. The initial experimentation with

these drugs began in the early 1950s insofar as their use in treating depression is concerned and evolved out of a serendipitous finding that iproniazid (Marsilid) had mood-elevating effects in the patients to whom it was administered for the treatment of tuberculosis. These drugs have been classified as monamine oxidase (MAO) inhibitors despite the fact that phenelzine (Nardil) and tranylcypromine (Parnate) and others are heterogeneous pharmacologically and chemically, and it has not been proven that their effect on depression is related to MAO inhibition in the central nervous system. Several of the MAO drugs are related structurally to amphetamines. In the treatment of depression, they ordinarily take several weeks to manifest their effects and therefore objective measurements or comparisons become difficult. The usual dosage of Nardil is 45 milligrams daily for up to six weeks, or until benefit occurs, at which point the dosage is slowly reduced until the person is maintained on 15 milligrams or less each day, taken by mouth. Parnate is usually given orally in doses of 20 milligrams per day for several weeks and then, if favorable results occur, the drug is continued at a dosage level of from ten to 20 milligrams daily, usually, because of side effects, being administered to hospitalized patients only. The drugs are also used in treating hypertension and angina. Since they have general enzyme-inhibiting properties in the body, this interferes with the normal metabolic breakdown of other drugs that might be administered concurrently and thus there is a prolongation or intensification of actions of barbiturates, alcohol, other antidepression drugs, and narcotics, particularly Demerol. This drug interaction has resulted in a number of fatalities, in some instances from a hypotensive crisis or a respiratory depression when depressant drugs are given concurrently; and in other cases a hypertensive crisis when the combination is with stimulant drugs or with natural or aged cheeses such as cheddar, Camembert and Stilton, which contain large quantities of tyramine, a substance having a marked effect on blood pressure. Acute overdosage of the MAO inhibitors produces hyperexcitability, restlessness, hallucinations, convulsions, and other serious symptoms. Severe liver damage, with a high incidence of fatalities, occurred with one of the earlier MAO inhibitors subsequently withdrawn from the market and a hepatitis-like picture continues to occur infrequently with those in current use. Overstimulation of the central nervous system is another important side effect and it includes agitation, confusion, insomnia, tremors, and dizziness. Some of the toxic effects, such as those occurring in the liver, are not correlated with dosage or the length of time the person has been taking the drug. At least several million patients have been treated with these drugs, particularly Parnate, but there are no composite statistics on the numbers of deaths and disabilities, temporary and permanent, from this use.

A second group of "new" antidepression drugs are the dibenzozepine compounds and these, particularly imipramine (Tofranil) and amytriptyline (Elavil), have become the most extensively used of the formal antidepression chemicals. Because it is safer than the MAO inhibitors and is more popular with patients, Tofranil, in gradually increasing oral doses from 200 to 250 milligrams daily for several weeks, has become the most widely prescribed. If significant improvement takes place, the individual is maintained on the drug for a number of months or longer, but with gradual reduction of the dosage to a maintenance level of 50 to 100 milligrams daily. The drug structurally is quite similar to the phenothiazines, was first synthesized in 1948 and clinically investigated since 1958. How the drug works to relieve depression is poorly understood but seems to be qualitatively different from the production of euphoria as seen with the MAO inhibitors. A number of its pharmacological actions are similar to the phenothiazines with such end products as fatigue, dry mouth, blurred vision, and difficulty in thinking and concentrating. The drug produces a hypotensive effect on the cardiovascular system. In addition to the side effects already mentioned, weakness, headache, tremors, dizziness, hallucinations, delusions,

manic excitement, skin rashes, and the more serious conditions of myocardial infarctions (coronaries), heart failure,
agranulocytosis, allergic jaundice, and grand mal convulsions have been reported. There is no physical dependency
(although a withdrawal-like syndrome has been reported
in a few patients taking more than 250 milligrams daily
for long periods of time when the drug is abruptly discontinued) but psychic dependency and tolerance to some of
the effects do occur.

The natural history of episodes of depression must
always be considered in evaluating the effectiveness of
particular drugs. Apparently more than three-quarters
of depressed patients ultimately have spontaneous remis-
sions or recoveries without specific treatment, although, of
course, this might take much longer and involve greater
dangers than when one of these drugs is used. A certain
number of mild to moderate depressions, particularly in
direct response to personal, family, and social tragedies,
are a normal part of existence and should not be looked at
with a pathological frame of reference. When a depression
is overwhelming in terms of insomnia, loss of concentration, feelings of hopelessness, inability to function, suicidal
preoccupations (some suicidal ideas probably occur in most
if not all normal people sometime during their lives), then
a drug such as Tofranil, or sometimes electroconvulsive
therapy, should be instituted as soon as possible.

The imprecision and crudeness of the designations
"psychotomimetic," "hallucinogen" and *"psychedelic"*
have already been commented upon, yet these terms and
others, such as "psychotogenic," are the ones generally
used in pharmacology and in law to describe a group of
drugs with mixed effect that do not fit the other, relatively
clear categories. Categorization of people or things seems to
be a particularly American obsession, although it is quite
possible and preferable to deal with individual people and
things and refer to them by specific names. Thus, one could
call the more poorly understood drugs the "wastebasket
drugs" or "miscellaneous drugs," but in this sense I think

the term "LSD-type" drugs is the best for the family including not only LSD but mescaline, psilocybin, STP, and the others already covered. It makes even less sense to lump together in these vague categories drugs such as marijuana, whose pattern of use internationally and effects are vastly different. No clear line of demarcation exists between the LSD-type drugs and the other mind-altering drugs, in terms of either chemical structure or psycho-pharmacological effects, particularly when one remembers the importance of the individual psychology in determining drug effect. Since its accidental discovery in 1943, LSD has come to be the most widely used of these substances, generally in an oral dosage of 150 to 250 micrograms (an ordinary aspirin tablet contains 300,000 micrograms), but as little as 25 micrograms can produce some discernible effects. Like most of the other drugs in this grouping, LSD has an indole nucleus and is structurally similar to the naturally occurring chemical mediator in the brain, serotonin. LSD exerts a strong antagonism with serotonin (5-hydroxytryptamine) and some investigators consider this to be the basis for its actions, but other neurochemical findings cast doubt on this and it must be said again that the exact mechanism of action is unknown. Tolerance develops rapidly to LSD if used daily (a highly unusual pattern of use), there is cross-tolerance to mescaline and psilocybin, and this tolerance rapidly disappears when the drug is discontinued. There is no physical dependence, and psychological dependence, as it is understood with the other mind-altering drugs, would be much less common with the LSD group. There have been no deaths or damage to body organs from the direct physical effects of LSD even with large doses or chronic use. Its significance lies mainly in the quantitative dimension, that is, in the intensity and pervasiveness of its perceptual and psychological effects on the central nervous system. The underlying personality, mood, attitudes, expectations, and setting in which the drug is taken have proven to be far more important as determinants of an LSD experience than with drugs such as alcohol, marijuana, barbiturates, or amphetamines. Guidance by a trained, trusted person is another important factor, and dosage, because of the great potency of this drug, is a more important variable than with the others. With an average dose the effects begin within 30 to 45 minutes and usually last 8 to 12 hours. Mild physical sensations, particularly in the limbs, occur, but the main dimensions of the drug reaction are perceptual, cognitive (thought), and affective (mood). The perceptual changes are primarily visual but also include the other individual sensory modalities and sometimes a blending or synesthesia so that one "hears" something seen or "tastes" something touched. With the eyes closed, kaleidoscopic colors and a wide array of geometric shapes and specific objects, such as cathedrals, are often seen. With the eyes open, a particular object, painting, or leaf that would not ordinarily be seen because of the forest will receive considerable attention extending over a period of many minutes. As an example, one may see subtle undulations of the configuration of the leaf and many variations in the shades of greenness that would ordinarily not be apprehended. Illusions can occur and sometimes, depending on the interaction of the many important human and drug variables, hallucinations. Thoughts which are ordinarily suppressed or repressed from consciousness come into focus and previously unseen relationships or combinations between these are recognized. Either this aspect or the perceptual phenomena can be upsetting and disruptive to the individual if he is unprepared for them or unable to cope with them even if prepared. This sometime enhancement of awareness or sensitivity and new synthesis of ideas are the basis for the beneficial effects that have been reported in some creativity and problem-solving experiments, and also the main basis for the religious-mystical or "consciousness-expansion" experiences that have been reported by some. Ordinary boundaries and controls between the self and the environment and within the self are loosened, resulting in seeing oneself as an outside observer might see one (and sometimes not liking that which is seen). Mood changes or swings can occur and sometimes intense pleasurable or esthetic experiences, such as marked enhancement of appreciation of a piece of music, poetry, or a love relationship. On other occasions or with other individuals, the mood changes can be highly unpleasant and labile. The main effects occur during the first several hours of the experience and gradually dissipate as the drug effect wears off. Throughout the experience the normal individual has insight, is fully aware that he is experiencing a drug effect, and is able to respond to the reality of telephones, doorbells, etc., although he will usually be less inclined to do so because of a feeling that these things are not so important. Because of the intensity and complexity of the experience, it can certainly be disorganizing and upsetting to an individual as well as having some of the specific serious consequences mentioned earlier in the book. LSD, like other drugs found in the ergot fungus, has a contracting effect on the uterus, but, unlike ergotamine, it does not produce significant constriction of blood vessels. The seeds of at least four species of morning-glory plants contain isolysergic acidamide, having effects similar to but less potent than LSD-25. Also closely related in structure and effects are dimethyltryptamine (DMT), psilocybin, and others. DMT, which is usually inhaled, has a rapid onset of action, effects coming on within minutes, and a shorter duration (one to two hours) than LSD. Psilocybin is in between, lasting about six hours with an average dose of 25 milligrams and having less intense effects than LSD.

Another subgroup of LSD-type drugs contains a phenyl group rather than indole and includes mescaline and STP, which is 2,5-dimethoxy-4-methyl-amphetamine. This illustrates the continuum between these drugs and the central-nervous-system stimulants. Not only STP but MDA, MMDA, and others have been directly derived from the amphetamine structure. The usual oral dose of mescaline is 350 milligrams, its effects last 12 to 14 hours and are roughly the same as the changes brought about by LSD.

Experimentation with mescaline and peyote dates back to the 1890s, but they were used much earlier by American Indians in their religious ceremonies. The exact structure of mescaline was not determined until 1918. Unlike the situation with LSD or mescaline there has not been the extensive animal and human pharmacological and psychological research with STP, MDA, etc. These from the beginning have circulated on the black market and been used nonmedically so that even basic pharmacological data do not exist. When STP, for example, first began to be distributed, no one had the slightest idea of what the proper dosage was and people were taking large amounts that gave two- or three-day "trips," many panic reactions, and other untoward side effects. As the dosage was worked out informally (now appearing to be five milligrams on the average), bad reactions seemed to decrease even though the purity of any given black-market supply of either STP, LSD, or any of the others always remains in question and can greatly influence the reaction. When taken by injection rather than orally the effects come on more quickly and are usually more intense.

With all these drugs, the most common side effect is an acute anxiety or panic state brought on by the intense psychological experience and clearing up as the drug wears off, or more quickly if the person is given a phenothiazine drug such as Thorazine either by injection or orally (although with STP sometimes its effects are augmented); and/or reassurance and understanding. Since the phenomenon has been driven underground and stigmatized, it is impossible to determine with any degree of precision the exact incidence of complications but probably they are of the order of one in a thousand "trips" and the more serious ones, such as accidental death or suicide and prolonged psychotic reactions, on probably the order of one in 10,000 to one in 100,000 drug experiences.

The full medical and scientific use of LSD-type drugs has been greatly slowed if not prevented by the hysteria and overreaction to "the psychedelic revolution." However, these drugs have been and will continue to be valuable tools for researching the physiology and chemistry of the brain and nervous system; treating alcoholism, certain sexual problems, and childhood schizophrenia; helping knowledgeable, motivated, already creative people to overcome certain problems or blocks; having religious and mystical experiences; and managing terminal illness where a person's pain can be relieved and his attitudes toward life and death altered. The psychotherapy that has been done with alcoholism, and also to a lesser extent with neuroses and personality or character disorders, is of two kinds, psychedelic and psycholytic. The latter involves giving an average dose of up to 150 micrograms in conjunction with an already established psychotherapeutic relationship between the patient and the therapist, using the drug to help bring out repressed material and new associations, and then continuing the nondrug psychotherapy, utilizing the material added from the LSD experience. The psychedelic psychotherapy uses a higher dose, of up to 1,000 micrograms, given once or a few times in an attempt to dissolve the old self and develop a new person through a transcendental experience. The practice of the two techniques may well overlap and a transcendental experience may be temporary or permanent, or may be interpreted by still another individual as psychotic disorganization. The research of Unger, Savage, and Pahnke using psychedelic therapy with terminal-cancer patients was reported as follows:

> Based on the apparent safety of the procedure and the encouraging impressions obtained with these six patients, it would appear that the earlier the use of psychedelic therapy is initiated in a patient with a malignancy, the more meaningful the psychological effects which may bring about a sense of lessened distress associated with the sense of fulfillment. The patient may be able to reach out much more directly to express his emotions and feeling toward his family, who are helped to resolve some of the guilt originating from their defensiveness and fears.

By now the reader will have some comprehension of the enormous range of substances being used for mind-alteration, but the list is not yet complete and, before dealing with marijuana, our current drug preoccupation, a few *others* require mention. In the past, gases, such as ether, chloroform, and nitrous oxide (laughing gas), have all been sought out for pleasure, euphoria, and relaxation by the ordinary citizen and by scientists such as Sir Humphrey Davy, who is reported to have inhaled nitrous oxide as he walked through London on his way to preside at meetings of the Royal Society. This same substance is being used today by some who divert it from aerosol cans containing everything from deodorants to foods. Another form of mind-altering substance use and abuse involves organic solvents also taken by inhalation and including toluene in glues ("glue sniffing"), plastic cements, and lacquer thinner; naphtha in lighter or cleaning fluid; gasoline; acetone in fingernail-polish remover; chlorinated hydrocarbons as used by dry cleaners; and benzene. Not being standard "drugs" and being used only clandestinely, relatively little is known about the extent of use or incidence of side effects, but it is well understood that these substances are capable of producing sudden death and severe damage to the liver, kidneys, and central nervous system. Then there are the amphetamine-like substances, such as mephentermine and several others, found in nasal inhalers; there is the belladonna or scopolamine found in plants such as the jimson weed and in over-the-counter preparations such as Compoz; antihistaminics, several of them related structurally to the phenothiazine tranquilizers, found in both over-the-counter and prescribed cold and allergy preparations; amyl nitrite ampoules used ordinarily to revive someone who has fainted; pain remedies containing caffeine, phenacetin, and aspirin; numerous plants that have been mentioned; and common kitchen spices such as nutmeg (often used in prisons to alter consciousness and escape from reality) and mace.

Even then the story is not ended, for almost monthly if not weekly, there are "scientific" reports in our newspapers about some new dangerous substance, such as "sex juice," which gave an Eastern health officer front-page attention when he claimed it was being widely used and causing great harm to youth. Some days later, when someone bothered to do a chemical analysis, it was found that the substance was none other than oil of peppermint and had no mind-altering effect whatsoever. A variety of reports circulated about STP in which doctors who should have known better rushed into print to indicate that the drug was serotonin triphosphate, because "obviously" that's what the letters "STP" stood for. The drug is, of course, an amphetamine derivative with LSD-type effects and was actually named after a widely advertised automobile engine additive, as a "put down" of our society by "hippies" sensing some of our absurdities. It later came to be talked about as "serenity, tranquility, and peace." Even more ludicrous and satirical was the banana hoax of two years ago, which could well have been an advertising gimmick of the United Fruit Company seeking to dispose of a surplus of bananas, but was actually a clever theater-of-the-absurd play carried out by a few "hippies" and the underground press. Within days the dry scrapings from the inside of the banana peel (bananadine, or, as Donovan had called it, "Mellow Yellow") were being prepared and smoked by thousands, widely written up in the mass media, investigated by narcotics policemen, and denounced by politicians. In the San Francisco area I saw those who had smoked innumerable cigarettes made from banana scrapings in hopes of getting high, but instead, getting sore throats and irritated lungs. The substance was even available by mail for five dollars a half ounce and could be purchased in stores for approximately a quarter a cigarette. Government and private research grants were sought and obtained to study the pharmacology and sociology of this phenomenon, and one such report actually was published in the *American Journal of Psychiatry* in 1967. Although some users reported getting high or even having visual hallucinations, no active LSD-type (or any other mind-altering) substance has been found with chemical analysis, and any effects that

occurred were the result of suggestion, expectation, and
lack of sophistication combined with a desire to ridicule
the Establishment. If all of this, plus the knowledge of the
extreme ease of preparation of certain drugs such alcohol, or of concealment of other drugs such as LSD, has not
been convincing enough about the impossibility of controlling such a complex and widespread phenomenon through
the criminal law, let us attempt a *reductio ad absurdum*.
Suppose that we somehow managed to eliminate the use of
all of these mind-altering chemicals and drugs, or at least
those considered undesirable by the rule makers, by passing more criminal laws, increasing penalties, hiring more
drug police, placing informants and spies in every classroom and neighborhood, tapping all phones, eliminating all
privacy, forbidding purchase of airplane glue, and locking
all gasoline tanks (allowing them to be opened only at
registered service stations so that none would be diverted
to inhalation). Despite all of that, we would still not have
eliminated the "danger" of mind or consciousness altera-
tion or the danger of disapproved pleasure seeking. Nondrug phenomena, such as hypnosis, meditation, the arts,
sexual relationships, and human love in general, would
require attention because, sometimes with some people,
each is capable of producing a possibly "dangerous"
change in consciousness. Finally, we would need breathing
police, environment police, and sleep police because
sensory deprivation, sleep deprivation, and carbon-dioxide
accumulation (as from holding one's breath) can all produce
varying degrees of mind-alteration ranging up to hallucinations and temporary "psychoses." As an alternative to
jailing everybody, perhaps some would continue to accept
the recommendation of one of the 1968 Presidential candidates, that we run over all these people with our automobiles, although some would perhaps wonder whether we
should take the advice of a man discharged from the armed
services because of mental illness, and some might even
wonder whether we had not arrived at the Orwellian world
of *1984* some 15 years early.

Coming now to cannabis or *marijuana* and its active principle, tetrahydrocannabinol (THC), we find a drug which is not clearly a member of any of the categories of mind-altering drugs detailed above, shares some aspects of several, and in terms of present knowledge is best described as a mixed sedative-stimulant drug. It is not a narcotic, it is not a hallucinogen or psychedelic, and it is not a tranquilizer, although some aspects of its actions in some people are tranquilizing, sedating, "psychedelic," intoxicating, and many other labels that could be applied. The resin containing THC is found mainly in the female plant, particularly in the tops, leaves, and shoots. Only recently has THC been synthesized, although very similar synthetic substances, synhexyl and pyrahexyl, have been known for years and were formerly experimented with. Cannabin was available and used in medical practices as a sedative-hypnotic, pain reliever, and "tranquilizer" until the 1940s, when stigmatization and powers of the Federal Bureau of Narcotics and local narcotics-police agencies forced it out of medical circulation and also, with very rare exceptions, prevented any research being done with the drug, so that their one-dimensional picture of its evil attributes would remain untarnished by knowledge. This also accounts for the unavailability of answers to many really simple questions about the drug's effects. During the time cannabis was in the U.S. Pharmacopeia, bioassay methods were used to standardize it, since its chemistry was not fully understood. At that time the dosage was 60 to 200 milligrams for medical practice and, in extract form, 15 milligrams taken by mouth. Presently in the United States the drug is used almost entirely by inhalation in the form of homemade cigarettes, with the individual user on any given occasion usually smoking between a half and one cigarette using a process of self-titration to determine when the optimal effects have been achieved, and then stopping. Heavier doses frequently produce a diminishing of the pleasurable sensations sought. The effects come on within a few minutes after smoking and 30 to 60 minutes after oral ingestion, lasting somewhere between two and four hours. The main effects are on the brain, but there are also a mild increase in pulse rate and blood pressure, dryness of the mouth and throat (perhaps because of the irritating effect of smoke in general), and increased appetite. No evidence has been found of damage to body organs from either short-term use or long-term use, and no deaths have occurred, even with large doses. In ordinary doses, it acts on the brain and interacts with the mind to bring about in the average person mild euphoria, relaxation, increased flow of ideas, sometimes increased volubility and hilarity, and specific changes in the perception of time, with minutes sometimes seeming to be hours. With large doses of the delta-9-THC or of the crude marijuana, temporary illusions, hallucinations, and personality disorganization can occur as with large doses of a number of other drugs detailed earlier. Psychological dependence can occur with regular use, but there is no addiction and probably no tolerance developing from use of the drug. As a part of the La Guardia-sponsored study, *The Marijuana Problem in the City of New York* in 1944, certain psychological tests were carried out on 77 subjects (without a control group or a double-blind design using a placebo or another drug). The study found impairment of equilibrium and hand steadiness and adverse effects on the speed and accuracy of performing various intellectual tasks, but no effect on reaction time, auditory acuity, or estimation of time and distance. There was marked individual variability irrespective of dosage. More sophisticated measures and research designs as well as a purer substance for testing are now available, and, hopefully, as public pressures force an opening up of research by the bureaucracies of the Bureau of Narcotic and Drug Abuse and the National Institute of Mental Health, we will have much more information, although such data is not relevant to our present policies.

A careful review of the anthropological and medical literature from around the world combined with the pre-Prohibition experience in this country would indicate that cannabin preparations have potential usefulness in treating depression; anxiety and tension; poor appetite; headache and other forms of pain; possibly some symptoms of the withdrawal illness from alcohol or narcotics addiction; cough; impaired respiration, and hypertension. It may also be valuable as an investigative tool for understanding brain function; accelerator of psychotherapy, and antibiotic (the non-THC components of the plant). Whether or not such utility is confirmed by future objective research, the self-prescribed, nonmedical, social, or recreational use of the drug is not going to abate in the near future unless the underlying causes, to be discussed in the next chapter, are somehow remedied.

CHAPTER 9

Why? Perchance To Dream

Whether 'tis nobler in the mind to suffer
The slings and arrows of outrageous fortune,
Or to take arms against a sea of troubles,
And by opposing end them?

To sleep: perchance to dream

For who would bear the whips and scorns of time,
The oppressor's wrong, — the law's delay,
The insolence of office, —

And enterprises of great pith and moment
With this regard their currents turn awry,
And lose the name of action.

— SHAKESPEARE

Why do people use and abuse drugs? How such questions are answered has always depended on the education or lack thereof of the individual commentators, the biases of their particular occupation or profession, their understanding of what is included under the rubric of "drugs," and by opportunism and expediency. The questions we ask determine the kind of answers we arrive at, and if, for example, a person is equating use with abuse in terms of a specific drug, he will never understand the full picture. Obviously a person cannot become a drug abuser without first being a user of that drug, but there are many factors which bring about abuse that are not involved in the reasons for ordinary use. To one person, possession by the devil or by evil spirits may be the "explanation"; to another, always thinking in a one-dimensional, oversimplified manner, it is "overpermissiveness" or bleeding-heart professors, communists, drug pushers, mental illness. Although we will examine some specific theories, there is actually no one cause of either drug use or drug abuse, but rather the phenomenon that we are seeking to understand in this book is multifactoral in origin, involving a complex interweaving of sociological and psychological factors, with perhaps an element of chance.

We must begin our answer with the understanding that we live in a *drug-ridden, drug-saturated society,* in which from infancy onward we have been taught to accept and live the industrial slogan of "Better Living Through Chemistry." We are taught that there is a pill, a drink, or a cigarette for every real or imagined pain, trouble, or problem, and that the more of these substances we use, the better off we will be. Both the alcoholic-beverage industry and the tobacco industry spend between one and two million dollars every single day in the United States alone to promote and encourage the earliest possible use of their drugs by the greatest possible number of people, and hopefully in large quantities. The imagery which is used to disseminate these drugs, and which is beamed particularly to young people by the use of space or time in publications or programs of special interest to them, e.g., sports events on TV, stresses (eternal) youthfulness, sexual pleasure, and happiness to be obtained, supposedly, from the drug. Sex is, of course, used to sell everything from deodorants to automobiles to the over-the-counter pseudosedatives, such as Compoz, which has been advertised in multimillion-dollar campaigns as the "little gentle blue pill" which makes women presidents of their clubs and men successful executives. The company marketing this substance and its advertising agency go one step further, by featuring on their packages as an ingredient of the substance extract of passion flower, thereby communicating that, in addition to all the other imagined benefits to be obtained by using it, there will also be an aphrodisiac effect. A typical Scotch whisky, vodka, or cigarette ad will show an attractive miniskirted woman standing with her legs spread seductively apart holding the drug in her hand with such lines of print as "The first thing about a holiday bash is don't be bashful." "Wade in, straight on," "Don't stand there, get with them." Another one says, "Must a Girl Really Prove Herself to Earn Her [a particular brand of whiskey]," showing a partially clad man and woman facing each other in a manner having obvious sexual overtones. According to Madison Avenue you can't be a man, a woman, or have fun without these substances being a prominent part of the setting. With alcohol and tobacco, even though their use is illegal for most people under twenty-one, the advertising is beamed equally to teenagers and "grown-ups."

In addition to this fully legal advertising, there is a less explicit kind of advertising going on about the totally illegal drugs marijuana, heroin, and LSD. The advertising, propagandizing, and *glorification* are free, being done, if not systematically, quite thoroughly by drug policemen, certain politicians, and the mass media, who day after day, week after week, feature pot, acid, and "dope," exaggerating the properties of these drugs as well as their importance in the total context of our society, but very successfully arousing interest and curiosity, leading to ever-widening patterns of use.

Perhaps more important even than the overt and covert proselytizing for drug use is the *role-model* presented by the older generations of America. It is both ironical and hypocritical that the same parents and other respectable adults who ask why young people are using drugs are themselves using three to five mind-altering drugs daily and providing a regular model of drug use for their children to identify with and imitate. The average middle-class bathroom medicine cabinet contains somewhere around 40 drugs, a goodly number of which are mind-altering substances. A typical drug-using day for housewife, businessman, or factory worker begins with the stimulant caffeine, goes on to include the stimulant nicotine, then some alcohol, not uncommonly a tranquilizer, perhaps a sleeping pill at night, and sometimes a prescription stimulant the next morning to overcome the effects of the previous evening's sleeping potion. Every time these supposedly law-abiding, drug-hating adults socialize with each other, whether at a wedding or a funeral, every time they relate to other human beings, and every time they work or play at being happy or having fun they use drugs. Why indeed do young people become interested in drugs?

Closely related to this is the matter of *peer-group pressure* to conform, to go along with the crowd if one wants to be accepted and be "in." Think, for example, of the plight of the poor teetotaler at a cocktail party or other common event focused around the use of the drug alcohol. At the very least, this individual is a source of anxiety for those around him, for he represents the most dangerous thing in American society, a noncomformist, and this person may well become an object of suspicion and hostility, with considerable pressures being exerted to join in the elbow-bending and backslapping, the getting plastered, and the often associated sexual promiscuity. One shows that he is a man, one of the boys, and a good American by drinking along with everyone else. Many young people are rightly condemning the conformity and overconformity of their elders, yet, at the same time, they are often responding to similar peer-group pressures and conforming to their crowd by illegal alcohol, tobacco, or marijuana use. Rarely is an individualistic, independent decision made by either young or old as to whether a particular mind-altering drug is really important, necessary, or desirable for them to use. Among other things, this fact shows us how little this society's institutions, including the families and schools, have inculcated individualism, or made it possible, despite the sometime lip-service that is given to this as an American ideal.

The availability and indeed the *overavailability* of practically all of the mind-altering drugs, whether legal or illegal, is certainly another important factor in their widespread use. This availability involves production, distribution, numerous legal or illegal outlets, and minimal to moderate taxation. In the larger cities of California and most other states, alcohol, as one example, is easily obtained at package liquor stores, bars, restaurants, grocery stores, and drugstores, sometimes six places in one block. Marijuana is also readily available in most neighborhoods of the bigger American cities and in a surprising number of the smaller cities, despite the fact that it circulates on an entirely underground basis.

Once one has learned to use one drug, the experience or mode of use can *carry over* to other substances, not because of a direct pharmacological or psychological relationship, but for other, more complicated reasons. Thus, the drug police, by ever lobbying for criminal prohibitions against certain drugs, drive each of the drugs together in the illicit-distribution chain, so that an individual coming into contact with one of them ordinarily is exposed to others, which he may decide to sample or be pressured into doing so. Also, the pattern of drug-law violation established with teenage use of alcohol or tobacco may make it much more acceptable and no more "deviant" to use still other illegal drugs. Another example is the *interrelatedness* of tobacco smoking and cannabis smoking. If our society had not been taught over a period of decades that it was somehow harmless, necessary, and pleasurable to put a dried plant leaf in one's mouth, set it on fire, and inhale the toxic fumes into one's lungs, to be followed by exhalation that pollutes the air for other people, all of this with tobacco smoking, we would not have the widespread smoking of marijuana today. Since smoking is learned behavior, and since we were not born with chimneys in our heads, once we learn to smoke one kind of cigarette, it becomes much easier to smoke other kinds, entirely apart from the specific drug effects.

Some anthropologists, on the basis of studies of "primitive" societies, have stated that drinking (and I think this would apply equally to other patterns of drug use) varies directly with the level of *anxiety* in the particular society, and varies inversely with counteranxiety occurring from painful experiences during or after drinking. If we extrapolate from this finding, it would mean that when people

are anxious, or the society in general has a great deal of
anxiety, there is more drug use, but that when the drug use
causes unpleasantness for the individual, this works in the
opposite direction to reduce the phenomenon. Various attempts have been made to relate alcohol use to *national or
religious characteristics:* drinking by the French is attributed to a belief that this provides strength and virility and
the economic dependence of about a third of the population
on the alcoholic-beverage industry; the Irish are said to
have a high tolerance for drunkenness and to use drinking
as an outlet for guilt, anxiety, and aggression because of
overdependency; the Italians supposedly have a lack of
ambivalence in their attitudes toward drinking, take alcohol
only with meals and within the family, condemn inebri-
ation, and are uninhibited in their expression of emotion and
aggression; the Chinese, for whom drinking is important in
formal social functions, stress self-control and consider
drunkenness silly; the Jews are thought to have a ritualis-
tic attitude toward drinking, strongly condemning excessive consumption and attaching a high value to alertness
and control; and the Moslems (of most countries) have a
religious prohibition against drinking. Comparable *sociocultural studies* about other drugs and other groups are
sadly lacking. It is generally believed that drinking and
alcoholism correlate significantly with urbanism, affluence,
and education, and to some extent with the male sex.
Throughout the underdeveloped world of Africa, Asia, and
Latin America, there are large heterogeneous populations
migrating to cities, hoping for better opportunities and
adding to overcrowding, slums, unemployment, the loosen-
ing of family and tribal ties, and other factors which can be
expected to produce more use and abuse of mind-altering
drugs. As far back as 1934, detribalization was found to be
related to extensive production and consumption of illicit
beer in a Johannesburg, South Africa slum. We need a much
deeper understanding of the processes of aculturation,
social integration, and attitude formation. In addition to the
factors already mentioned, secularization, homogenization,

assimilation, industrialization, and family disruption, all of which are occurring significantly in the United States and throughout the world, will undoubtedly influence the drug scene.

Some have postulated a so-called theory of *ethnic specificity* which states that alcohol is beloved by Western man because it satisfies a need for action and extroversion; opium is sought by those of the Eastern world because they value contemplation and passivity; and cannabin is preferred by the African and Near Easterner who seeks fantasy and collective emotion. Carstairs studied the cultural differences and attitudes within a large Indian village toward the two most popular intoxicants, one an alcoholic beverage and the other a cannabin beverage. The warrior and ruler caste being one of the few Hindu castes permitted to drink alcohol was generally a strong partisan of the drug, often consuming it in large quantities. They used cannabin occasionally, but it was neither strongly approved nor disapproved. The Brahmin caste, in contrast to the aforementioned Rajputs, were strong partisans of cannabin, claiming it enhanced religious life, but unanimously and strongly denounced the use of alcohol. Members of both groups at various times were observed to be deeply intoxicated, although describing quite different subjective experiences and seeing no similarity between their intoxication and that of those using the other drug. Obviously a Westerner who was unfamiliar with the psychological and physical effects of cannabin, in addition to having a quite different cultural heritage, might approach the drug experience with fear of cannabin or possibly fear of "unsanitary" preparations of either drug. In this study, the author also points out that there are alternative ways of dealing with sexual and aggressive impulses other than repressing them or using alcohol for an outlet for them (a theory suggested by several anthropologists). The Brahmin seems to deemphasize all feelings and interpersonal relationships in obedience to an impersonal set of rules of right behavior as he seeks a more profound contact with reality, while the Rajput, more like the Westerner, seems committed to a life of action, regarding individual achievement as important and accepting actual indulgence, as with alcohol, only if it is within socially prescribed limits. All of the cultural associations to the two drugs, the psychological and physical effects, the differing values and attitudes of the two castes are shown to be involved in the dichotomy in choice of intoxicant.

The Blums, in their study of alcohol use in *rural Greece*, also demonstrate the complex interrelationships of drug use with culture and personality. Despite the disintegration of their historical centers of power and wealth and successive subjugation by Romans, Goths, Slavs, Albanians, Venetians, Turks, and Germans, there persists in the villagers studied an ideal of manly excellence, *levendi*, and a national sense of honor, *philotomo*, which would be damaged in their eyes by drinking excessively. Alcohol is used in the Greek village in a variety of social settings, including meals, coffeehouses, family celebrations, festivals, religious rites, and the treatment of illness. Wine is rarely taken without something to eat and drinking occurs in a group context. Learning about the drug begins in childhood with tasting and consuming small amounts at mealtimes. Women drink as commonly as men but in smaller amounts and less often. No one abstains because of social position, although a few are more careful to be moderate because of this. Income and leisure are important determinants of what beverage one drinks and how much one can drink consistently. Consumption appears to follow a J-curve, with most individuals in the low-consumption end of the continuum and decreasing numbers extending to the high consumption end. Conscious efforts to seek altered states of mood or consciousness are rare. On the contrary, alcohol is considered a facilitator of social and natural processes. On special occasions, such as festivals, the effects of the drug show two major trends: enhancement of fun behavior and release or intensification of aggressive competitive impulses, sometimes leading to quarrels and violence.

Wine is believed by the Greeks to have definite food value and is thus good for one's health (second only to milk in their estimation). Both wine and ouzo (a distilled grape product containing 46 percent alcohol) are also considered special healing powers (ranking third to herb teas and milk). Conversely, wine and ouzo to excess rank first and second among liquids believed to be health-endangering. Attitudes toward alcoholic beverages are closely linked to the attitudes toward solid foods and nonalcoholic liquids, and in different amounts and different contexts the same substance can be considered both good and bad. Since parents were found to use food as a reward and rarely to punish children by food deprivation, it is postulated that children do not project onto foods or wine elements of badness or forbidden desirability and they do not become objects for rebellion. Because it is believed that alcohol contains power which may be magically managed to serve as a means of propitiating other powers, it follows that it must be handled with more than usual caution. Thus, attitudes are engendered which lead to restraint in drinking. The Greek life style in general stresses moderation as an ideal. The typical Greek values wine as one of the most important elements in his life and sometimes shows his superiority through ability to drink, but always uppermost is the maintenance of pride and avoidance of shame. There were a small number in the villages studied who drank too much by local standards and by Western standards would be considered alcoholics, but the concept of alcoholism did not exist. The person defined as a confirmed drunk by community opinion was rejected, ridiculed, and sometimes physically attacked but was never thought of as a social or health problem.

Numerous concepts or hypotheses have been put forward by sociologists and criminologists to explain *deviant behavior* in general, including certain forms of mind-altering-drug use and abuse that have been looked at from this perspective. These theories of causation include: anomie, alienation, and retreatism; status-seeking among peers;

differential association; blocked opportunity in the legitimate opportunity structure followed by access to illegiti-
mate opportunity; the specific effects of lower-class culture;
family disorganization; personality inadequacy leading to
escapist behavior, and a variety of others. Any or all of
these factors might in a given instance be involved in the
development of a certain pattern of mind-altering-drug use
or abuse, but all of the theories are nonspecific, incomplete,
and rest upon unexamined assumptions about what is use
and what is abuse, and which drugs represent deviancy
and which do not.

The word *"alienation"* has come into increasing usage
as a capsule summary of the human condition, most particularly the American condition. Someone once said that
America is the only country that moved from infancy to
senility without passing through a period of maturity. In
any event, alienation embraces the sociological concept of
anomie (retreat from life as a result of the gap between the
cultural norms and the abilities of individuals to act in ac-
cord with them), despair, depersonalization, loneliness,
rootlessness, a sense of meaninglessness, atomization,
hopelessness or pessimism, and a loss of values or beliefs.
So many individuals and groups have been described by
various writers and academics as alienated that, in some
senses, we can say that practically everyone out of infancy
is alienated. Man has lost control over his own environment, is increasingly separated from his work and his fel-
lows, is dehumanized and routinized, has lost a sense of
community, and is living a life of noisy desperation. To
put it more succinctly, meaning and identity have been lost
as individualism and inner-directiveness have been replaced by an other-directed, marketing orientation. While
the condition of alienation is intense and pervasive in our
times, it cannot be said to be unique. The fifteenth-century
French poet Deschamps said, "Why are the times so dark?
Men know each other not at all, but governments quite
clearly change from bad to worse. Days dead and gone
were more worthwhile, now what holds sway? Deep gloom

and boredom, justice and law nowhere to be found. I know no more where I belong." The mass society and the bureaucratic-political process dominated by bigness, mediocrity, authoritarianism, expediency, and anonymity have destroyed the individual and provided a fertile climate for escapist, pleasure-seeking behavior, with drugs from alcohol to LSD becoming the most common "answer." Let it not be misunderstood that all of this drug use involves seeking (temporary) oblivion, for there are other, more selective objectives as well. Thus, some use of some drugs in response to alienation involves a search for meaning, feeling, authenticity, and self-realization. The fact that this quest is but rarely satisfied by drug use does not minimize it as a motive and should not blind us to looking at the multitudinous alienating forces in the society.

As we come to *psychological explanations,* we find a veritable quagmire of confusion and arbitrariness. To illustrate this, suppose for a moment that you were seeking to explain psychologically why people drink, or use the drug alcohol. One common response to such a question would be that they drink to relax and feel good, implying in a sense that, prior to drinking, they were tense and felt bad. This could then be pursued to build a superstructure of psychopathology and arrive at a psychiatric diagnosis of sickness for all users. It would be equally foolish to ascribe the use of any other mind-altering drug, whether marijuana or tranquilizer, solely or even primarily to individual psychopathology. Yet modern medicine and psychiatry and psychology have done just that by accepting the police concept and including all illegal drug use (except alcohol and tobacco by those under twenty-one) as mental illness, using the diagnoses of drug addiction or character disorder while ignoring distinctions between use, abuse, and addiction.

In Freudian psychoanalytic theory, drug abuse is spoken of as "the addictions," classified as an impulse neurosis, and addicts are seen as people who use the effects of alcohol, morphine, or other drugs to satisfy archaic oral longings, including sexual satisfaction, a need for security, and a need for self-esteem. The drug means a fulfillment of primitive desires, represents food and warmth to the person, and genital sexuality (the theoretical end point of psychosexual development in Freudian theory) becomes uninteresting for them. Psychoanalytically, the addict is intolerant of tension, pain, or frustration, and his overwhelming oral dependence leads to the bottle's or needle's supplanting all other interests and reality. The specific pleasure from alcohol is said to be due to its removal of inhibitions and reality considerations from consciousness so that a person may satisfy instinctual impulses and have care banished. Thus, the super-ego has only half facetiously been defined as "that part of the mind that is soluble in alcohol." Some analysts have stated that chronic alcoholics specifically have had a pathological family situation which created oral fixations and (latent) homosexual tendencies.

Other personality theories characterize the alcoholic (the most studied drug abuse) as suffering from inadequacy, emotional immaturity, self-destructive impulses, striving for power, or feelings of inferiority. Other descriptive, not really diagnostic or ideologic, terms applied at different places in the scientific literature to drug abusers and sometimes to illegal users include the following: psychopath, passive-aggressive personality, narcissist, sociopath, hedonist, rebellious, hostile, infantile, neurotic, self-indulgent, and a variety of other similarly nonspecific, vague, and confusing terms.

Alfred R. Lindesmith, a courageous pioneer with both theory and social policy regarding narcotics addiction, pointed out decades ago the importance of the withdrawal illness in explaining the continuance of addiction. He has stressed that the process of addiction is not explained in terms of psychological motives or sociological theories of retreatism and social failure, but rather that the craving for opiates comes from the experiencing of relief from withdrawal distress. Abraham Wikler has proposed a similar theory, which he calls a *"pharmacodynamic theory* of addiction," emphasizing that once physical dependency has developed to the narcotic, this becomes a basic biological drive, supplanting sexual and aggressive impulses which the individual may ordinarily be unable to cope with. In talking about narcotics, Wikler has also stated that the normal person uses them only for relief of pain while the psychopath uses them for euphoria.

We have now shifted from discussing social and psychological causes of drug *use* to a discussion of theories of that segment of use constituting drug *abuse,* particularly alcoholism and narcotics addiction, which have been the prototypes. The groups of drug abusers from which most generalizations come are very specialized ones seen in captivity in hospitals or prisons. Thus most illicit narcotic (heroin) users and addicts who have come to public attention in America are young, unemployed males of Negro, Mexican, or Puerto Rican ancestry, living in large urban ghettos and products of broken, culturally deprived homes and inadequate schools from which they dropped out prior to getting a high school diploma. Isadore Chein's studies of heroin addiction in New York showed it to be highest where income and education were lowest and where there was the greatest breakdown of normal family life. Most had tried heroin before the age of fifteen and had previously seen someone take it. Also around this age, most had left school and there was no major social institution involved in their lives. Heroin became a natural social activity free of conflict within this social milieu or subculture. Despite this, it cannot be said that there is any one preaddiction personality even when the discussion is being restricted to heroin addiction. The effects of our legal processing system actually make the addicts that we know about seem much more similar than they are and in fact we see a post-addiction and post-law-enforcement personality and sociology. In one sense, considering the full context of drugs and of the society, it can be said that everyone is potentially a drug abuser.

Anthropologists sometimes claim that where the drinking customs, values, sanctions, and attitudes of a society are well established, accepted, and consistent with the overall culture, there will be a low rate of alcoholism. It seems also that the rate of alcoholism in a given culture is influenced by the degree to which the culture operates to bring about inner tensions in its members; the attitudes toward drinking which the culture produces in its members; and the degree to which the culture provides suitable substitute means of satisfaction. It has also been found that first-generation Americans of Irish and Anglo-Saxon descent have higher rates of alcoholism, and those of Italian, Jewish, and Chinese descent have lower rates, apparently due to child-rearing practices, including the way alcohol is used and introduced in the home as a part of meals and normal family life, as opposed to being given undue and unique emphasis. As these subcultural groups become assimilated into basic American society, the alcoholism rate becomes the same as in the general population.

Over the years, many physical causes have been suggested for alcoholism and sometimes for narcotics addiction or other drug abuses, but all of these have been based upon either research with lower animals which was not borne out in man, or a confusion of effects from alcoholism with causes. It has been postulated, for example, that the alcoholic is someone who is allergic to the corn, wheat, or rye grains from which alcoholic beverages are distilled; has a metabolic or hormonal deficiency which alcohol satisfies; or suffers from nutritional abnormalities. No physical basis, including genetic or constitutional, has been found to explain any form of drug abuse, although it is certainly conceivable that such factors could play a role along with the interplay of sociological and psychological factors, the availability of the drug, and chance circumstances. Many people seem to prefer to believe in a physical explanation so that they need not look within themselves, their family, or their society and also, once more, because of the drive for oversimplification.

We see, then, many drugs, many causes, many factors, and many dimensions which must be taken into account if we are to understand and cope with mind-altering-drug use and abuse. We might well turn the usual question around to ask why, with the enormous pressures toward drug usage and the widespread availability of so many drugs, more people aren't using and abusing these substances.

CHAPTER 10
Youth, American Society, and Drugs

> "Our youth today love luxury. They have bad manners, contempt for authority, disrespect for older people. Children nowadays are tyrants. They contradict their parents, gobble their food and tyrannize their teachers."
> — SOCRATES, circa 425 B.C.

Many people today, including a number of highly successful politicians, discuss American youth as though it were one homogeneous entity of tens of millions simultaneously smoking pot, dropping acid, copulating in the streets, and rioting. Although it is clear that we live in a society obsessed with youthfulness, there is no clear definition of "young" or "youth." Several things are clear, however, including the fact that, as one grows older, the upper limit of being young becomes more flexible. Roughly half the population of the United States is now under the age of twenty-five, but a more significant figure is that there are approximately four million people at each of the age levels around twenty: four million eighteen-year-olds, four million nineteen-year-olds, etc. There are also some seven million students in our thousands of colleges and universities.

When we are talking about young people as opposed to children or older people, we are encompassing a group frequently stereotyped with such labels as "adolescent," "juvenile," or "teenager." After applying such labels, many people will react to their attitudes and prejudices toward the label just as they might react to a stereotype of "Negro" or "cop." In turn, the people being reacted to in this stereotypical manner are likely to feel hostility and comparable intolerance toward those discriminating against them. It would be far better if we thought of young people as individual human beings who happen to be age fifteen or age eighteen or age twenty-one. Conventional wisdom attributes maturity and wisdom to age, although there is little to support such a belief. From a biological standpoint, adolescence is considered the period between the first appearance of secondary sexual characteristics and full physical maturity. The process is initiated between the ages of eight and fourteen by the hypothalamus and the anterior pituitary gland, leading to an orderly sequence of changes, but a sequence with great individual variation between the sexes in the time of appearance, and in different parts of the body. Psychological and philosophical maturity is far more complicated to define, but there are certainly many young people who are as mature as, if not more mature than many older people, and there are many older human beings who show no evidence of maturity.

As the survey data summarized in early sections of the book made clear, the pattern of youthful drug use in many respects duplicates the pattern of the older American's drug use, with alcohol and nicotine (along with caffeine) leading in the popularity parade and marijuana next in line. Thinking of youth in terms of the age range fifteen to twenty-five, most subgroups are showing extensive interest in and use of marijuana (more so than with the older ages), including college and high school students, ghetto dwellers, soldiers and sailors in Vietnam, Peace Corps volunteers, hippies, and artists. The use of other drugs, such as LSD and heroin, is also proportionately more common among young people; but sedatives and stimulants, while used and abused by many, are used much less frequently by the young than by older middle-class Americans.

Just as it is commonly asked why the young are interested in drugs, it is also asked about them, and about black people and other minorities, "What do these people want?" Something of what they want and many of the influences being exerted on them have already been covered in some depth, but life and society as seen from the young person's perspective requires further amplification.

Most young people are not manning the ramparts, fighting for social change and progress, but rather, like their elders, are apathetic, accepting, or resigned to things as they are. They are peacefully allowing the schools and the broader society to assimilate them into the middle-class, achievement-oriented society of older America. Although the activists or so-called New Left (and New Right) receive considerable attention and are thought by many to represent American youth, they probably number no more than tens of thousands in such groups as the Students for a Democratic Society (SDS), antiwar and antidraft groups, student power advocates, and some elements of the hippies and Yippies. Then there are the equally radical groups of special minorities within the minority of youth, namely the Black Panthers, Brown Berets, and others seeking power, dignity, and sometimes justice for racial and cultural minorities. There is a much larger group of our young who become involved in certain special issues that are of concern to them, such as participating in the election campaigns of Eugene McCarthy and Robert Kennedy, volunteering for the Peace Corps, and tutoring ghetto youth; and there is an even larger segment who, although not activists, express their underlying discontent with the status quo by their involvement in folk-rock. American pop culture today is probably for the first time determined by youth who, with folk-rock, acid-rock, raga-rock, light shows, poster art and the psychedelic scene in general, have determined the cultural values for the society.

Many heroes come from such imaginative and absurdly titled groups as Big Brother and the Holding Company, the Grateful Dead, the Quicksilver Messenger Service, the Fugs, the Buffalo Springfield, the Mothers of Invention, the Peanutbutter Conspiracy, the Byrds, the Rolling Stones, the Beatles, Country Joe and the Fish, Jefferson Airplane (and Bob Dylan). The Beatles' albums *Sergeant Pepper's Lonely-hearts Club Band* and *Revolver* have numerous songs with drug themes, and there are also "Let's Go Get Stoned," "Rainy Day Woman," "Eight Miles High," "Hey, Mr. Tambourine Man," "Can't Get High," "Flying High," "Mind

Gardens," "Lucy in the Sky with Diamonds," "A Little
Help from My Friends," "Mother's Little Helper," "Connection," "Crystal Ship," and many others. The records
bought by the millions by American youth and listened to
incessantly include the following words (warily listened to
by the older generation who usually hear only the music
while complaining of its loudness): "There's something
happening here. What it is ain't exactly clear. There is a
man with a gun over there telling me I've got to beware. I
think it's time we stopped. Children what's that sound.
Everyone look what's going down." (—The Buffalo Springfield); "Mr. America, walk on by your supermarket dream,
Mr. America, walk on by the liquor store supreme, Mr.
America, try to hide the emptiness that's you inside."
(—The Mothers of Invention); "And you ask why I don't
live here, hey, how come you have to ask me that?" (—Bob
Dylan); "All the lonely people, where do they all come
from? All the lonely people, where do they all belong?"
(—The Beatles); "He's as blind as he can be, just sees what
he wants to see, nowhere, man, can you see me at all?"
(—The Beatles); "Slow down, you've got to make the morning last." (—Simon and Garfunkel); "All I want is just be
free and live my life the way I want to be. All I want is to
just have fun and live my life like it just begun. But you're
pushing too hard on me." (—The Seeds); "Come, mothers
and fathers throughout the land, and don't criticize what
you can't understand. Your sons and your daughters are
beyond your command. Your old road is rapidly aging,
please get out of the new one if you can't lend your hand.
The times they are a-changing." (—Dylan); "All you need
is love, love is all you need." (—The Beatles); and finally,
"We were talking about the space between us all. With
our love we could save the world if they only knew. Try to
realize it's all within yourself. No one else can make you
change. And to see you're only really very small and life
goes on within you and without you." (—The Beatles).
Most young people have no heroes in the conventional
sense. Less than half in one national poll held any living

public figure in high regard. They are increasingly disillusioned and disappointed by the country's leaders and
by the Vietnam war. During President Johnson's reign, less
than one out of 20 of the young people surveyed held him
in any esteem. The whole older generation is held in contempt by most for their hypocrisy, incompetence, and moral
and intellectual dishonesty. Perhaps just as the black problem is mainly a white problem, the youth problem is mainly
an adult problem. As Margaret Mead once said, the young
have become "scapegoats for adult apathy, indifference,
lack of responsibility, and lack of imagination." Another
apt comment is, "The denunciation of the young is a necessary part of the hygiene of older people, and greatly assists
the circulation of their blood."

The perceptive social psychologist Kenneth Keniston
has especially emphasized the strong pressures on American students to perform — that is, play a role — to do well aca-
demically, getting grades and passing tests, while ignoring
feeling, courage, art, and emotional satisfactions. Once
professional competence is attained, he may or should
realize that more important questions remain unanswered,
such as the meaning of life, what to stand for as a person,
and what is significant and relevant. A second major
pressure youth is subject to is what Keniston calls "stimu-
lus flooding" leading to "psychological numbing." He
refers to the sheer quantity, variety, and intensity of external stimulation, imagery, and excitation to which they
and most Americans are subjected — sights, sounds, and
people, all actively clamoring for a response. To survive,
an armor is developed which sometimes walls off the
person from all experience and people. A reaction against
this numbing effect sometimes leads to a pursuit of experience for its own sake, a private quest for identity or meaning. For many students, traditional sources of meaning
such as religion, political ideology, campus activities, and
upward mobility have evaporated. A focus on direct experience and the here and now is the defining characteristic
of many, a hang-loose or situation ethic, a find-your-thing-

and-do-it. Many college students and hippies have become concerned with authenticity, love, intimacy, sincerity, and directness, rather than phoniness and hypocrisy. Many are alienated or disaffiliated, rejecting on esthetic and humanistic grounds the prevalent American values. They see the United States as ugly, cheap, commercial, dehumanizing, and arbitrary, and they feel estranged from their own experience.

This view is in marked contrast to the feeling of exhilaration expressed by Joseph Conrad, "I remember my youth and the feeling that will never come back—the feeling that I could last forever, outlast the sea, the earth, and all men." Erik Erikson has emphasized that the great task of the second decade of life is to determine who you are and what you want to be; to find identity and love. He distinguishes eight stages of psychosocial development, each having a specific conflict: basic trust *versus* basic mistrust; autonomy *versus* shame and doubt; initiative *versus* guilt; industry *versus* inferiority; identity *versus* role confusion; intimacy *versus* isolation; generativity *versus* stagnation; and ego-integrity *versus* despair. If the essential strengths evolve properly, they result in the emergence of basic virtues that Erikson considers necessary: hope, will power, purpose, competence, fidelity, love, care, and wisdom.

The quest for identity is greatly hampered by the ambiguities and frustrations encountered along the road, by the generation and communication gaps, and by the frequent killing of the spirit by the bureaucratic-educational process which the brilliant sociologist and educational philosopher Edgar Z. Friedenberg has said is geared to assimilating youth into the middle class as benignly as possible and also designed to keep them off the streets and out of competition in the labor market. Individuality, freedom, originality, and nonconformity are curbed, thus greatly narrowing the world rather than opening it up. Then there is the problem that many adults, including parents and teachers, resent and envy youth for the many years they have ahead of them and for their apparent freedom.

Friedenberg clearly indicates how hostile a mass society is to the positive goals of growth, including the commitments through which different identities can be tried and accepted or rejected by young people. He puts it nicely, albeit tragically, when he says, "The most serious threat to self-esteem is the possibility of meeting someone who really is qualified, thus opening limitless vistas of inferiority."

A recent study of college students found that they sought love and affection, development of their personal identity, time for thinking, and a meaningful career. Quietly dropping into place was seen as being as serious as dropping out of school and suggests that the academic program does not adequately relate to students' personal motivation.

Badges or buttons have become another means of expressing the aspirations and dissatisfactions of young people: "I am a human being, do not fold, spindle, or mutilate"; "I only followed orders" (with a picture of Adolph Eichmann); "I am anonymous, help me"; "Up the Establishment"; "Teen Power"; "Help, I am having an identity crisis"; "Caution, Military Service May Be Hazardous to Your Health"; "Kill for Peace"; "War is good business, invest your son"; "The Marine Corps Builds Oswalds"; "Death Is Camp"; "Jesus Wore Long Hair"; "Support Mental Health or I'll Kill You"; "No Being, Thinking, Loving, Just Killing—It's the American Way"; "Is there a life after birth?"

Social critic Paul Goodman has repeatedly emphasized that most young people have no meaningful employment to look forward to; there simply are not enough worthwhile jobs by even ordinary standards, and when one considers the inefficiency and underemployment with which most organizations operate, and the already high and growing unemployment rates, the picture becomes even bleaker, particularly for the relatively uneducated (meaning, more and more, anyone with less than an MD or PhD) in an increasingly technological society. Friedenberg sees American youth as a colonial population controlled by an imperialistic power, while Goodman tells us that colleges have become only extensions of dreary, regulation-bound high schools, models of the great rat race, in which grades are pursued rather than knowledge in order to ensure good jobs and a rich life.

There are many youthful life styles, including what we could call ordinary middle-class; activist; hippie; racial minority; student; soldier; and other specialized styles of living, a number of which, of course, overlap in many respects. In some of these life styles an absence of hope or an underlying sense of desperation leads to a variety of drug-using behaviors; in others a more prominent aspect is the quest for meaning and feeling; and in still others "simple" pleasure seeking is the prime motive. White as well as black youth are seeking not only acceptance, integration, and equal opportunity, but justice, dignity, and pride. We will never know what might have been the full results and benefits of the hippie movement because of the successful war waged on these young people by the health and police departments of San Francisco and by public officials in other communities which got up-tight about such terribly un-American and un-Christian (despite Jesus) things as long hair and sandals. The core group of hippie philosophers believe that one must change oneself in order to change society, or, as Socrates said, "Let him that would move the world first move himself." They thus reminded us that everyone of us is in a sense a model for others to identify with and imitate. Many of the hippie ideals, often unarticulated, continue to circulate in a kind of underground through folk-rock themes and the underground press and movies, and include such "bizarre" ideas as love, nonviolence, peace, and a contempt for hypocrisy (shared by the activist youth). As with Christianity, one can say it's a wonderful thing, but it's too bad it has never been tried. Another specific component of the hippie philosophy was a dissatisfaction with "structure freaks," referring to people who are prisoners of the bureaucratic-political process, those accepting as a given of the day-to-day life the Establishment structure around them.

Strangely to some, many young people feel a sense of

outrage well expressed by a quotation from Henry Miller: "If we were wide awake, we would be instantly struck by the horrors that surround us. We would drop our tools, quit our jobs, deny our obligations, pay no taxes, observe no laws." They immediately understand the story about Thoreau being in a Boston jail for nonpayment of taxes as a protest against a specific injustice of the time. Emerson came to visit him and is supposed to have asked, "What are you doing in there?" To which Thoreau responded, "What are *you* doing out there?" To some readers these statements will seem to lack pertinency, but remember the poignant comment of Julian Bond at the 1968 Democratic National Convention as he looked out at the assembled delegates of a stacked and atavistic assemblage and said, "You people don't even know what we're talking about." It is a mistake indeed to equate profound dissatisfaction, discontent, and criticism with "adolescent rebellion" which will be outgrown. There are, of course, similarities between any generation of youth and past generations, but today we live in a world of unprecedented technological and social change; affluence for the many in America and poverty for most of the rest of the world and for a large number of Americans; and the ever imminent possibility of total annihilation from one or a thousand hydrogen bombs. We see increasing bureaucratization and increasing totalitarianism, while at the same time there is a unique mass expectation of selfhood, justice, and subsistence recognized to be possible of attainment, but being kept from those who want it (and should have it) by our social pathology. Two issues have become particularly symbolic and representative of the generation conflict: the Vietnam war, and marijuana.

Few of our youth favor an inequitable, unjust, and unnecessary draft law feeding them into the hopper of an unsuccessful, illegal, and immoral war while helping communism and totalitarianism — all to save face for Johnson, Rusk, Nixon, Ky and other politicians who refuse to admit their tragic mistakes, even now that they have been repudiated by the American voter.

As young people have become increasingly sensitive to

the gap between things as they are and as they can and should be, and between what adults say they believe in and what they show by their actions that they really believe in, marijuana has become a way of striking out against the overwhelming hypocrisy of American society even more than the protests against the Vietnam war.

The moral authority of adults in general and the assumption that wisdom and leadership will actually accrue with increasing age are both being challenged by youth who recognize the ineffectiveness and ineptitude of most of our elected and appointed "leaders." The Tweedledums and Tweedledees who run for public office (and get elected); the senile men who control most of our institutions; the pervasive mediocrity and resistance to change; the fragmentation and unnecessary complexity of government (in New York City, more than 1,500 separate governmental units, and in the San Francisco Bay area more than 1,000); the amorality, dehumanization, and continuous abuses of authority which characterize bureaucracies; the lies and the irrelevancy of much that takes place, all communicate frustration and hopelessness and foster extremism or pleasure seeking with drugs or sex. The people who have made our problems are absurdly put in charge of solving them; those who have fostered drug usage, lobbied for ever more fanatical laws, and made drugs seem more important than anything else in life have arranged to be assigned to "stamping it out."

The sense of urgency felt by many young adults is simply not comprehended by the power structure or formal leaders of the society. Change and conflict are inevitable as we are forced to adapt our social organization and institutions to new knowledge, changing aspirations, and the fluctuating environment. Some of these changes not already commented on which are engendering conflict are: urbanization, with America moving from 80 percent rural to 80 percent urban over a relatively brief period with consequent overcrowding, noise, traffic congestion, air and water pollution and slums; the poverty of 30 million Americans and the daily hunger of ten million of these; the mass media, particularly its electronic components, which have made the world into a global village and in a sense led to the Americanization of the world; secularization and a general absence, or defying, of moral and ethical values with "Why not?" and "situation ethics" becoming the standard; family disintegration; racism and discrimination in general against women, youth, and the better-known minorities; overpopulation; and growing irrationality and unpredictability. We are not free to avoid change biologically or sociologically and are faced with the choice of letting all of these things run us over or accepting unpleasantness, facing reality, and seeking to control the change so that it becomes progress which solves our problems and enriches our lives. Both the young and the old have been victimized by society, but the burden falls on the young, since adults have all of the power. The typical "teenager" is more enraged by the weakness and emptiness of his parents and other adults than by their tyranny. Acquiescence, superficial attributes of status and achievement, being "liked," and not getting caught in violations of the rules or legal codes are no longer seen as sufficient, as is demonstrated by the enormous popularity of the film *The Graduate* and the much earlier popularity of the book *The Catcher in the Rye*. Why, indeed, should somebody be made to feel a failure for finishing second, for not getting an "A," or not measuring up to various other arbitrary norms.

It may well be said that inconsistency, injustice, and hypocrisy are inherent characteristics of human nature, but it can be replied that idealism, morality, compassion, honesty, and justice are possible and desirable replacements for these existing standards. Large numbers of our young are practicing intimacy and openness between black and white, male and female, and rich and poor. Many seek something that the broader society assumes it has, but really does not, namely, participatory democracy and consent of the governed. Some turn inward with various drugs or meditation, or go and live in remote areas, having come to

feel that for them there are no alternatives, that the system
can't be changed, and it is not worth changing. For most,
however, drug use, although involving a variety of motives
and a panoply of sociological causes, is like their sexual
behavior, only one component of a far more complicated
and complete life style. Youthful drug use, like that of other
segments of the population, is a barometer and a com-
mentary on the society, reflecting the failure of the family,
the schools, and the "leaders" to provide meaningful
ingress for youthful energy, intelligence, and altruism—one
more of the many tragic and totally needless wastes of mankind's creative potential. Our youth are herded, processed,
harassed, coerced, infantilized, rejected, drafted, criminalized, and otherwise prevented from self-realization and
maximization of their potential. And the society is kept
from reform and progress, moving ever closer to internal
and external moral and physical destruction.

There are a few latent or secondary functions of the drug
scene and drug laws which bear particularly upon young
people and are revealing of American society. One of these
is a *smokescreening function,* particularly utilized by
politicians, editors and publishers, and administrative
bureaucrats, who seek, sometimes desperately, for subjects
or issues which can easily be oversimplified and distorted,
talked about widely, and not antagonize powerful financial
or voting blocs. Drugs are ideal for this. The more they are
talked about and used to monopolize public attention, the
less the candidate or office holder needs to talk about the
real criminal, social, and health problems of the society.
Reality in effect is obscured by a cloud of smoke or hot air.
Many other phenomena in American life are, of course,
used in a similar manner as smokescreens, but probably
none so consistently or so effectively as a few drugs such
as marijuana, heroin, and LSD.

Then there is the *scapegoating function.* There are those,
such as the Reagans and the Wallaces, who, judging from
their pre- and post-election statements, would, if they
could, make it illegal to be young in America, but are

unfortunately (from their standpoint) barred from doing so by such "irrelevant and outmoded" institutions as the Bill of Rights. They then seize upon certain practices most prevalent among the young, or sometimes other minorities, including political activism and certain forms of drug use as a way of attacking and silencing dissent and nonconformity. In the 1930s it was particularly easy to pass our present drug laws without any medical or scientific testimony and without any public expression of concern because the use of marijuana was essentially confined to outgroups or outcasts of American society, Negroes, Mexican Americans, jazz musicians, and a few intellectuals, people without any significant access to political or social influence. The heroin laws have also had a similar scapegoating function, with black and Puerto Rican youth in big-city ghettos. These functions, of course, go well beyond the actual properties of any given drug and help to account for the deep-seated nature of many of our attitudes and procedures.

Closely related to the smokescreening and scapegoating functions is the use of the drug phenomenon as an *anti-intellectual device*, with knowledge and intellect being completely disregarded in policy formulation, and drug use being used to attack and denigrate our schools and the whole educational process. Extremist candidates for offices in California and other political subdivisions of the country often imply that all students are drug users and attack all "pointy-headed intellectuals."

It is fitting to conclude this chapter interrelating drugs, youth, and American society with a quotation from the sociologist Simmel: "The deepest problems of modern life derive from the claim of the individual to preserve the autonomy and individuality of his existence in the face of overwhelming social forces."

CHAPTER II

Beyond Drugs: The Real Problems and How to Solve Them

> "I went down into my inmost self, I found a bottomless abyss at my feet, and out of it came . . . the current which I dare call my life." — TEILHARD DE CHARDIN

It is clear that the *social and legal policies*, if ostensibly developed to control or prevent the use of some mind-altering drugs, are the cause of the main social problems that we find with those drugs. The time has long passed for us to refocus our attention and concern from drugs and drug laws to human beings, who, among the variety of things that they do between birth and death, engage in the seeking of pleasure and many other "strange" things through drug usage. The main question is not what to do about drugs, but what to do about people, and even for those who consider either pleasure or certain drugs to be inherently evil and vicious, the question would then become, what do you do with people who engage in this "evil" practice? What do you do to, and with, them that would be effective in reducing, controlling, or eliminating this practice and would avoid doing more harm than the practice itself? Obviously there are a number of people psychologically dependent on the marijuana issue and on the drug issue more broadly, particularly the drug-police agencies and certain politicians, and their psychological dependence on this issue is of such severity that it represents a religious mania. They will remain refractory to proposals that would ameliorate the situation or place it in perspective, in part because they see any attempt to bring rationality to bear as a threat to their power and security. These men and their Establishment allies in the medical profession will undoubtedly seek to perpetuate the status quo, and it is only a slight exaggeration to anticipate that they will escalate their efforts, perhaps by asking for the death penalty for the first offense of possessing one of the drugs they disapprove of and castration for the second offense. These men will certainly continue to ignore major problems involving drugs that they use, or drugs that are good for business, while singling out a few dimensions of other drugs to view with alarm and pretend to cope with. The real issue is not how harmful or harmless any particular drug is, since all drugs, including all mind-altering drugs, have certain risks or dangers and none of them, including marijuana, will ever be shown to be as dangerous as a nuclear bomb or even a loaded gun no matter how much research is funded by government agencies. Most of all, even where it is shown that there are major, frequent, "hard" effects and problems from particular drugs, especially alcohol and nicotine, there is absolutely no basis for the deeply ingrained assumption that the only way or the best way of attacking such problems is criminalization of all concerned. There are serious reservations about the whole effectiveness of criminal sanctions as deterrents against antisocial conduct, but in the drug area, as with the other crimes without victims, it is quite clear that with a police approach the overall situation has gotten much worse and caused enormous social and personal harm. From a moral standpoint, which should become our starting point, it is now, and has always been, inhumane to manufacture criminals out of private possessors or users of a drug no matter what that drug might be. The criminalization of drug users is in the same category as burning witches at the stake or putting mentally ill in dungeons, and I believe that within a decade my view will prevail that all drug use should be handled as a sociological and public health matter (and sometimes problem). The drug user should be taken entirely out of the criminal law. This would mean that neither federal nor state law would make it a criminal offense to use or possess a particular drug, but instead would focus the criminal law on antisocial behavior such as crimes against the person or crimes against property, whether or not these occur in association with a drug, most commonly alcohol. Secondly, the criminal law can focus, if felt desirable by society, on reducing the manufacture, cultivation, and distribution of drugs. This is only one of many selective, thoughtful, and individualized measures that are possible for a mature and intelligent society to institute rather than believing that they must either criminalize or legalize, legalization meaning turning a drug over to advertising and public-relations men, making it fully available and uncontrolled as we have mistakenly done with alcohol and tobacco. This selective concentration on the business end of drugs and on real crime would be a far more socially beneficial deployment of limited police resources, would increase respect and support for the policemen, and would end the social and psychological destruction of American youth from arrest records, expulsion from school, and indoctrination into crime and sexual "deviance" in our jails and prisons. Obviously, in terms of the tonnage of marijuana being imported each week and month from Mexico into the United States, all drug policemen seriously interested in stopping the drug traffic should be massed either at the Mexico-California border or in Mexico itself to cut this off literally at its roots, and also should be lobbying with the State Department and state legislatures to take action against this. The concepts of the old politics that all one must do is pass a law and that "control" means criminal sanctions are as outmoded and unworkable as most of their other ideas and actions.

It would be totally hypocritical to concern oneself with reducing the availability and use of drugs such as marijuana without expressing even greater concern about the availability of alcohol and tobacco, which are the "hardest" and most dangerous mind-altering drugs in terms of scientific evidence and total numbers affected.

Believing as I do that both the individual and the society are giving far too much attention to mind-altering drugs and that, for the society as a whole, the more people depend on such drugs, the less likely they are to involve themselves in creative social change, it is important to move the society *beyond drugs*. However, if one takes up only one drug, such as marijuana, to focus on, and considers the objective evidence of what it does and doesn't do as compared to other widely used substances, if we indeed had only a choice between continued criminalization and legalization, we would probably be better off to have the legalization because of the far greater harm that will continue to derive from our present policies. Many so-called authorities, of course, state that this would simply add the same quantity and quality of problems as we have with drugs such as alcohol. The evidence presently available does not bear that out, but in any case, people often substitute one drug for another, or use them different times in different ways, and there is not a simple additive use or abuse phenomenon. Fortunately, however, we do have far more varied policy choices open to us including a variety of civil as opposed to the criminal measures, and the broader approach already discussed.

The alcohol and tobacco problems justify a higher priority in every respect than the marijuana problem, but dealing with the total context of the drugs sought for pleasure is the ideal way of approaching the matter. All advertising of alcohol, tobacco, and over-the-counter pseudosedatives, pick-me-ups, and tension relivers should be banned, or until that can be brought about, there should be high taxation on advertising space and time devoted to these drugs. The number of retail outlets where these drugs are pushed or made readily available should be steadily reduced through licensing restrictions. Subsidization of the growing of tobacco or of grain crops utilized for alcohol production should cease forthwith. All packages, bottles, cartons, or containers in places where these are sold or served should have prominent and explicit signs about the dangers to health such as cancer and heart disease, drunk driving, and cirrhosis. Stricter penalties with quick and implacable action should be instituted against drug-induced or associated antisocial behavior, particularly drunk driving, which, even when it involves killing someone, presently results in little more than a slap on the wrist as punishment. Specialized drug-police agencies, because of their gross ineffectiveness, destructiveness, and corruption, should be disbanded, and the more selective drug-enforcement activities recommended above should be carried out by general police intelligence and detective work, and internationally by the U.S. Customs. Not the least of the benefits to accrue from all of these reforms would be the savings of hundreds of millions of dollars for the taxpayers in reduced police, court, institutional, and other direct and indirect costs of our drug policies.

Before passing on to the other components of my master plan for moving beyond drugs, it requires emphasis that all of the measures recommended here should be done concurrently, since there is no one simple solution to any complex problem. To illustrate the stupidity of the legalization-criminalization dichotomy, an analogy can be made to child-rearing practices. If a parent or other adult was seeking to influence a child's behavior and was distressed by some action of the child, he would assume that he had only two alternatives, one, to totally ignore what the child had done and allow it to do anything it wanted ("legalization"), or physically to brutalize it and throw it out of the house forever ("criminalization"). Seen that way, the illogic should be self-evident.

Education, including efforts to teach people to think and to alter their attitudes, has never been utilized in American society to attack the drug problem. Just as we label "education" an expensive building (our edifice complex) staffed by administrators and teachers, without looking at the details of what takes place inside, we have assumed that a scare lecture about heroin by narcotics police or a crash lecture by an unprepared English or physical-education teacher was satisfactory drug education. We need immediately to institute, beginning no later than sixth grade and possibly even in kindergarten, objective, factual pro-

grams of drug education dealing with the full context of
mind-altering drugs from alcohol through narcotics presented by specially trained, knowledgeable teachers. The
program should be carefully planned, should last over a
period of weeks rather than just one day or one week, taking
up at least an hour and a half each week and utilizing a
combination of lectures, small and large group discussions,
audiovisual materials (films, slides, exhibits, programmed
instruction), and then continuing each year through high
school, with the material upgraded to the age level, knowledge, and sophistication of seventh graders, tenth graders,
and twelfth graders. Even if some teachers and other older
persons in the society are biased against the inclusion
of alcohol and nicotine in this program, it is absolutely
necessary to include them if they want the kids to listen
to, and accept, the program, for they will no longer tolerate the hypocrisy of leaving out of any discussion the
enormous social, health, and criminal problems from the
accepted drugs. Additional goals of a drug-education program should be to desensationalize and demythologize
drugs, in other words, to counter the glorification and exaggeration of drugs by advertisers, drug policemen, politicians, and Learians.

By their behavior and own life style, in addition to what
they communicate directly in the classroom, the teachers
should seek to convey that it is possible and usually desirable to relate to others, and seek meaning, happiness, and
achievement without alcohol, tobacco, marijuana, or the
rest. College campuses should sponsor drug-education
seminars for students, faculty, and administrators similar
to those that have been carried out in recent years by the
U.S. National Student Association and the National Association of Student Personnel Administrators. Many professional groups, including most physicians, require much
more information than they presently have about mind-
altering drug use and abuse and should arrange for special
programs through their organizations locally or nationally.
Special national conferences should be held to bring to-

gether the country's best experts to assess the present state of knowledge and make recommendations to the public and to legislative bodies. An example of what is needed was summarized in a statement circulated at the 1967 meeting of the American Sociological Association and signed by, among others, Professors Alfred Lindesmith, Howard Becker, and the writer:

> We the undersigned medical and social scientists, having national and international experience with the problems and challenges of marijuana use, wish to indicate our agreement that the present extreme laws imposing criminal penalties on users of marijuana require drastic and immediate reform through judicial and legislative action. Social and legal policies in the United States regarding this substance should recognize possession or use as a sociological and public health matter, removing this from the criminal law and reserving such criminal penalties solely for antisocial behavior and, if necessary, illicit manufacture and distribution. Present marijuana laws were based almost entirely on self-serving hearsay testimony presented in an artificially created climate of emotionalism, and fail to reflect or consider scientific knowledge or thinking. Such legislative action in the 1930s has defeated the purposes for which it was supposedly intended, and has brought about far more extensive drug use, and has done far more social and individual harm than marijuana itself. Clinical and social research, which is practically nonexistent at the present time due to current repressive policies of narcotics agencies, should be urgently accelerated and broadened. State and national conferences of true experts in the pharmacological, psychological, sociological, and other aspects of marijuana use should be convened in the near future to provide guidelines to government for future policies of regulation and control.

The goals of any educational program need to be clearly

articulated, and if possible they should include some
built-in techniques for evaluating accomplishment or failure. It would be a totally unrealistic goal for the educational component of the overall master plan to hope to
eliminate *all* mind-altering drug usage, and in fact this
would not be desirable, since, at the very least, a certain
amount of such drug usage is extremely important in relieving human suffering as part of medical practice.

Like education, treatment and rehabilitation have been
greatly neglected by our society. There have been several
token institutional treatment programs for narcotics addicts,
particularly at the federal prison-hospitals in Lexington,
Kentucky, and Fort Worth, Texas (prior to their being
transformed into research institutions); there have been
some specialized parole, methadone, and self-help or extramural programs for narcotics addicts; and there are a large
number of specialized clinics for alcoholics throughout
the country. The only comprehensive rehabilitation program for drug abusers is San Francisco's Center for Special
Problems, which deals with the full context of drug abuses
including alcoholism, chronic cigarette smoking, amphetamine abuse, narcotics addiction, etc., as well as with several other special social and health problems which are
either ignored or dealt with solely through repressive measures. Treatment services are appropriate only for the drug-
abuse segment of drug use, and even the most ideal treatment program, one which makes available in one setting a
humane and acceptable (by the consumers) combination of
traditional and innovative methods provided by both professionals and nonprofessionals, will be no more than a
small finger in a big dike. The major approach to both drug
abuse and the broader drug use must be one of education,
prevention, and attacking the complex sociocultural roots.
Treatment of drug abuse must include case-finding or early
detection of illness through public information programs;
availability of specialized programs: detoxification and
withdrawal treatment for those addicted to alcohol, sedatives, or narcotics, this ordinarily requiring a period of

in-patient hospital care; still more important, long-term out-
patient help, including group and individual psychotherapy, social work services, vocational counseling and
placement, special medications such as Antabuse for the
alcoholic, behavior therapy, self-help approaches such as
Alcoholics Anonymous, Daytop Village, or Synanon, hypnosis, methadone maintenance, LSD, and other experimen-
tal-drug treatment; halfway houses; and, still more important, full acceptance by private practitioners and public programs of drug abuse as a chronic illness requiring the same
understanding and long-term care as would hopefully
be provided for any individual, rich or poor, with other
chronic illnesses such as peptic ulcer or schizophrenia. The
traditional attitudes of rejection and animosity must be
overcome, for the real problem is not money or buildings,
but rather the development of a sufficient number of trained
and experienced personnel and the use of imagination in
reorganizing already existing private and public-health-
care institutions. Wherever possible, two or more avenues
of help should be made available to each drug user, since
there is no one method of treatment, whether it be psychotherapy or Synanon, that helps more than a minority with
this problem, and the chances of success are greatly improved by stressing several different methods in a total
approach individualized in terms of the individual's symptoms, problems, and desires in terms of help. A good
treatment program should also have available services for
nondrug-abusing relatives or family members ranging from
educational efforts to direct treatment services in some instances, where this will indirectly benefit the alcoholic
or narcotics addict.

Belatedly, many kinds of research projects are now going
on with a number of the mind-altering drugs. But research
has no direct relevance to social policy, and we know quite
clearly from the tobacco research particularly that overwhelming scientific findings of harmfulness are not even
sufficient to bring about minimal efforts to control and suppress this almost uniformly destructive drug habit, while,

on the other hand, there is a paucity of research data about other drugs for which people are sent to prison for indefinite periods simply for being in a room where the drug is present, or for possessing it. The main concentration of research should not be, as it is now, on chromosomes, biochemical changes, and sociological survey data, but instead should be concentrated on attitude change; developing drugs with fewer side effects and less overall risk for those who will continue to seek pleasure or otherwise desire or "need" mind-alteration through drugs; and most of all finding acceptable and practicable alternatives to drug use that take into account both the noble and ignoble motives and reasons for drug usage. Among the attitudes that require changing, of course, are those of our mediocre and incompetent public officials so that our social policies can be modernized and humanized. Among other things we can perhaps teach our representatives is that it is often better to do nothing in terms of passing laws than prematurely to respond to vitriolic pressure groups by enacting far-reaching, dangerous, and probably unconstitutional legislation that in any case drastically impinges on traditional American ideals, if not practices. Additionally, using civil fines rather than criminal imprisonment, and making distinctions between the user and the trafficker (whether the drug be marijuana, alcohol, or heroin) need to be communicated to legislative and judicial bodies who presently use as their sole sources of information the self-serving and false statements of drug-police agencies whose main motive is to gain larger budgets, exaggerate the importance and effectiveness of what they are doing, and aggrandize their status. They should no longer ignore alcohol- and tobacco-induced killings and other deaths, or the death and disability toll from the unrestricted availability of guns because of the machinations of the merchants of death, including the National Rifle Association. The President's Commission on Law Enforcement says,

> Excessive reliance upon the criminal law to perform tasks for which it is ill-suited has created acute prob-

lems for the administration of criminal justice. The use of criminal law to enforce morals has tended both to be inefficient and to produce grave handicaps for enforcement of the criminal law against genuinely threatening conduct. It has served to reduce the criminal law's essential claim to legitimacy by inducing offensive and degrading police conduct, particularly against the poor and the subcultural, and by generating cynicism and indifference to the criminal law. It has also fostered organized criminality and has produced possibly more crime than it has suppressed.

We must learn to recognize, accept, and cope with the complexity and ambiguity of life and the diverse manifestations of life, such as mind-altering-drug use. As part of this, we must learn to think through and understand what problems are in reality and how they can best be coped with, if at all. Putting things in relevant and appropriate context and assigning priorities seem to me to be essential ingredients of a civilized and productive life. Both young and old will hopefully soon recognize that there are many more important, interesting, and valuable things in life than mind-altering drugs; learn to choose other battle grounds of greater significance; and move beyond drugs to full involvement in the world around them. Instead of the "psychedelic ethic" which received wide publicity, a better model would be to: turn on to people and the world, tune in to knowledge and feeling, and *drop in* to changing and improving life and society. There are indeed also some pied pipers playing seductive, illusionary tunes and they are being headed off at the wrong pass by sheriffs using atomic bombs. But neither drugs nor power are where it's at. The price we are paying for our hypocrisy, illusions, and hatreds is far too great.

Thoreau once prophetically commented that "there are a thousand people hacking away at the branches of evil for every one striking at the roots." The roots of mind-altering-substance use and abuse are deeply imbedded in a sick, corrupt, and mediocre society, yet a society that offers greater hope for progress than any other. What is it about the American way of life that is so far making it impossible for the majority of our population, young and old, to relate to each other or to find any sense of purpose without using drugs; why are so many bored and disillusioned; and why are so many without hope, even from an early age? Some of the answers are more obvious than others. A total program for dealing with the many drug problems involving the many drugs and chemicals must certainly include an end to racism, poverty, injustice, and bureaucratic totalitarianism. Other roots are more complicated to dig out, but require a major improvement in the overall quality of American life, facilitating the pursuit of excellence; encouraging individuality; tolerating and channeling nonconformity and rebellion into constructive directions; reestablishing family life to include mutual trust, compassion, and communication; making the entire education process (and life itself) an exciting, mind-expanding experience; replacing our present obsolete bureaucratic institutions with self-directing, adaptive, problem-solving, goal-oriented systems able to cope with rapid change and with complexity, and in general developing a thinking, feeling kind of people power, including youth power and full voting rights and full social and political participation from the age of eighteen onward. Anyone who does not become part of the solution is in effect part of the problem, and the penalties for not speaking out and acting are death of the spirit, alienation, and ultimately destruction of our society. Lives of significance, relevance, and meaning can be developed which include love for people, beauty, art, literature, music, nature, and other facets of a rounded, full, and creative life. When these goals are even partially accomplished, drugs will pale into relative insignificance, remaining to be used only on a highly selective basis. All progress ultimately comes from individualism, ideally a socially concerned and compassionate individualism. As Andrew Jackson said, "One man with courage makes a majority." It is people, not drugs, that must decide our destiny.

A Frenchman who liked America, de Tocqueville, said, "I am tempted to believe that what we call necessary institutions are often no more than institutions to which we have grown accustomed. In matters of social constitution, the field of possibilities is much more extensive than men living in their various societies are ready to imagine."

COMPARISON CHART OF MAJOR SUBSTANCES USED FOR MIND ALTERATION

	1 — OFFICIAL NAME OF DRUG OR CHEMICAL	2 — SLANG NAME(s)	3 — USUAL SINGLE ADULT DOSE	4 — DURATION OF ACTION (HOURS)	5 — METHOD OF TAKING
A	Alcohol Whiskey, gin, beer, wine	Booze Hooch Juice	1½ oz. gin or whiskey, 12 oz. beer	2–4	Swallowing liquid
B	Caffeine Coffee, tea, Coca-Cola ® No-Doz ®, APC	Java	1–2 cups or 1 bottle 5 mg.	2–4	Swallowing liquid
C	Nicotine (and coal tar) Cigarettes, cigars	Fag	1–2 cigarettes	1–2	Smoking (inhalation)
D	Sedatives Alcohol—see above Barbiturates Nembutal ® Seconal ® Phenobarbital Doriden ® (glutethimide) Chloral hydrate Miltown ®, Equanil ® (meprobamate)	Downs Yellow jackets Red devils Phennies Goofers	50–100 mg. 500 mg. 500 mg. 400 mg.	4	Swallowing pills or capsules
E	Stimulants Caffeine—see above Nicotine—see above Amphetamines Benzedrine ® Methedrine ® Dexedrine ® Cocaine	Ups Bennies Crystal, Speed Dexies or Xmas trees (spansules) Coke, snow	2.5–5.0 mg. Variable	4	Swallowing pills or capsules or injecting in veins Sniffing or injecting

		Downs			
F	Tranquilizers				
	Librium® (chlordiazepoxide)		5-10 mg.		Swallowing pills or capsules
	Phenothiazines				
	Thorazine®		10-25 mg.	4-6	
	Compazine®		10 mg.		
	Stelazine®		2 mg.		
	Reserpine (rauwolfia)		1 mg.		
G	Cannabis (marijuana)	Pot, grass, tea, weed, stuff	Variable—1 cigarette or 1 drink or cake (India)	4	Smoking (inhalation) Swallowing
H	Narcotics (opiates, analgesics)				
	Opium	Op	10-12 "pipes" (Asia)		Smoking (inhalation)
	Heroin	Horse, H, skag	Var.—bag or paper w. 5-10% heroin	4	Injecting in muscle or vein
	Morphine		15 mg.		
	Codeine		30 mg.		
	Percodan®		1 tablet		
	Demerol®		50-100 mg.		
	Cough syrup (Cheracol®, Hycodan®, etc.)		2-4 oz. (for euphoria)		Swallowing
I	LSD	Acid, sugar	150 micrograms	12	Swallowing liquid, capsule, pill (or sugar cube)
	Psilocybin		25 mg.	6	
	Mescaline (peyote)	Cactus	350 mg.	4	Chewing plant
J	Antidepressants				
	Ritalin®		10 mg.	4-6	Swallowing pills or capsules
	Dibenzapines (Tofranil®, Elavil®)		25 mg., 10 mg.		
	MAO inhibitors (Nardil®, Parnate®)		15 mg., 10 mg.		
K	Miscellaneous				
	Glue		Variable	2	Inhalation
	Gasoline				
	Amyl nitrite	Poppers, snappers	1-2 ampoules		
	Antihistamines		25-50 mg.		Swallowing
	Nutmeg		Variable		
	Nonprescription "sedatives"				

		6	7	8	9	10
		LEGITIMATE MEDICAL USES (PRESENT AND PROJECTED)	POTENTIAL FOR PSYCHOLOGICAL DEPENDENCE[1]	POTENTIAL FOR TOLERANCE (LEADING TO INCREASED DOSAGE)	POTENTIAL FOR PHYSICAL DEPENDENCE	OVERALL POTENTIAL FOR ABUSE[2]
A	Alc.	Rare Sometimes used as a sedative (for tension)	High	Yes	Yes	High
B	Caf.	Mild stimulant; treatment of some forms of coma	Moderate	Yes	No	None
C	Nic.	None (used as an insecticide)	High	Yes	No	Moderate
D	Sed.	Treatment of insomnia and tension. Induction of anesthesia	High	Yes	Yes	High
E	Stim.	Treatment of obesity, narcolepsy, fatigue, depression. Anesthesia of the eye and throat	High	Yes	No	High
F	Tran.	Treatment of anxiety, tension, alcoholism, neurosis, psychosis, psychosomatic disorders and vomiting	Minimal	No	No	Minimal
G	Can.	Treatment of depression, tension, loss of appetite, sexual maladjustment, and narcotics addiction	Moderate	No	No	Moderate
H	Nar.	Treatment of severe pain, diarrhea, and cough	High	Yes	Yes	High

	6	7	8	9	10
	LEGITIMATE MEDICAL USES (PRESENT AND PROJECTED)	POTENTIAL FOR PSYCHOLOGICAL DEPENDENCE[1]	POTENTIAL FOR TOLERANCE (LEADING TO INCREASED DOSAGE)	POTENTIAL FOR PHYSICAL DEPENDENCE	OVERALL POTENTIAL FOR ABUSE[2]
I LSD Psi.	Experimental study of mind and brain function. Enhancement of creativity and problem solving. Treatment of alcoholism, mental illness, and the dying person (Chemical warfare)	Minimal	Yes (rare)	No	Moderate
	Mes.				
J A-dep.	Treatment of moderate to severe depression	Minimal	No	No	Minimal
K Misc.	None except for antihistamines used for allergy and amyl nitrite for some episodes of fainting	Minimal to moderate	Not known	No	Moderate

[1] The term "habituation" has sometimes been used to refer to psychological dependence, and the term "addiction" to refer to the combination of tolerance and an abstinence (withdrawal) syndrome.

[2] Drug abuse (dependency) properly means: (excessive, often compulsive) use of a drug to an extent that it damages an individual's health or social or vocational adjustment; or is otherwise specifically harmful to society.

	11	12
	REASONS DRUG IS SOUGHT BY USERS (DRUG EFFECTS AND SOCIAL FACTORS)	USUAL SHORT-TERM EFFECTS[3] (PSYCHOLOGICAL, PHARMACOLOGICAL, SOCIAL)
A Alc.	To relax. To escape from tensions, problems and inhibitions. To get "high" (euphoria). Seeking manhood or rebelling (particularly those under twenty-one). Social customs and conformity. Massive advertising and promotion. Ready availability.	CNS depressant. Relaxation (sedation). Sometimes euphoria. Drowsiness. Impaired judgment, reaction time, coordination and emotional control. Frequent aggressive behavior and driving accidents.
B Caf.	For a "pickup" or stimulation. "Taking a break." Social custom and low cost. Advertising. Ready availability.	CNS stimulant. Increased alertness. Reduction of fatigue.
C Nic.	For a "pickup" or stimulation. "Taking a break." Social custom. Advertising. Ready availability.	CNS stimulant. Relaxation (or distraction) from the process of smoking.
D Sed.	To relax or sleep. To get "high" (euphoria). Widely prescribed by physicians for both specific and nonspecific complaints. General climate encouraging taking pills for everything.	CNS depressants. Sleep induction. Relaxation (sedation). Sometimes euphoria. Drowsiness. Impaired judgment, reaction time, coordination and emotional control. Relief of anxiety-tension. Muscle relaxation.
E Stim.	For stimulation and relief of fatigue. To get "high" (euphoria). General climate encouraging taking pills for everything.	CNS stimulants. Increased alertness, reduction of fatigue, loss of appetite, insomnia, often euphoria.
F Tran.	Medical (including psychiatric) treatment of anxiety or tension states, alcoholism, psychoses, and other disorders.	Selective CNS depressants. Relaxation, relief of anxiety-tension. Suppression of hallucinations or delusions. Improved functioning.
G Can.	To get "high" (euphoria). To relax. To socialize. To conform to various subcultures which sanction its use. For rebellion. Attraction of behavior labeled as deviant. Availability.	Relaxation, euphoria, increased appetite, some alteration of time perception, possible impairment of judgment and coordination. (Probable CNS depressant.)

| | 11 | 12 |
	REASONS DRUG IS SOUGHT BY USERS (DRUG EFFECTS AND SOCIAL FACTORS)	USUAL SHORT-TERM EFFECTS[3] (PSYCHOLOGICAL, PHARMACOLOGICAL, SOCIAL)
H — Nar.	To get "high" (euphoria). As an escape. To avoid withdrawal symptoms. As a substitute for aggressive and sexual drives which cause anxiety. To conform to various sub-cultures which sanction use. For rebellion.	CNS depressants. Sedation, euphoria, relief of pain, impaired intellectual functioning and coordination.
I — LSD Psi. / Mes.	Curiosity caused by recent widespread public-ity. Seeking for meaning and consciousness-expansion. Rebellion. Attraction of behavior recently labeled as deviant. Availability.	Production of visual imagery, increased sensory awareness, anxiety, nausea, impaired coordina-tion; sometimes consciousness-expansion.
J — A-dep.	Medical (including psychiatric) treatment of depression.	Relief of depression (elevation of mood), stimulation.
K — Misc.	Curiosity. To get "high" (euphoria). Thrill seeking. Ready availability.	When used for mind alteration, generally produces a "high" (euphoria) with impaired coordination and judgment.

[3] Always to be considered in evaluating the effects of these drugs is the amount consumed, purity, frequency, time interval since ingestion, food in the stomach, combinations with other drugs, and, most importantly, the personality or character of the indi-vidual taking it and the setting or context in which it is taken. The determinations made in this chart are based upon evidence with human use of these drugs rather than upon isolated, arti-ficial-experimental situations or animal research.

	13	14
	USUAL LONG-TERM EFFECTS (PSYCHOLOGICAL, PHARMACOLOGICAL, SOCIAL)	FORM OF LEGAL REGULATION[a] AND CONTROL
A Alc.	Diversion of energy and money from more creative and productive pursuits. Habituation. Possible obesity with chronic excessive use. Irreversible damage to brain and liver, addiction with severe withdrawal illness (DT's).	Available and advertised without limitation in many forms with only minimal regulation by age (twenty-one or eighteen), hours of sale, location, taxation, ban on bootlegging and driving laws. Some "black market" for those under age and those evading taxes. Minimal penalties.
B Caf.	Sometimes insomnia or restlessness. Habituation.	Available and advertised without limit with no regulation for children or adults.
C Nic.	Lung (and other) cancer, heart and blood-vessel disease, cough, etc. Habituation. Diversion of energy and money. Air pollution. Fire.	Available and advertised without limit with only minimal regulation by age, taxation, and labeling of packages.
D Sed.	Irritability, weight loss, addiction with severe withdrawal illness (like DT's). Diversion of energy and money. Habituation, addiction.	Available in large amounts by ordinary medical prescription which can be repeatedly refilled or can be obtained from more than one physician. Widely advertised and "detailed" to MD's and pharmacists. Other manufacture, sale, or possession prohibited under federal drug-abuse and similar state (dangerous) drug laws. Moderate penalities. Widespread illicit traffic.
E Stim.	Restlessness, irritability, weight loss, toxic psychosis (mainly paranoid). Diversion of energy and money. Habituation. Extreme irritability, toxic psychosis.	Same as Sedatives, above. Same as Narcotics, below.
F Tran.	Sometimes drowsiness, dryness of mouth, blurring of vision, skin rash, tremor. Occasionally jaundice, agranulocytosis.	Same as Sedatives, above, *except* not usually included under the special federal or state drug laws. Negligible illicit traffic.

	13	14
	USUAL LONG-TERM EFFECTS (PSYCHOLOGICAL, PHARMACOLOGICAL, SOCIAL)	FORM OF LEGAL REGULATION[4] AND CONTROL
G Can.	Usually none. Possible diversion of energy and money.	Unavailable (although permissible) for ordinary medical prescription. Possession, sale, and cultivation prohibited by state and federal narcotics or marijuana laws. Severe penalties. Widespread illicit traffic.
H Nar.	Constipation, loss of appetite and weight, temporary impotency or sterility. Habituation, addiction with unpleasant and painful withdrawal illness.	Available (except heroin) by special (narcotics) medical prescriptions. Some available by ordinary prescription or over the counter. Other manufacture, sale, or possession prohibited under state and federal narcotics laws. Severe penalties. Extensive illicit traffic.
I LSD Psi. Mes.	Usually none. Sometimes precipitates or intensifies an already existing psychosis; more commonly can produce a panic reaction when person is improperly prepared.	Available only to a few medical researchers (or to members of the Native American Church). Other manufacture, sale, or possession prohibited under state and federal narcotics laws. Extensive illicit traffic.
J A-dep.	Basically the same as Tranquilizers, above.	Same as Tranquilizers, above.
K Misc.	Variable — some of the substances can seriously damage the liver or kidney.	Generally easily available. Some require prescriptions. In several states, glue banned for those under twenty-one.

[4] Only scattered, inadequate health, educational, or rehabilitation programs (usually prison hospitals) exist for narcotics addicts and alcoholics (usually out-patient clinics), with nothing for the others except sometimes prison.

Bibliography

Abramson, H. *The Use of LSD in Psychotherapy and Alcoholism.* Indianapolis: The Bobbs-Merrill Co., Inc., 1967.

Alpert, R., Cohen, S., and Schiller, L. *LSD.* New York: The New American Library, Inc., 1966.

Altizer, Thomas J. J., and Hamilton, William. *Radical Theology and the Death of God.* Indianapolis: The Bobbs-Merrill Co., Inc., 1966.

American Bar Association and the American Medical Association on Narcotic Drugs. *Drug Addiction: Crime or Disease?* Bloomington: Indiana University Press, 1963.

Barber, Bernard. *Drugs and Society.* New York: Russell Sage Foundation, 1967.

Barron, Frank. "Creativity and Psychological Health." *Origins of Personal Vitality and Creative Freedom.* New York: D. Van Nostrand Co., Inc., 1963.

Barron, Frank, et al. "The Hallucinogenic Drugs." *Scientific American,* 1964, 210 (4), pp. 29-37.

Becker, H. S. *Outsiders.* The Free Press, 1963.

Blum, R. H. "Mind Altering Drugs and Dangerous Behavior" in *Task Force Report: Narcotics and Drug Abuse.* President's Commission on Law Enforcement and Administration of Justice.

Blum, R. H., and Associates. *Students and Drugs and Society and Drugs,* San Francisco: Jossey-Bass, 1969.

Blum, R. H., and Associates. *Utopiates: The Use and Users of LSD-25.* New York: Atherton Press, 1964.

Braden, William. *The Private Sea: LSD and the Search for God.* Quadrangle Books, 1967.

Brotman, R., and Freedman, A. *A Community Mental Health Approach to Drug Addiction.* U.S. Government Printing Office, Washington, D.C., 1968.

Bruce, Lenny. *How to Talk Dirty and Influence People.* New York: Playboy Press, 1967.

Bugental, James F. T. (Ed.). *Challenges of Humanistic Psychology.* New York: McGraw-Hill Book Co., 1967.

Carey, James T. *The College Drug Scene.* Englewood Cliffs, N. J.: Prentice-Hall, Inc. (Spectrum Books), 1968.

Chein, I., Gerald, D. L., Lee, R. S., and Rosenfeld, E.: *The Road to H.* New York: Basic Books, Inc., 1964.

Cohen, A. K. *Deviance and Control.* Englewood Cliffs, N. J.: Prentice-Hall, Inc., 1966.

Cohen, John (Ed.). *The Essential Lenny Bruce.* Ballantine Books, Inc., 1967.

Cohen, Sidney. *The Beyond Within: The LSD Story.* New York: Atheneum Publishers, 1964.

Cohen, S., and Ditman, K. S. "Complications Associated with Lysergic Acid Diethylamide (LSD-25)." *Journal of the American Medical Association,* 1962, 181 (2), pp. 161-62.

Cornell, P. H. *Amphetamine Psychosis.* London: Chapman and Hall, Ltd., 1958.

Cutting, W. C. *Handbook of Pharmacology: The Action and Uses of Drugs* (Third Edition). New York: Appleton-Century-Crofts, 1967.

Daedalus: Journal of the American Academy of Arts and Sciences. "Toward the Year 2000: Work in Progress." Boston: Summer, 1967.

De Ropp, R. S. *Drugs and the Mind.* New York: Grove Press (Evergreen Black Cat), 1957.

Drug Arrests and Dispositions in California. Bureau of Criminal Statistics, State Department of Justice, 1967.

"Drug Use and Crime." Issues in *Criminology* 2, No. 2, Fall, 1966.

Ebin, D. *The Drug Experience.* New York: Orion Press, 1961.

Eldridge, Wilbur B. *Narcotics and the Law: A Critique of the American Experiment in Narcotic Drug Control.* American Bar Foundation, 1962.

Farber, L. H. "Ours Is the Addicted Society," *New York Times Magazine,* December 11, 1966, p. 43.

Fiddle, Seymour. "Portraits from a Shooting Gallery: Life Styles from the Drug Addict World." Harper & Row, 1967.

Fort, Joel. "The AMA Lies About Pot," *Ramparts*, August 24, 1968.

Fort, Joel. "Comparison Chart of Major Substances Used for Mind-Alteration." National Sex and Drug Forum, 330 Ellis St., San Francisco, 1967.

Fort, Joel. "FTW: A Motto for Our Times," *Psychiatry and Social Science Review*, 2, No. 6, June 1968, pp. 16-19.

Fort, Joel. "Giver of Delight or Liberator of Sin: Drug Use and 'Addiction' in Asia." *Bulletin on Narcotics*, Vol. 17, 3 and 4, 1965.

Fort, Joel. "Marijuana: The Real Problems and the Responsibilities of the Professions in Solving Them." *Psychiatric Opinion 5*, No. 5, 1968, pp. 9-16.

Fort, Joel. "The Problem of Barbiturates in the U.S.A." *Bulletin on Narcotics*, 1964, 16 (1), pp. 17-35.

Fort, Joel. "A Public Health Approach to Drug Abuse."*Wisconsin Pharmacy Extension Bulletin*, 11, No. 9, September, 1968.

Fort, Joel. "Recommended Future International Action Against Abuses of Alcohol and Other Drugs." *British Journal of Addiction*, 1967.

Goldstein, Richard. *1 in 7*, New York: Walker & Co., 1966.

Goodman, L. S., and Gilman, A. *The Pharmacological Basis of Therapeutics* (Third Edition). New York: The Macmillan Co., 1965.

Haggard, Howard W. *Devils, Drugs and Doctors*. New York: Pocket Books, 1946.

Harris, Sara. *Skid Row U.S.A.* New York: Belmont Books, 1956.

"The Health Consequences of Smoking: A Public Health Service Review, 1967." U.S. Government Printing Office, 1968.

Huxley, Aldous. *Doors of Perception and Heaven and Hell*. Harper & Row, 1963.

Huxley, A. *Island*. New York: Bantam Books, Inc., 1963.

Hess, Albert G. *Chasing the Dragon: A Report on Drug Addiction in Hong Kong*. North-Holland, 1965.

Hesse, H. *Journey to the East.* New York: The Noonday Press, 1957.

Johnson, George. *The Pill Conspiracy.* New York: Signet, 1967.

Keniston, K. *The Uncommitted.* Harcourt, Brace & World, 1965.

Krieg, Margaret. *Black Market Medicine.* Englewood Cliffs, N. J.: Prentice-Hall, Inc., 1967.

Krieg, Margaret. *Green Medicine.* New York: Bantam Books, Inc., 1966.

La Barre, Weston. *Peyote Cult.* Hamden, Conn.: The Shoe String Press, Inc., 1954.

Larner, Jeremy, and Tefferteller, Ralph. *The Addict in the Street.* Zebra Books, 1966.

Laurie, Peter. *Drugs.* Baltimore: Penguin Books Inc., 1967.

Leary, T. "Playboy Interview." *Playboy,* September, 1966.

Lewin, L. *Phantastica: Narcotic and Stimulant Drugs.* New York: E. P. Dutton & Co., Inc., 1964.

Lindesmith, A. *The Addict and the Law.* Bloomington: Indiana University Press, 1965.

Lowes, P. D. *The Genesis of International Narcotics Control.* Librairie E. Droz, 1966.

Lucia, Salvadore P. *Alcohol and Civilization.* New York: McGraw-Hill, Inc., 1963.

"Marijuana: Turned-On Millions." *Life,* July 7, 1967, p. 16.

Masters, R. L., and Houston, Jean. *The Varieties of Psychedelic Experience.* Holt, Rinehart, & Winston, 1966.

Mathison, Richard. *The Shocking History of Drugs.* New York: Ballantine Books, 1958.

Mayor's Committee Report on Marijuana. Lancaster, Pa.: Jaques Cattell Press, 1944.

McCarthy, Raymond G. (Ed.). *Drinking and Intoxication: Selected Readings in Social Attitudes and Controls.* Glencoe, Ill.: The Free Press, 1959.

McGlothlin, W. H. "Hallucinogenic Drugs: A Perspective," *Psychedelic Review,* 1965, No. 6, pp. 16-57.

McLuhan, M. *Understanding Media.* New York: Signet, 1964.

Metzner, Ralph. *The Ecstatic Adventure.* New York: The Macmillan Co., 1968.

Murphy, H. B. M. "The Cannabis Habit: Review of Recent Psychiatric Literature," *Bulletin on Narcotics*, 15 (1): 15-23, January-March, 1963.

Nowlis, Helen H. *Drugs on the College Campus*. New York: Anchor Books, 1968.

Pahnke, Walter N., and Richards, William A. "Implications of LSD and Experimental Mysticism." *The Journal of Religion and Health*, Vol. 5, No. 3, July, 1966.

"Peyote." *United Nations Bulletin on Narcotics*, IX, 1959.

Physicians' Desk Reference, Medical Economics, Inc., 1967.

Ploute, T. F. A. *Alcohol Problems: A Report to the Nation by the Cooperative Commission on the Study of Alcoholism*. New York: Oxford University Press, 1967.

The President's Commission on Law Enforcement and Administration of Justice, "Drunkenness." Task Force Report, U.S. Government Printing Office, 1967.

The President's Commission on Law Enforcement and Administration of Justice. "Narcotics and Drug Abuse," Task Force Report, U.S. Government Printing Office, 1967.

The President's Advisory Commission on Narcotic and Drug Abuse, Final Report. U.S. Government Printing Office, 1963.

Rexroth, Kenneth. "The Fuzz," *Playboy*, July, 1967, p. 76.

Roueché, Berton. *The Neutral Spirit: A Portrait of Alcohol*. New York: Little, Brown & Co., 1960.

Schoenfeld, Eugene. *Dear Dr. Hip-pocrates*. New York: Grove Press, Inc., 1968.

Schur, Edwin M. *Crimes Without Victims*. Prentice-Hall, Inc., 1965.

Simmons, J. L., and Winograd, B. *It's Happening*. Santa Barbara: Marc-Laird, 1966.

Sinclair, A. *Prohibition: The Era of Excess*. Boston: Little, Brown & Co., 1962.

Solomon, D. (Ed.). *LSD: The Consciousness-Expanding Drug*. New York: G. P. Putnam's Sons, 1964.

Solomon, David (Ed.). *The Marijuana Papers*. Indianapolis: The Bobbs-Merrill Co., Inc., 1966.

Stafford, P. G., and Golightly, B. H. *LSD: The Problem-Solving Drug*. New York: Award Books, 1967.

Starr, John. *The Purveyor*. New York: Holt, Rinehart & Winston, 1962.

State of California Narcotics Act, 1967, Division 10 and 10.5 of the Health and Safety Code. State Department of Justice.

Taylor, Norman. *Narcotics: Nature's Dangerous Gifts*. Dell Publishing Co., 1963.

Thompson, Hunter. *Hell's Angels*. Random House, Inc., 1966.

Unger, S. M. "Mescaline, LSD, Psilocybin and Personality Change." *Psychiatry* 26 (2), pp. 111-25, 1963.

Ungerleider, J. Thomas (Ed.). *The Problems and Prospects of LSD*. Springfield, Ill.: Charles C. Thomas, 1968.

Watts, Alan. *The Joyous Cosmology: Adventures in the Chemistry of Consciousness*. Pantheon Books, Inc., 1962.

White House Conference on Narcotic and Drug Abuse, *Proceedings*. U.S. Government Printing Office, 1962.

Wikler, Abraham. *The Relation of Psychiatry to Pharmacology*. Baltimore: The Williams and Wilkins Co., 1959.

Wolfe, Tom. *The Electric Kool-Aid Acid Test*. New York: Farrar, Straus & Giroux, Inc., 1968.

The World of Youthful Drug Use. Berkeley, California: University of California School of Criminology, 1967.

Yablonsky, Lewis. *Synanon: The Tunnel Back*. Penguin Books, Inc., 1967.

Index